Public Administration in Africa

Performance and Challenges

PUBLIC ADMINISTRATION AND PUBLIC POLICY
A Comprehensive Publication Program

EDITOR-IN-CHIEF
DAVID H. ROSENBLOOM
Distinguished Professor of Public Administration
American University, Washington, DC

Founding Editor
JACK RABIN

RECENTLY PUBLISHED BOOKS

Public Administration in Africa: Performance and Challenges, edited by Shikha Vyas-Doorgapersad, Lukamba-Muhiya. Tshombe, and Ernest Peprah Ababio

Public Administration in Post-Communist Countries: Former Soviet Union, Central and Eastern Europe, and Mongolia, Saltanat Liebert, Stephen E. Condrey, and Dmitry Goncharov

Hazardous Materials Compliance for Public Research Organizations: A Case Study, Second Edition, Nicolas A. Valcik

Logics of Legitimacy: Three Traditions of Public Administration Praxis, Margaret Stout

The Politics–Administration Dichotomy: Toward a Constitutional Perspective, Second Edition, Patrick Overeem

Managing Development in a Globalized World: Concepts, Processes, Institutions, Habib Zafarullah and Ahmed Shafiqul Huque

Cybersecurity: Public Sector Threats and Responses, Kim J. Andreasson

Government Budgeting and Financial Management in Practice: Logics to Make Sense of Ambiguity, Gerald J. Miller

Globalism and Comparative Public Administration, Jamil Jreisat

Energy Policy in the U.S.: Politics, Challenges, and Prospects for Change, Laurance R. Geri and David E. McNabb

Public Administration in Southeast Asia: Thailand, Philippines, Malaysia, Hong Kong and Macao, edited by Evan M. Berman

Governance Networks in Public Administration and Public Policy, Christopher Koliba, Jack W. Meek, and Asim Zia

Public Administration and Law: Third Edition, David H. Rosenbloom, Rosemary O'Leary, and Joshua Chanin

Public Administration in East Asia: Mainland China, Japan, South Korea, and Taiwan, edited by Evan M. Berman, M. Jae Moon, and Heungsuk Choi

Handbook of Public Information Systems, Third Edition, edited by Christopher M. Shea and G. David Garson

Available Electronically
PublicADMINISTRATION*netBASE*
http://www.crcnetbase.com/page/public_administration_ebooks

Public Administration in Africa

Performance and Challenges

Edited by
Shikha Vyas-Doorgapersad
Lukamba-Muhiya. Tshombe
Ernest Peprah Ababio

CRC Press is an imprint of the
Taylor & Francis Group, an **informa** business

CRC Press
Taylor & Francis Group
6000 Broken Sound Parkway NW, Suite 300
Boca Raton, FL 33487-2742

© 2013 by Taylor & Francis Group, LLC
CRC Press is an imprint of Taylor & Francis Group, an Informa business

No claim to original U.S. Government works

Printed on acid-free paper
Version Date: 20130220

International Standard Book Number-13: 978-1-4398-8880-3 (Hardback)

This book contains information obtained from authentic and highly regarded sources. Reasonable efforts have been made to publish reliable data and information, but the author and publisher cannot assume responsibility for the validity of all materials or the consequences of their use. The authors and publishers have attempted to trace the copyright holders of all material reproduced in this publication and apologize to copyright holders if permission to publish in this form has not been obtained. If any copyright material has not been acknowledged please write and let us know so we may rectify in any future reprint.

Except as permitted under U.S. Copyright Law, no part of this book may be reprinted, reproduced, transmitted, or utilized in any form by any electronic, mechanical, or other means, now known or hereafter invented, including photocopying, microfilming, and recording, or in any information storage or retrieval system, without written permission from the publishers.

For permission to photocopy or use material electronically from this work, please access www.copyright.com (http://www.copyright.com/) or contact the Copyright Clearance Center, Inc. (CCC), 222 Rosewood Drive, Danvers, MA 01923, 978-750-8400. CCC is a not-for-profit organization that provides licenses and registration for a variety of users. For organizations that have been granted a photocopy license by the CCC, a separate system of payment has been arranged.

Trademark Notice: Product or corporate names may be trademarks or registered trademarks, and are used only for identification and explanation without intent to infringe.

Library of Congress Cataloging-in-Publication Data

Public administration in Africa : performance and challenges / editors, Shikha Vyas-Doorgapersad, Lukamba-Muhiya Tshombe, Ernest Peprah Ababio.
 pages ; cm -- (Public administration and public policy)
 Includes bibliographical references and index.
 ISBN 978-1-4398-8880-3 (hardcover : alk. paper)
 1. Public administration--Africa. 2. Public administration--Africa--Personnel management. 3. Management--Africa. I. Vyas-Doorgapersad, Shikha.

JQ1875.P83 2013
351.6--dc23   2012050933

Visit the Taylor & Francis Web site at
http://www.taylorandfrancis.com

and the CRC Press Web site at
http://www.crcpress.com

Contents

Preface vii
About the Editors ix
Contributors xi

1 Governance Apparatus in South Africa: From Policy Design to
   Service Delivery 1
   GERRIT VAN DER WALDT

2 Public Administration in the Democratic Republic of Congo 27
   LUKAMBA-MUHIYA. TSHOMBE

3 Public Administration and Corruption in Uganda 45
   BENON C. BASHEKA

4 Public Sector Reforms in Nigeria: 1999–2009 83
   ADEWALE BANJO

5 Combating Poverty in South Africa: Understanding the Informal
   Sector in the Context of Scarce Opportunities 97
   LORAINE BOITUMELO "TUMI" MZINI

6 Media as a Catalyst for Good Governance in South Africa: An
   Expanded Vision of Public Administration 117
   SHIKHA VYAS-DOORGAPERSAD

7 Implementing Good Governance Reform in Ghana: Issues and
   Experiences with Local Governance 135
   PETER FUSEINI HARUNA AND LAWRENCE AKANWEKE KANNAE

8 Overview of the African Peer Review Mechanism in Selected
   African Countries 153
   ERNEST PEPRAH ABABIO

9   Lessons for Africa in Economic Policy Reform: The Mauritius
    Best Practice Case.. 167
    DANIEL FRANCOIS MEYER AND ANNELISE VENTER

10 A Comparative Analysis of Local Government in Ghana and
    South Africa... 187
    ERNEST PEPRAH ABABIO AND KWAME ASMAH-ANDOH

11 Integrating Traditional Leadership Structures with
    Contemporary Public Administration Machinery for Innovative
    Governance and Improved Service Delivery 209
    SHIKHA VYAS-DOORGAPERSAD AND LUKAMBA-MUHIYA. TSHOMBE

Index 223

Preface

The traditional field of public administration has always been wide. The phenomenon has been widened further with the surfacing of the additional concepts of management and governance. The shift in paradigm is currently on governance, the extent to which politicians and appointed officials join hands in utilizing resources to improve living conditions. Such is the complexity of the policy arena in the global world. With the advent of sophistication in education technology, creation of public awareness of what government does, participatory political culture in even the developing nations, and yet a tendency by politicians and officials to divert resources away from what they were intended for, alias corruption, the process of evaluating the art of governance on how governments perform has never been so complex. And such is the focus of this book on public administration in Africa. We regret that we could not provide features on all 54 states in Africa, precisely due to space limitation. It is our hope that remaining issues such as emerging political and administrative reforms in Angola, Libya, Egypt, and the Sudans will be explored in a later publication.

In its 11 chapters, *Public Administration in Africa* encompasses a wide range of issues on governance. Gerrit van der Waldt sets the tone with an analysis of the relationship between policy design and its destination, service delivery. The background locus is South Africa, which has embarked on a massive post-apartheid revolution on governance. On the Democratic Republic of Congo, Lukamba-Muhiya. Tshombe espouses an interesting historical development of a state that has gone through upheavals in governance. There is a trace of transition from a Belgian Congo, through governance in the leadership cult of Mobutu Sese Seko, to the current state of governance in a period of civil war upheavals. Corruption in Africa has become a common phenomenon in governance in Africa. The scientific analysis of this by Benon C. Basheka in the case of Uganda makes for interesting reading. A decayed political economy ultimately results in a need for sweeping measures to lift a smile on the human face. This is where the analysis by Adewale Banjo on public sector reforms in Nigeria becomes paramount. A chronic policy issue that emerging African policy makers have to tackle is poverty, its denial, and the lack of resources to maintain a dignified life. In the informal settlement case study in South Africa, Loraine Boitumelo "Tumi" Mzini paints a startling picture of the poverty scenario common in many African states, and draws recommendations for tackling it. Policy problems invariably become issues of governance through media sensitivity. On the South African policy scene, Shikha Vyas-Doorgapersad highlights the media as a catalyst for good governance in South Africa. Local government, normally as a ministry or a department, oversees the governance issues of municipalities as institutions closest to the people. Service delivery and the promotion of a good life as propounded by Aristotle become largely the function of municipalities in Africa. Interesting that the analytical aspects of local government are the form of structural streams that augur well for efficient and effective service delivery. Peter Fuseini Haruna and Lawrence Akanweke Kannae consequently provide analytical aspects of implementing good governance reforms on issues, experiences, and challenges in Ghana. This is further augmented by the comparative analysis of local government in Ghana and South Africa, in which Ernest Peprah Ababio and Kwame Asmah-Andoh succinctly engage the concepts of decentralization and devolution in measuring service delivery performance. The role of traditional leadership cannot escape the discourse of public administration debate in Africa, more especially where local government is under surveillance. Thus the overview of the integrative role of traditional structures with contemporary public administration by Shikha Vyas-Doorgapersad and Lukamba-Muhiya. Tshombe complements the holistic analysis of local government functioning in Africa. The relatively high economic growth of the island state of Mauritius is exemplary for emulation, as shown by Daniel Francois Meyer and Annelise Venter on Mauritius: Africa's economic success story—an analysis of best practice and lessons learned. A book on public administration in Africa may not be complete without a discourse on the regional integration of the continent. This oversight function is presented by Ernest Peprah Ababio in an overview of the African peer review mechanism in selected African countries.

With the above stimulating discussions and analyses, it is our hope that the reader stands to gain

- An understanding of governance as a concept in the context of policy development and implementation in Africa
- An appreciation of the extent to which policy issues on challenges such as poverty and corruption are being tackled
- Knowledge of local government functioning in Africa and the role of traditional leadership
- An assessment of public service reforms as provided by governments and the African Union
- An insight into the role of the media in galvanizing public awareness in the unique policy environment of Africa

We express our profound appreciation to our publisher, Taylor & Francis, for making this project a reality, and to all our readers, for the interest shown in our output.

About the Editors

Shikha Vyas-Doorgapersad is an associate professor in public management and administration at the Vaal Triangle Campus of North-West University of South Africa. She holds an MA, MPhil, and PhD in public administration from the University of Rajasthan (India). Her lecturing and research interests are in public policy, gender issues, and municipal governance. She has presented research findings at international conferences worldwide. Vyas-Doorgapersad has published two books, contributed chapters in books, has 19 articles in refereed accredited journals, and 5 articles in international peer-reviewed journals. She serves as a reviewer to several accredited journals in South Africa. Vyas-Doorgapersad has supervised 14 master's dissertations and promoted one doctorate. She serves as external moderator/examiner for MA and PhD degrees for several universities in South Africa.

Lukamba-Muhiya. Tshombe is a senior lecturer in public management and administration at the Vaal Triangle Campus of the North-West University in South Africa. He is the research coordinator in the Department of Public Management. Tshombe holds a BA honors degree in public administration, an MPhil (energy policy) from the University of Cape Town, and a PhD in public management from the Cape Peninsula University of Technology. His lecturing interests are in public management, disaster risk, public sector reform, public–private partnership, waste management, and energy security. About these, Tshombe has presented five research papers at international conferences in Uganda, Mozambique, Ethiopia, Indonesia, Brazil, and Italy. He has published 10 articles in refereed accredited journals. He is currently supervising MA and PhD students in the field of public management and administration. Tshombe serves as an external examiner for MA and PhD degrees for several universities in South Africa.

Ernest Peprah Ababio is a professor in public management and administration at the Vaal Triangle Campus of North-West University of South Africa, and chair of public management. He holds a BA honors in political science from the University of Ghana, and a BA honors, MA, and DLitt et Phil in public administration from the University of South Africa. His lecturing and research interests are in public finance, public policy analysis, regional integration, and municipal government and administration. About these, Ababio has presented several conference papers worldwide and has published 25 articles in refereed accredited journals. He is a community sponsor and engages in several workshops and training in public finance and policy for municipal counselors and officials. He sits as member and chair of a number of municipal committees. Ababio has supervised 35 master's dissertations, has promoted 6 doctoral candidates, and serves as an external moderator/examiner for several universities in South Africa and internationally.

Contributors

Ernest Peprah Ababio
North-West University
Vanderbijlpark, South Africa

Kwame Asmah-Andoh
Nelson Mandela Metropolitan
   University
Port Elizabeth, South Africa

Adewale Banjo
University of Zululand
Kwadlangezwa, South Africa

Benon C. Basheka
Uganda Management
   Institute–Kampala
Kampala, Uganda

Peter Fuseini Haruna
Texas A&M International University
Laredo, Texas

Lawrence Akanweke Kannae
Ghana Institute of Management and
   Public Administration
Accra, Ghana

Lukamba-Muhiya. Tshombe
North-West University
Vanderbijlpark, South Africa

Daniel Francois Meyer
North-West University
Vanderbijlpark, South Africa

Loraine Boitumelo "Tumi" Mzini
North-West University
Vanderbijlpark, South Africa

Gerrit van der Waldt
North-West University
Potchefstroom, South Africa

Annelise Venter
Fezile Dabi District Municipality
Sasolburg, South Africa

Shikha Vyas-Doorgapersad
North-West University
Vanderbijlpark, South Africa

Chapter 1

Governance Apparatus in South Africa: From Policy Design to Service Delivery

Gerrit van der Waldt

Contents

Introduction..2
State, Society, and Constitutionalism...2
The Architecture of Government's Apparatus 4
From Policy Design to Service Delivery: Clarifying the Value Chain 8
    Policy and Service Delivery 10
    Service Delivery Innovations..12
South Africa's Governance Scene at a Glance...14
Apparatus of the South African Government..16
    The Executive Authority 17
    The Legislative Authority 20
    The Judiciary 21
Value Chain Integration: The System of Cooperative Government...................22
Conclusion..23
References 24

Introduction

Most modern conceptions about the ideal state began with the reflections of Greek philosophers such as Plato and Aristotle. In the long history of statehood and political thought, the meanings ascribed to such ideals, however, have been variously modified and should be understood within the context of a particular state. The dominant culture and ideology prevalent in a state will, for example, ultimately influence the way a government structures itself in order to reflect the conceptions and conventions that the public attaches to the ideal or best way government should govern. Should the government not reflect these conceptions and conventions, the public will usually replace the ruling party in government—peacefully at the ballot box or violently through a *coup d'etat* (revolutionary overthrough of government). It is thus critical for any government to utilize its apparatus optimally to adhere to the social contract between those that govern and those who are governed.

The purpose of this chapter is to explore the apparatus that governments, in general, and South Africa, in particular, utilizes in order to perform those roles and functions assigned to it. In the context of this chapter, the term *apparatus* should be understood in its widest application referring to organizational arrangements and systems, structures, processes, equipment, methods, and operations utilized by government institutions, agencies, and entities to perform their governance functions. It thus refers to the totality of means by which a system of government performs its functions. The application of such an apparatus enables government to unpack the processes in a value chain from policy design to service delivery. The apparatus of government thus makes it possible to bridge the gap between policy intent and actual changes to the conditions of people on grassroots level.

A brief reflection of the role of the state in society will first be provided to set the governance scene. An overview of the South African constitutional dispensation—the architecture of government—will follow to clarify the system of cooperative government and the way government interacts on national, provincial, and local spheres, as well as between legislative, executive, and judiciary tiers. An exploration of the value chain from policy design to policy implementation (service delivery) will follow to highlight the significance of governance apparatus in the process.

Lastly, a brief synopsis of the South African government's apparatus on the respective spheres and tiers of government will be provided.

State, Society, and Constitutionalism

An analysis of public affairs is incomplete without contemplating the role of the state and its governance structure, the government, in society. The origin of a state can typically be traced back to its traditions, culture, ideology, history, environmental conditions, and so forth. Public officials and political representatives can only meaningfully fulfill their obligations if they appreciate the role that public institutions should play in society. Furthermore, any judgment of the "goodness" of a government is only possible if the criteria to measure its performance are known. Clarification of the role of a state, and its government apparatus to govern, should thus expose the criteria that citizens ascribe to the goodness of it.

Debates about the role of the state in society emerged with philosophers like Plato and Cicero. One theory about how political authority can arise is social contract theory. According to the original proponents of this theory, John Locke, David Hume, and Jean-Jacques Rousseau, consent is the basis of government. It is because people have agreed to be ruled that governments are entitled to rule. Citizens of a country come together and form contracts that serve their interests, and these contracts establish rule (Jenks 1900). In other words, people agree that they need a collective body, a state, to maintain social order in its broadest sense. This implies that people give up some of their rights to a government in order to maintain order. Locke's political philosophy holds that citizens enter into a social contract under which the state provides certain services to its citizens. This contract, however, works both ways: not only must the state govern according to certain acceptable conventions, but also it prescribes how citizens should behave. If they disobey certain conditions of civil order and rule of law, the state has the right to intervene with its apparatus to maintain order (Barker 1960). The apparatus typically utilized in this respect includes the police service, the judiciary, and in more severe cases, the defense force and intelligence services. This contract principle lies at the foundation of public administration as discipline. As an applied social science public administration must equip civil servants to serve the people. People place government, and its officials, in their trust to provide them with services and products.

The social contract usually results in a constitution for the state. The design of a constitution is the next step in the development of societal order. Its purpose is to establish principles, values, institutions, procedures, duties, and structures that persist from one ruling party to the next (see Carneiro 1967). With the constitution, as the highest authority of the state, elected representatives of the people establish laws, and permanent public officials are appointed to implement and uphold these laws. In the case of South Africa, no apparatus of the state may exercise any powers not duly delegated to it, or do so in a way that is not consistent with shared values, ideology, established structures, or procedures defined by the constitution. The constitution of the Republic of South Africa Act 108 of 1996 came into effect on February 4, 1997. This is the highest law in South Africa, and no other law or government action can overrule the constitution or be in conflict with it. South Africa's constitution is regarded as one of the most progressive in the world and is based on the values of dignity, equality, and freedom.

Any breaches of the social contract in society could lead to conflict and even civil war. Sustaining the social contract therefore depends in large part on so ordering the constitution and laws as to avoid unbalanced or excessive concentrations of power, whether in the public or the private sector. In framing the constitution of

South Africa, for example, political representatives had to address the problem of avoiding unbalanced or excessive concentrations of power in government by adopting a constitution in which legislative, executive, and judicial powers are largely divided among separate branches, with each having some power to check the potential abuses of the others. This is known as the *trias politica* principle, which refers to the separation of state powers. In statehood these powers typically refer to legislative (policy making), executive (policy execution), and judiciary (legal) powers.

Constitutional rule in a state is further connected with the question whether it is better to be ruled by the best man (represented by a political party) or the best laws, since a government that consults the good of its subjects is also a government in accordance with law. The supremacy of law is generally accepted as a mark of a good state. In Plato's work the *Statesman*, he makes government by law and government by wise rulers alternatives. It could be argued, however, that even the wisest ruler cannot dispense with law because the law has an impersonal quality that no man, however good, can attain. In this regard Aristotle argued that law is "reason unaffected by desire."

From the perspective highlighted above, the notions of rule of law and constitutional supremacy arose. This means that the highest authority in a truly democratic country is not the president, ruling party, or parliament, but the constitution. The validity of all decisions taken by political representatives or officialdom is tested against the spirit and stipulations of the constitution. In a constitutional dispensation the constitution itself is the yardstick and indispensable condition of a moral, just, and civilized society. A constitution can thus be regarded as the fundamental principles and rules according to which a state is governed (Pylee 1997).

A constitution further prescribes the basic human rights of citizens and the powers of government. Fundamental rights usually revolve around *life*, *liberty*, and *property*. In maintaining these rights in society, the functioning of government apparatus may sometimes come into conflict with the exercise of the rights of members of society. To maintain the common good, it is therefore critical that an independent judiciary judge the legality of any government action—or inaction.

The Architecture of Government's Apparatus

As ascertained in the previous section, a state exists to facilitate the common good in society. To facilitate adherence to the common good, that is, the welfare, prosperity, and safety of civil society, a government needs to structure itself in such a way that it could utilize resources optimally, distribute services and products fairly and equitably, and accomplish certain strategic objectives. As a collective entity, it is vital that government institutions pursue collective goals. To pursue these goals the macro organizational design of government is critical.

There is significant terminological diversity and a general lack of clarity regarding the concept governance—mainly attributed to the wide scope of its potential applications. Governance is further applied in many different settings and disciplinary domains. Hirst (2000), for example, unpacks at least five versions of governance, or five different areas in which it is applied:

- Governance in economic development and in the context of international development agencies such as the World Bank and the International Monetary Fund
- Governance in terms of international relations and international regimes
- Corporate governance or governance in private corporations
- Governance as new public management
- Negotiated social governance that is representative of networks, partnerships, and various deliberative forms

It is evident that the content ascribed to governance could vary in relation to the details of its application, purpose, context, as well as the instruments utilized to govern. On the basis of this, good governance could be taken to refer to the efficient and effective management of public resources and problems in dealing with the critical needs of the society (Kjaer 2004). Kaufmann, Kraay, and Zoido (1999) argue that good governance and sound public sector management constitute the major mechanisms of social order and prosperity.

On the African continent, the United Nations Economic Commission for Africa (UNECA) has been in the forefront of the good governance debate. This debate typically centers around the interrelationship between good governance and economic development. UNECA, in partnership with the United Nations Development Program (UNDP), the World Bank, and other agencies, has developed indicators to determine the level of goodness of countries. Among these indicators are

- The extent to which the state minimizes the impact of civil strife and communal violence and institutes mechanisms for promoting peace, political stability, and security.
- The extent to which the key governance institutions of the judiciary, legislative, and executive are functioning effectively and exercise institutional check and balance.
- The extent to which the public management system is perceived to be effective, accountable, transparent, and has integrity.
- The level of freedom of association and expression; existence of a conducive and enabling environment for citizen's initiatives and activities and for encouraging the development of viable civil society organizations.
- The ready availability and free flow of information to permit informed public discussions on national issues and policies. This will make it possible for accountability to be practiced, laws to be fairly and correctly applied, and watchdog institutions to function freely.

Furthermore, Hyden and Braton (1993), Batley and Larbi (2004), and Van der Waldt (2004) identified various characteristics of good governance that include elements such as the degree of trust in government, the degree of responsiveness to needs, the degree of transparency and accountability, as well as the nature of authority exercised by government over society. In this regard, the Mo Ibrahim Foundation developed 84 indicators (such as economic prosperity, safety, human rights, and development) to measure the goodness of countries on the African continent. The UNDP, through its Global Program on Capacity Development for Democratic Governance Assessments and Measurements, furthermore in 2005 published different governance indicator frameworks within the Global Barometer, including the World Values Survey, the World Governance Assessment, the Public Integrity Index, and the Afrobarometer. Through these frameworks the UNDP seeks to assist developing countries to produce disaggregated and nonranking governance indicators to enable the monitoring and measurement of governments' performance.

Globally, various mechanisms and initiatives are in place to measure the successes and failures of governance. These mechanisms and initiatives include

- World Bank governance surveys: Country-level governance assessment tools that use information gathered from a country's own citizens, business, and public sector workers to diagnose governance vulnerabilities.
- World Governance Index (WGI): Use composite indices such as peace and security, rule of law, human rights and participation, sustainable development, and human development.
- Sustainable governance indicators (SGIs): Systematically measure the need for reform and the capacity for reform within (OECD) countries. The project examines to what extent governments can identify, formulate, and implement effective reforms that render a society well equipped to meet future challenges, and ensure their future viability.
- The African Peer Review Mechanism (APRM), which is an instrument that member states of the African Union (AU) voluntarily acceded to as a self-monitoring mechanism. Its mandate is to encourage conformity in regard to political, economic, and corporate governance values, codes, and standards, among African countries and the objectives in socioeconomic development within the New Partnership for Africa's Development (NEPAD).

From the orientation provided above, it is evident that a government can only be labeled as good if its architecture—that is, its institutional arrangements and functional structures—functions effectively to promote the common good in society. A government must therefore organize its machinery in such a way that all the core responsibilities of a government (i.e., protection, welfare, education, etc.) are available where and when they are needed. These macro organizational arrangements refer to the way public institutions in all spheres and tiers of government are arranged through a process known as departmentalization for the benefit of society. The concept of organization is derived from the Greek word *organon* meaning "tool." It could be argued that public institutions are therefore the tools that a government utilizes to operationalize its respective responsibilities in society. These tools should be systematically structured and designed according to statutory prescriptions and regulatory frameworks that the government must establish.

Organizations are formed when a group of individuals unite to accomplish specific objectives. They are responsible for creating a work environment that best utilizes resources such as people, finances, information, and technology. But, in order to meet these objectives, they will need to create appropriate organizational structures. Just like any organization should organize itself, a government should also organize itself and consider aspects such as structure, design, work specialization, departmentalization, chain of command, span of control, centralization and decentralization, and the advantages of certain organizational designs. Burton, Obel, and DeSanctis (2011) explain how organizations should be designed. Typical steps include

- Define the scope of the organization and assess its goals.
- Develop its strategy given the particular environment.
- Configurate the structure of the organization.
- Design appropriate processes.
- Obtain human resources, design their tasks, lead, and incentivize them.
- Establish coordination, control, and information systems.

The establishment of any public institution, as apparatus of the state, typically follows these steps.

A government's macro organization is an extremely complex activity that is typically influenced by issues such as political ideology, level of constitutionalism, demography of society, economic considerations, and geographical variables. Some of the functions of government are centralized in national government, while other functions are decentralized to regions and localities that are closer to the people that need it.

From a macro perspective a government should address societal problems and achieve particular objectives. In order to achieve this, it must consider especially four things:

- The most effective way to establish order, cooperation, and coordination between organizations on different tiers and spheres of government
- The establishment of a chain of command and resource allocation within a system of cooperation and intergovernmental relationships
- The allocation of authority, powers, and resources to perform certain functions to particular entities on national, provincial, and local spheres
- The manner in which an institution will be organized into line and support functions

In a democratic society public policy should be designed in such a way that a framework is provided for the establishment of public institutions as well as providing a framework for how these institutions should function. Such frameworks should be designed with due recognition of the needs and aspirations of society and contain prescriptions on these needs, and aspirations should be addressed. In this regard, Hanekom (1987) stated that public policy concerns the directional intention of a government in ensuring service delivery for the population of a state. It is therefore all about the political direction in which a government steers a country and the way in which available resources are to be allocated and utilized by the various organs of state.

From the above orientation it can be deduced that the state has to design the architecture of its apparatus in such a way that resources are optimally utilized and fairly distributed to society. Only if this process is successfully completed and executed can a government be regarded as good. In the next section the value chain in the process from policy design to service delivery will be explored.

From Policy Design to Service Delivery: Clarifying the Value Chain

A value chain refers to the interlinked activities that convert resources (input) into outputs (services or products). The chain of activities gives the service or products more added value than the sum of the independent activities' values. Similarly, in government, the architecture of the interaction *between* public institutions as well as the architecture of activities *within* public institutions should be designed in such a way that value is added for the common good. Such architecture is typically the result of a policy framework within which public institutions organize themselves and perform certain functions. Figure 1.1 illustrates this value chain in a policy-making and policy implementation context.

Of all the pressing issues that demand a government's attention, only a small number will receive serious consideration by public policy makers. Due to limited resources and time, each problem must compete for official attention. Decisions to consider some problems mean that others will not be considered, at least for the time being (Anderson 2000). Agenda setting is, accordingly, the deliberate act of selecting issues that merit serious consideration for formulating or reformulating policy (Baumgartner, Green-Pedersen, and Jones 2006).

Setting the policy agenda requires a look at how problems developed, how they were defined, the legitimization of one course of action over another, and the appearance of policy systems to act on such problems over a continuous basis (Jones and Baumgartner 2004). To achieve agenda status, a problem must be converted into an *issue*, or a matter that requires government attention. An issue arises when

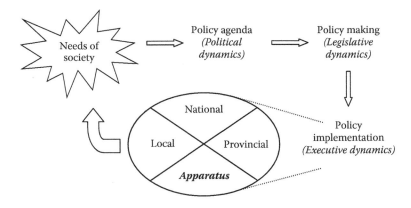

Figure 1.1 Policy-making/policy implementation value chain.

society demands governmental action, and there is public disagreement over the best solution to the problem (Anderson 2000).

As the policy formulation process moves toward the final stage, some provisions will be rejected by stakeholders, others accepted, and still others modified; differences will be narrowed; negotiations will be struck; until ultimately, the final policy decisions will be a formality, or the policy will be adopted by a vote in the legislature (Anderson 2000).

The policy-making process—from agenda setting to policy evaluation—in each country will follow unique paths. Within the South African context public policy typically emanates from international frameworks such as the Millennium Development Goals, international treaties, and continental and regional cooperation, such as the various programs of the African Union and the Southern African Development Community (SADC). Nationally, policy originates from the goals of statehood stipulated in the constitution of the Republic of South Africa Act 108 of 1996, the state of the nation address, as well as the annual government's program of action, the new growth path, Vision 2030 of the National Planning Commission, and the so-called apex priorities stipulated by the ruling party.

During cabinet *lekgotlas* (strategic sessions), the ministers in cabinet decide how the executive authority will operationalize the issue through national legislation. Various cluster committees will then debate a plan of action and will refer the policy issue to a particular department or agency within the cluster for the preparation of a green paper, white paper, and eventually, a draft bill.

After a decision has been made on the policy for dealing with a particular issue, the department concerned prepares a draft bill on the issue, in consultation with the minister. The relevant government ministry, which will ultimately be responsible for the implementation of that policy, would then be requested to formulate a discussion document in a form of a green paper to allow for public debate in input from interested parties and stakeholders. Parliamentary committees, portfolio committees in the National Council of Provinces, as well as provincial legislatures provide opportunities for public participation on these papers.

On approval by the minister, the draft bill is submitted to a cabinet committee for recommendations. The cabinet discusses the draft bill and ensures that it does not contradict any other policy (especially the constitution). Once it is satisfied, the bill is submitted to the state law advisers at the Department of Justice. The officials, from a legal point of view, will check and ensure that the draft bill is consistent with the constitution. The bill is then made available to the legislation and proceedings section of parliament, and is ready for printing.

The printed draft bill is proofread by parliamentary officials and state law advisers. The draft bill may first be tabled at either the National Assembly, or at the National Council of Provinces. These bodies will refer it to the relevant portfolio committee. This committee would review the bill and invite public comments. The bill will then be discussed at committees, and other parties may lobby for changes or protest the principles or stipulations of the bill, after which it is sent back to the National Assembly for consideration and voting. Once both houses of parliament agree on the bill, it is then sent to the president. After the president has signed the bill it becomes national legislation. It receives an act number and is taken up in the *Government Gazette* for publication. The law will be implemented by the national and provincial ministries and departments. The provincial and national legislatures and local authorities may pass subordinate legislation that gives detail on certain matters contained in the law. When the adoption phase of the policy process has been completed with the signature of the president, one can refer to it as public policy.

Policy making, however, does not end when the processes become law. The purpose of making the policy was to address a problem identified (Sabatier and Mazmanian 2005). Consequently, the adopted policy must take a new form; it must be implemented.

Public policy implementation has been described as "what happens after a bill becomes law" (Anderson 2000). During implementation the intentions, the objectives, and the course of action selected by policy makers are operationalized.

Policy and Service Delivery

On the implementation side, public policy materializes and is the result of the legislative and executive activities in a specific sphere of government. As far as levels of policy within these spheres of government are concerned, Cloete, Wissink, and De Coning (2000) differentiate between geographical and hierarchical perspectives. From a geographical vantage point, for example, one could distinguish between policies on local, provincial, national, and international levels. A hierarchical perspective relates to levels of policy within government institutions that are primarily focused on the utilization of resources. It is important to appreciate this multitiered and multidimensional nature of policy to understand the way in

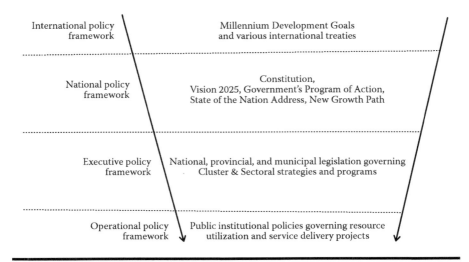

Figure 1.2 Hierarchical and geographical perspectives of public policy.

which public institutions are designed to render the correct quality and quantity of services. Figure 1.2 illustrates the layered vantage points of policy. It illustrates the hierarchical levels of policy, juxtaposed on the geographical (spheres of government) perspective.

In the design of policy, policy makers need to clearly formulate the problem and determine goals, objectives, and alternative policy options. Relevant information pertaining to the formulation of government policy is crucial to enable a thorough analysis and to present meaningful and rational solutions to societal challenges.

In terms of territorial integrity South Africa covers a large geographical area. The key objective of government is to improve service delivery by bringing its institutions closer to the people. In terms of bringing service delivery institutions closer, Chapter 3 of the constitution provides for the division of government structures into three distinct, interdependent, and interrelated spheres. It is through these spheres of government that public policy must be operationalized with the end objective of effective service delivery to the population. The spheres are therefore empowered to formulate (legislative authority) and implement (executive authority) public policy within the boundaries of their respective jurisdictions as stipulated in the constitution (Venter 2001).

In terms of the stipulations of Chapters 5 to 7 of the constitution, the service delivery powers and functions of the three spheres can briefly be summarized as follows.

The national sphere is the highest sphere of government and makes decisions on, and has legislative authority over, matters of national interest. It is in this sphere of government where party political policy is transformed into national public policy. Existing national policies in South Africa can be directly linked to the constitution. The main responsibility of the national sphere of government is to design policies (national legislation) that will act as a framework within which service delivery must occur. The national sphere is further responsible to monitor, support, and ensure the implementation of the above policies. Policy decisions that are taken within the provincial or local spheres of government must always be guided and are always subjected to the legislative boundaries established through national policy.

The provincial sphere of government has legislative and executive authority over matters of provincial interest. The legislative authority of the provinces is vested in the premiers and the provincial cabinets. The executive authority is vested in the provincial government departments, which fall under the jurisdiction of the various provincial members of executive committees. Within this sphere of government national public policy is in most cases translated into executive public policy (Venter 2001). The powers and functions of this sphere of government naturally impact on the local sphere of government. The annual state of the province address made by the respective premiers, as well as the provincial growth and development strategy, can be regarded as the core frameworks for policy design to deal with economic, social, and community development.

The local sphere of government is commonly known as the sphere closest to the people. This sphere, consisting of local, district, and metropolitan municipalities, is responsible for developmental issues within a designated local area. The legislative and executive authority of a municipality is vested in its council. Policy approved by a municipality is known as by-laws and applicable to a specific town or city. Integrated development plans (IDPs) can be regarded as the ultimate framework for such by-laws and direct all service delivery initiatives. Furthermore, municipalities make use of so-called top-layer (council-wide) service delivery and budget implementation plans (SDBIPs) as well as departmental (operational) service delivery and budget implementation plans.

Service Delivery Innovations

Access to public services is a right enshrined in the United Nations Declaration of Human Rights, in particular Article 21(2), which states: "Everyone has the right to equal access to public service." Around the globe, there are renewed drives in government to contemplate how to give effect to this human right. Renewal thinking involves rethinking the government's business and trying to improve service delivery to achieve government objectives. Government has been criticized for being overly bureaucratic, slow to respond, inefficient, and unimaginative. In South Africa, the announced intention is to shift to smaller and more flexible program delivery arrangements and to decentralize authority so that government operations become more client-oriented and innovative in delivering public services.

In determining the appropriate role for government a frequent analogy is that government should focus on "steering," not "rowing" (Osborne and Geabler 1992). This suggests that government should concentrate only on policy and regulatory functions (steering society) and rely on the outside (i.e., private enterprise) for the delivery of programs (rowing). There is thus a general trend internationally for the state to play a minimalist, managerialist role. This means removing itself from direct service delivery, i.e., provision of services, cutting the size of the state/public sector, and cutting the state budget—which means cutting spending in the public sector and on welfare areas.

The language of reinventing government draws heavily on the vocabulary of business. Government programs are seen as serving clients and not citizens. An important consequence of reinvention has been the changing nature of state-society interaction and exchange. Reforms such as privatization or contracting out of public services, the introduction of private sector-type management strategies and objectives into the public sector, the allowance for private involvement in the delivery of public services, and the perception of the recipients of such services as customers have contributed to this change in the relationship between the public and private sectors.

Service delivery improvement remains one of the urgent priorities of government. It requires the building of a more modern, people-centered public service—a public service that accepts both the challenges and opportunities presented by innovation, collaboration, and service. Despite the investment of resources, both human and capital, in transforming the public service and its institutions, there are still challenges facing government in its efforts.

Within the context described above, so-called alternative models or modes of service delivery emerged. The Canadian government, for example, championed the so-called alternative service delivery (ASD) model. ASD proposes a range of service delivery options involving a spectrum of public, private, and nongovernmental agencies. As a result, various alternative service delivery mechanisms have become available to government apparatus for service delivery. Some of these mechanisms include

- E-government and m-government: The use of information and communication technology, including mobile (cell phone) technology, to bring services closer, and more efficiently, to society.
- Outsourcing and contracting out: The outsourcing of certain services and projects to third parties when public institutions lack staff, financial, and other capacities to deliver them themselves. Institutions may also competitively contract with a private organization, for-profit or nonprofit, to provide a service or part of a service.
- Partnering through public-private partnerships (PPPs): Government partners with the private sector to render certain services or products.
- Shared service delivery: Various institutions collaborate to render services at a particular location, such as "one-stop shops."
- Commercialization (service shedding): Government stops providing a service and lets the private sector assume the function.
- Franchising: A private firm is given the exclusive right to provide a service within a certain geographical area.

- Privatization: Various options are available, such as long-term leasing, where the government retains ownership of the asset, but leases its use to the private sector; the government retains a minority interest in the risks and benefits of ownership; or it can also mean a sale to a not-for-profit entity.
- Corporatization: Government organizations are reorganized along business lines, focusing on maximizing profits and achieving a favorable return on investment.

This concludes a brief overview of the policy-making/policy implementation value chain. In the next section, the context within which the South African government must design and execute policy is explored. That will be followed by the apparatus available to it on the different spheres and tiers of government to facilitate operations within this value chain.

South Africa's Governance Scene at a Glance

As stated earlier, the specific environmental conditions, demographics, and dominant culture and ideology prevalent in a state will ultimately influence the way a government structures itself. To reflect on the apparatus of government in South Africa, it is therefore necessary to obtain a brief synopsis of South Africa as a country.

At the most southern tip of the African continent, South Africa is characterized by high levels of diversity and inequality. Although the country is known for a well-established economic sector, with mining, transport, energy, manufacturing, tourism, and agriculture as key areas, the majority of the population of approximately 49 million lives in poverty. High levels of inequality, characterized by extreme wealth on the one hand and desperate poverty on the other, are prevalent. The eradication of poverty is therefore one of the apex priorities for the government, as well as various other sectors of South African society. Statistics South Africa conducts an annual income and expenditure survey (IES) of households and an annual general household survey. These surveys portray that there are several distinct aspects to poverty in South Africa. They reflect that 47.1% of South Africa's population does not have adequate means for essential food and nonfood items. The poverty rates of South Africa's nine provinces differ significantly, as do those of the urban and rural areas of the country. The poverty rates typically range from 24.9% in Gauteng and 28.8% in the Western Cape to 57.6% in the Eastern Cape and 64.6% in Limpopo. The incidence of poverty, however, is much higher in the rural areas of South Africa—59.3% of poor individuals are rural dwellers despite the fact that the rural areas housed well below one-half of the South African population (Statistics South Africa, mid-year population estimates of 2011).

South Africa is further characterized by large-scale unemployment in the formal sector of the economy. The unemployment rate was reported at 23.9% in the fourth quarter of 2011. From 2000 until 2008, South Africa's unemployment rate averaged 26.38%, reaching a historical high of 31.20% in March 2003 and a record low of 23.00% in September 2007. The increasing growth rate of the economically active population in conjunction with a declining or stagnant rate of growth of the gross domestic product (GDP) implies that the level of unemployment is set to increase still further. A grim picture is that the unemployment rate among all 15- to 24-year-olds is 51%, more than twice the national unemployment rate of 25%, according to the latest South Africa survey published by the South African Institute of Race Relations (2012). The survey also found that an increasing number of South Africans rely on social grants, with the number of beneficiaries increasing by more than 300% in the past nine years. Also, the survey found that the average job created by a government program lasted just 46 days. Other key demographical indicators are indicated in Table 1.1.

Based on the above perspectives it is critical that South Africa's government apparatus is geared in such a way that both urban and rural settings receive services and goods at affordable service charges. Especially the 9 provincial governments and the 283 local, district, and metropolitan municipalities have a significant role to play to bring services such as water, electricity, housing, and health closer to the people. As in many African countries, much of South Africa's rural space is sparsely populated. The manufacturing base is weak due to poorly developed infrastructure. Local government has little or no tax base and weak human capacity. Agriculture and other natural resource-based activities provide the basis for many livelihoods. Many rural people live isolated from economic opportunities, necessitating high costs of transport for jobs and to accomplish basic tasks of daily life. Policy agenda setting and resource distribution priorities should reflect these social conditions and service delivery realities.

In spite of significant challenges, as highlighted above, South Africa remains the dominant player in geopolitics on the African continent. South Africa is an influential and active member of the African Union (AU) and regional institutions, such as the Southern African Development Community (SADC). Due to

Table 1.1 Key Demographical Indicators

Key Indicators	Rating
Population growth (% per annum)	1.0
Life expectancy (years)	50.0
Urban population (%)	60.3
UN Education Index	0.84
Gini Index	57.8
GDP per capita ($)	9,768.0

Source: UNDP, *Human Development Report,* World Bank, World Development Indicators, 2009.

its economic strength, it is also regarded as the key driving force behind the South African Customs Union (SACU).

Most Western governments view South Africa as a cornerstone for achieving peace and stability on the continent. The country is a driving force and one of the main sponsors of regional and continent-wide integration. The government was involved in a number of initiatives for conflict resolution, including the Democratic Republic of Congo (DRC) and Ivory Coast, and participated in peacekeeping missions such as in Burundi. As an upper-middle-income country according to the classification of the Development Assistance Committee (DAC) of the Organization for Economic Cooperation and Development (OECD), South Africa is regarded as the economic hub in the SADC. Compared to most African countries, South Africa is in a privileged position, since it is not dependent on foreign aid. The fact that a European Union (EU)–South African free trade agreement was established illustrates the strong position of South Africa.

Other success stories include the fact that all South African citizens enjoy the same civic rights, regardless of race and religion. All forms of discrimination are forbidden by the constitution and violations are prosecuted. The Constitution of the Republic of South Africa Act acknowledges 11 official languages, and there are significant levels of tolerance and harmony in the so-called rainbow nation.

Apparatus of the South African Government

South Africa has a constitutional multiparty, three-tier (local, provincial, national) democracy. South Africa further has a parliamentary system of government with formal separation of powers. As a result, the country has three capitals: Pretoria (administrative), Cape Town (legislative), and Bloemfontein (judicial). South Africa's administrative structure is geographically differentiated into local (municipal), regional (provincial), and national administrative bodies. The South African state is characterized as a national democratic and developmental state whose primary role is the transformation of society. The content of such transformation includes the democratization of state and society, building the economy, meeting the basic needs of society, and developing human resources.

Several institutions for monitoring, oversight, advice, research, and further improvement of government policies have been established by the constitution. The constitution provides for a constitutional democracy and lists the rights to which the people of this country are entitled. To give substance to these constitutional rights, independent institutions have been established to promote rights and to strengthen constitutional democracy. Chapter 9 of the constitution states that a number of "state institutions supporting constitutional democracy" be provided for. These are

- Public Protector
- South African Human Rights Commission

- Commission for the Promotion and Protection of the Rights of Cultural, Religious, and Linguistic Communities
- Commission for Gender Equality
- Auditor-General
- Electoral Commission
- Independent Authority to Regulate Broadcasting

The task of these institutions is to promote and protect those rights within the bill of rights that fall within their particular area. They should be impartial, independent, and subject only to the constitution and the relevant laws made in terms of the constitution. They should also exercise their powers and perform their functions "without fear, favour or prejudice" (Section 181(2), Chapter 9 of the Constitution).

In addition to the commissions described in Chapter 9, the constitution sets up other structures in South Africa to make sure that human rights are protected and a constitutional democracy is guaranteed. These are:

- Constitutional court
- Independent Complaints Directorate (ICD)
- Commission for Conciliation, Mediation, and Arbitration (CCMA)
- National Prosecuting Authority (NPA)
- Judicial Service Commission
- Financial and Fiscal Commission
- Public Service Commission
- Pan South African Language Board (PANSALB)

In the sections that follow a brief synopsis of the three tiers of government, namely, the executive, legislative, and judiciary, within the three spheres (national, provincial, and local) is made. This synopsis encapsulates the total governance apparatus of the state and portrays the value chain in the processes associated with policy design and policy implementation (service delivery). To facilitate the synopsis, Figure 1.3 illustrates the main governance apparatus of government.

The Executive Authority

The primary responsibility of the executive is to govern the country through the execution of national legislation. It consists of the president, the deputy president, and the cabinet ministers at the national sphere, and the premier and members of the executive councils (MECs) at the provincial sphere. It also includes government departments and civil servants. They are empowered to implement legislation, develop and implement policy, direct and coordinate the work of the government

18 ■ *Public Administration in Africa*

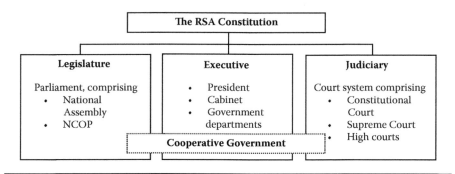

Figure 1.3 South African government's apparatus.

departments, prepare and initiate legislation, and perform other functions as called for by the constitution or legislation.

The executive cannot pass laws, but may propose to the legislature new laws and changes to existing laws (refer to the politics/administration dichotomy in Public Administration theory). The president is head of state and head of the national executive or cabinet. He or she is entrusted with maintaining the supremacy of the constitution as the guiding law of the country, and is also required to promote the unity and interests of the nation. As head of the national executive, the president is also the commander in chief of the defense force. The National Assembly elects one of its members to be president during the first sitting of the National Assembly.

The cabinet comprises the president (as its head), the deputy president, and ministers who are appointed by the president from the National Assembly. The president assigns powers and functions to ministers and may dismiss them. The president allocates specific responsibilities known as a portfolio to each minister to supervise. Currently South Africa has the following portfolios:

Agriculture, Forestry, and Fisheries	Human Settlements	Science and Technology
Arts and Culture	Independent Complaints Directorate	Social Development
Basic Education	International Relations and Cooperation	South African Police Service
Civilian Secretariat of Police	Justice and Constitutional Development	South African Police Revenue Service
Communications	Labor	State Security Agency

Cooperative Governance	Military Veterans	Sport and Recreation South Africa
Correctional Services	Mineral Resources	Statistics South Africa
Defense	National Treasury	Tourism
Economic Development	Police	Trade and Industry
Energy	Public Administration Leadership and Management Academy	Traditional Affairs
Environmental Affairs	Public Enterprises	Transport
Government Communication and Information System (GCIS)	Public Service and Administration	Water Affairs
Health	Public Service Commission	Women, Children, and People with Disabilities
Higher Education and Training	Public Works	Presidency
Home Affairs	Rural Development and Land Reform	

Each minister has a ministry that consists of a small team of advisors. The ministry and a department, headed by a director general, assist the minister in developing and implementing policy and laws. Ministers are accountable to the National Assembly for their actions and for those of their departments, and they must act according to government policy. They must also provide parliament with regular and full reports about matters for which they are responsible.

The executive in each province is called the executive council and is headed by the premier. Members of executive councils (MECs) are accountable to their legislatures in the same way as the cabinet is accountable to parliament. The premier is elected by the members of that provincial legislature (MPLs) from among themselves at the first sitting of that legislature after the election. The premier appoints the members of the executive council (MECs) from among the MPLs. MECs are accountable to their premiers. Like ministers, MECs are responsible for departments. These provincial departments deal only with those matters that provinces are allowed to control or those over which they share control with national government.

It is the responsibility of national government to build the administrative capacity of the provinces. If a province is not performing properly, national government can take over a province's responsibilities to maintain established service standards, economic unity, or national security or to prevent a province from acting in ways that harm the interests of another province or the country as a whole. In the same way, provincial governments are allowed to administer the affairs of local government that are not performing properly. Here, too, the National Council of Provinces (NCOP) is responsible for monitoring such an intervention (Section 139 of the constitution).

The Legislative Authority

The term *legislature* refers to a body of elected representatives that makes laws. The prime function of legislatures, therefore, is to formulate, debate, and pass legislation that is needed for the government and the country to function. The legislature also provides a forum in which the public can participate in issues and watch over the executive arm of government.

In South Africa the national legislature is parliament and each of the nine provinces also has a legislature. These 10 legislatures function autonomously and cooperatively within the framework provided by the constitution, particularly Section 3, which outlines the obligations of cooperative government.

Parliament has two houses: the National Assembly and the National Council of Provinces (NCOP). The National Assembly is elected to represent the people and to ensure government by the people under the constitution. It does this by providing a national forum for public consideration of issues, passing legislation, and scrutinizing and overseeing executive action.

Members are elected to the National Assembly through an electoral system based on proportional representation. The constitution makes it clear that the current electoral system can be changed by a new law, provided that the new electoral system results, in general, in proportional representation. This means that candidates are appointed from party lists in proportion to the number of votes the party wins in the elections.

The NCOP ensures that the nine provinces and local government have a direct voice in parliament when laws are debated. The NCOP represents the provinces to ensure that provincial interests are taken into account in the national sphere of government. It does this mainly by participating in the national legislative process and providing a national forum for public consideration of issues affecting the provinces.

The NCOP also has an important role to play in promoting national unity and good working relations between national, provincial, and local governments. While the delegates in the NCOP represent their political parties, they also have the important duty of representing their provinces.

Each province has a legislature, the size of which varies depending on the population levels in the province. According to the constitution the minimum size of a legislature is 30 members and the maximum size is 80 members. Members are elected from provincial lists on the basis of the number of votes received by a political party.

A provincial legislature is responsible for passing the laws for its province as defined in the constitution. These laws are only effective for that particular province. Parliament may intervene and change these laws if they undermine national security, economic unity, national standards, or the interests of another province. Like parliament, provincial legislatures have the responsibility of calling the members of their executive to account for their actions.

Provincial legislatures are bound only by the national constitution and by their own constitution, if they have one. The legislative authority of provinces as vested in provincial legislatures gives them the power to pass a constitution for the province, or amend any constitution passed by it (Sections 142 and 143 of the constitution); to pass legislation for the province with regard to any matters within a functional area listed in Schedules 4 and 5 of the constitution, outside those functional areas that are expressly assigned to the province by national legislation, and for which a provision of the constitution envisages the enactment of provincial legislation; and to assign any of its legislative powers to a municipal council in that province.

The recognition of local government in the constitution as a sphere of government has enhanced the status of local government as a whole and of municipalities in particular, and has given them a new dynamic role as instruments of delivery. The constitution provides for three categories of municipalities. As directed by the constitution, the Local Government: Municipal Structures Act 117 of 1998 contains criteria for determining when an area must have a category A municipality (metropolitan) and when its municipalities fall into category B (district municipalities) or C (local municipalities).

Municipalities are there to provide services to the inhabitants of the area of jurisdiction. Just like any other form of government, they need an organizational structure (apparatus) within which these services can be delivered. Since municipalities are autonomous, the local legislative (municipal council) can decide to a large extent how they want to structure their municipal departments. This means they can decide which departments they want to create to deliver the necessary services.

The Judiciary

Judicial authority is vested in the courts, which are independent and subject to the laws of the constitution. The courts are

- The constitutional court
- The supreme court of appeal
- The high courts
- The magistrates' courts
- Various other courts

The constitutional court is the highest court for constitutional matters. It is located in Johannesburg and presided over by a maximum of 11 judges. The court guarantees the basic rights and freedoms of all persons. Its judgments are binding on all organs of government, including parliament, the presidency, the police service, the army, the public service, and all other courts. It is also the only court that may decide upon disputes between organs of state in the national and provincial spheres. The disputes may concern the constitutional status, power, or functions of any of those organs of state; the constitutionality of any national or provincial bill or act; the constitutionality of any amendment to the constitution; or the possible failure of the parliament or the president to fulfill a constitutional obligation.

The supreme court of appeal is the highest court of appeal except in constitutional matters, and may hear only appeals, issues connected with appeals, and other matters that may be referred to it in circumstances defined by an act of parliament.

When people are not satisfied with the decision of a high court, they may take the matter further to the supreme court of appeal. The supreme court of appeal is located in Bloemfontein. It is presided over by five judges. High courts used to be called supreme courts and are primarily intended for more serious criminal and civil cases. They may hear some constitutional matters—with the exception of those matters that only the constitutional court may decide. Each province has a high court that is usually situated in the capital.

Magistrates' courts are the usual entry point for the majority of people who go to court. There are two kinds of magistrate courts: regional courts and district courts. Regional courts are higher in rank, which means that they hear more serious cases than the district magistrate courts and may impose heavier sentences. magistrates' courts and other courts may decide on any matter determined by an act of parliament, but may not inquire into or decide about the constitutionality of any legislation or any conduct of the president.

There are various other courts that are located at varying levels in the court hierarchy:

- Small claims courts, which consider minor cases
- Electoral court, which deals with electoral issues, for example, when there is a dispute among political parties concerning election results
- Labor court, which deals with issues pertaining to labor relations
- Land claims courts, which deal with matters of land redistribution

Value Chain Integration: The System of Cooperative Government

The public policy objectives of any democratic government should be to tend to the well-being of its population. As stated, service delivery can only be successful if government as an institution is structured in an effective and functional way. The reason for this is that any government consists of numerous and intertwined service delivery components that are present within the various governmental spheres.

These service delivery components include national departments, provincial governments and departments, as well as local authorities and departments. In order to be effective there should therefore be a total and continued cooperative relationship between the various service delivery components in the various government spheres (Venter 2001).

The importance of cooperative governance and intergovernmental relations in South Africa is reflected in Chapter 3 of the constitution, which determines a number of principles. The principles focus on integration—a system of cooperative governance:

- Preserve the national unity and indivisibility of the republic
- Secure the well-being of the people of the republic
- Provide an effective, transparent, accountable, and coherent government for the republic as a whole
- Be loyal to the constitution and the people of the republic
- Respect the constitutional status, institutions, and powers and functions of other spheres of government
- Do not assume any power or functions except those conferred on them in terms of the constitution
- Exercise powers and perform functions in a manner that does not encroach on the geographical, functional, or institutional integrity of government in another sphere
- Cooperate with one another with mutual trust and good faith

To improve integration among all spheres of government in both policy development and implementation, the Intergovernmental Framework Act 13 of 2005 was promulgated. Furthermore, the Department of Cooperative Government and Traditional Affairs advises role-players on how to coordinate and improve development planning, and provides platforms for knowledge sharing. It has developed a supporting intergovernmental planning framework, which provides greater clarity as to the type and role of appropriate planning at each government level.

To conclude, cooperative government facilitates interaction between the various spheres of government, each of which has independent and unique roles to play, as well as the tiers within government, with the view to achieve common goals to the benefit and well-being of society.

Conclusion

The purpose of this chapter was to explore the apparatus that governments, in general, and South Africa, in particular, design to establish a value chain from policy making to service delivery. It was established that based on the principles of rule of law and constitutional supremacy, a constitution can be regarded as the fundamental principles and rules according to which a state is governed. A constitution can be regarded as the architect of the design of government apparatus in such a way that resources are optimally utilized and fairly distributed to society. Only if this process is successfully executed can a government be regarded as good.

Government's apparatus facilitates the development of a policy-making/policy implementation value chain. Various apparatus are available to the South African government, on different spheres and tiers, to facilitate operations within this value chain.

Based on the particular demographical and other profile realities of the state, it became clear that it is critical that South Africa's government apparatus is geared in such a way that both urban and rural settings receive services and goods at affordable rates. Especially provincial and local governments have significant roles to play to bring services such as water, electricity, housing, and health closer to the people.

References

Anderson, J.E. 2000. *Public policymaking*. New York: Houghton Mifflin Company.
Barker, E. 1960. *Social contract*. London: Oxford University Press.
Batley, R., and Larbi, G. 2004. *The changing role of government: The reform of public services in developing countries*. New York: Palgrave, Macmillan.
Baumgartner, F.R., Green-Pedersen, C., and Jones, B.D. 2006. Comparative studies of policy agendas. *Journal of European Public Policy* 13(7): 959–974.
Burton, R.M., Obel, B., and DeSanctis, G. 2011. *Organizational design: A step-by-step approach*. 2nd ed. Cambridge: Cambridge University Press.
Carneiro, R.L., ed. 1967. *The evolution of society: Selections from Herbert Spencer's Principles of Sociology*. Chicago: University of Chicago Press.
Cloete, F., Wissink, H., and De Coning, C. 2000. *Improving public policy*. Pretoria: Van Schaik.
Hanekom, S.X. 1987. *Public policy: Framework and instrument for action*. Braamfontein, Johannesburg: MacMillan South Africa.
Hirst, P. 2000. Democracy and governance. In *Debating governance: Authority, steering and democracy*, (pp. 13–35), ed. P. Jon. Oxford: Oxford University Press.
Hyden, G., and Braton, M., eds. 1993. *Governance and politics in Africa*. Boulder, CO: Lynne Riener.
Jenks, E. 1900. *A history of politics*. New York: Macmillan.
Jones, B.D., and Baumgartner, F.R. 2004. Representation and agenda-setting. *Policy Studies Journal* 32(1): 1–24.
Kaufmann, D., Kraay, A., and Zoido, P. 1999. *Governance matters*. Washington, DC: World Bank.
Kjaer, A.M. 2004. *Governance*. Cambridge: Polity Press.
Osborne, D., and Geabler, T. 1992. *Reinventing government: How the entrepreneurial spirit is transforming the public sector*. New York: Addison-Wesley.
Pylee, M.V. 1997. *India's constitution*. New Delhi: S. Chand & Co.

Sabatier, P., and Mazmanian, D. 2005. The implementation of public policy: A framework of analysis. *Policy Studies Journal* 8(4): 538–560.
South African Institute of Race Relations. 2012. *Employment and incomes*. Annual survey. Pretoria: SAIRR.
South Africa (Republic). *The constitution of the Republic of South Africa Act 108 of 1996*. Pretoria: Government Printer.
Van der Waldt, G. 2004. *Managing performance in the public sector: Concepts, challenges and considerations*. Kenwyn, UK: Juta.
Venter, A., ed. 2001. *Government and politics in the new South Africa*. Pretoria: Van Schaik.

Chapter 2

Public Administration in the Democratic Republic of Congo

Lukamba-Muhiya. Tshombe

Contents

Introduction 28
Background of the Country 28
   History and Political Context of Public Administration in the DRC 30
   Functioning of the Colonial Government in Brussels 31
   Colonial Governance in the Colony 31
      First Reform Measures in 1914 32
      Second Reform Measures in 1924 32
      Third Reform Measures in 1933 32
   Public Administration after Independence 33
      First Phase of Reform: 1960–1965 33
      Second Phase of Reform: 1965–1997 36
   Structure of Congolese Public Administration in 1981 36
   Transitional Period: 1990–2011 40
Conclusion 41
References 42

Introduction

The Democratic Republic of Congo (DRC), previously known as Zaire, is a country located in the center of the African continent. This nation has encountered considerable challenges of a political, administrative, and economic nature since independence. Formerly colonized by Belgium, the Congolese people were not well prepared to manage the affairs of government when they attained their independence on June 30, 1960. This was largely because of the poor preparation provided by the Belgian colonizers and a dearth of experience in working toward democracy. One of the main problems was a marked lack of the necessary skills to run the civil service efficiently (Vengroff 1983). Since the establishment of the postindependence public service in the DRC, the bureaucracy has become an agency of intimidation and petty repression, which has translated into great hardship at the hands of the ruling elite for the overwhelming majority of the Congolese. It is clear that after more than 50 years of independence, the public administration in the DRC is in dire need of transformation.

The DRC government needs to completely overhaul the administration so that all public servants and officials at every level become more effective. The Congolese people across the board are complaining bitterly about inadequate service delivery. Strong political and economic vision is required if this dire situation is to improve. Currently, the Congolese government is trying to stabilize the economy after 32 years of dictatorship under the late president, Joseph-Desire Mobutu. From 1965, when Mobutu took power in a *coup d'état* (a position he held until 1997), the Congolese public service completely collapsed and civil servants did not even receive a regular salary at the end of each month. Many of them were obliged to find a second job in order to sustain their families. Today, a full 51 years after independence, these problems still remain and many public servants are still not receiving a regular monthly pay packet. There is a crying need for the current government to rethink the transformation of the public administration to ensure that it becomes an instrument of development in the DRC.

Background of the Country

The structure of the DRC originally comprised 11 provinces in a fairly uniform administrative hierarchical arrangement. These provinces formed the basic organization of local government. Of the 11, Kinshasa was both a province and also the capital. The other provinces were Katanga, Bas-Congo, Bandundu, Equateur, Oriental Province, Nord-Kivu, Sud-Kivu, Maniema, Kasai-Oriental, and Kasai-Occidental. However, in terms of Article 2 of the DRC constitution of 2006, it is stipulated that the Democratic Republic of Congo shall comprise 26 provinces: Kinshasa, Bas-Uele, Equateur, Haut-Lomami, Haut-Katanga, Haut-Uele, Uturi, Kasai, Kasai-Oriental, Kongo-Central, Kwango, Kwilu, Lomami, Lualaba, Lulua,

Mai-Ndombe, Maniema, Mongala, Nord-Kivu, Nord-Ubangi, Sankuru, Sud-Kivu, Sud-Ubangi, Tanganyika, Tshopo, and Tshuapa (DRC 2006).

To understand this demarcation, it should be explained that a number of existing provinces were divided into four. This was the case in Katanga, Kasai-Occidental, Bandundu, and Oriental Province. The implementation of the new 2006 demarcation will take time because most of the new provinces lack adequate infrastructure. The government will have to improve this situation by building new roads, establishing services, etc., so that these provinces can become fully operational (Tshombe, Uken, and Ferreira 2008).

The DRC has a surface area of 2,344,845 square kilometers (905,365 square miles) and shares its boundaries with nine other countries. In the north it borders on the Central African Republic and Sudan, while to the east are Uganda, Rwanda, Burundi, and Tanzania. On its western boundary the DRC's neighbor is the Republic of Congo, and to the south lie Zambia and Angola (Central Intelligence Agency 2006). After Sudan, the DRC is Africa's second largest country in sub-Saharan Africa. Despite its vast area, it has a considerable natural advantage, with no undue geographical hazards. It lies across the equator and enjoys an equatorial climate with average temperatures ranging from 26°C in the coastal and basin area to as low as 18°C in the rainy season. In the northern areas (Uele) and Katanga in the south, the winter season is dry (Gourou 2004).

The population comprises 250 ethnic groups within separate internal boundaries. A similar situation is found in other African countries, such as the Bakongo people in Angola, and the Zande who reside in both the DRC and the Sudan. Other examples include the Chokwe, who live in three different countries: the DRC, Angola, and Zambia; and the Alure people, who are found in the DRC as well as in Uganda. The majority of the people in DRC speak Bantu-based languages. Those in the northwest speak Kiswahili, Kilokele, and Sudan languages. Kiswahili is a language group spoken in five different provinces, but others elsewhere are also able to communicate in these languages (Gourou 2004).

The majority of public officials speak a variety of languages because the government frequently moves them from one province to another. In general, the Congolese people are multilingual, because of the existing intermediary languages such as Kikongo, Lingala, Tshiluba, and Kiswahili. As with most previously colonized countries, the influence of the colonizer, in this case Belgian rule, has meant that French has been retained as the official language.

Approximately 80% of the population lives in the rural areas of the DRC. The population density in urban areas was 21.7% per kilometer in the year 2000, and is evenly distributed. The population density in the great forest is only approximately half the national average, which numbers tens of thousands. According to the DRC government, the capital city, Kinshasa, has an estimated population of 10 million, while Lubumbashi has approximately 2 million inhabitants. Other urban areas have, respectively, Mbuji-Mayi (2,500,000), Kananga (1,400,000), Kisangani (1,200,000), and Mbandaka (850,000) (DRC 2008). According to the

DRC electoral commissioner the bulk of the population lives in the eastern part of the DRC. There is also a need for the DRC government to undertake an accurate census countrywide in order to ascertain the exact population in each province (CENI 2008).

History and Political Context of Public Administration in the DRC

The implementation of public administration in the DRC began with the arrival of the European (Belgian) colonizers. There is evidence that as early as the fifteenth century, long before the arrival of the Europeans, the so-called Kingdom of Kongo was well governed, although the European type of public administration was unheard of. However, after the Berlin Conference of February 26, 1885, Belgium established the L'Etat Independent du Congo (EIC), which ruled the Congo from 1885 to 1908. This period saw the establishment of public administration in the country. As soon the EIC was formed, the Belgian government set up a two-tier structure of governance comprising a central government (with its headquarters in Brussels) and a local government with its headquarters in Vivi (Boma), now in the Bas-Congo Province (Ndaywel and Nzieme 1997).

Historians claim that public administration in the DRC began in 1888 when the central government based in Belgium reorganized the management of the colony. This was inaugurated by royal decree on August 1, 1888. In terms of this decree, the colony was divided into 11 districts (Ndaywel and Nzieme 1997). Each district was managed by an administrator who had one or two deputies to assist him in the daily running of the district. All the administrative institutions were operated primarily for the benefit of King Leopold II of Belgium. During that period the administrative entities worked with private companies such as the Anglo-Belgian Indian Rubber Company, for the exploitation of rubber.

The EIC occupied the entire territory that is now the DRC and took every opportunity to profit from the Congolese natural resources, such as ivory, rubber, and minerals, all of which were exported to Belgium. Moreover, the government was guilty of large-scale human rights abuses, including forcing the local people to work on the rubber plantations; if they refused to comply, their hands were amputated. Atrocities such as this brought widespread criticism of the colonial attitude in the EIC. Indeed, many scholars believe that Belgian rule in the Congo can be labeled as genocide of the Congolese.

International pressure from Britain, the United States, and other countries put an end to King Leopold II's private regime in 1908. The reins of power were transferred to the Belgian government on November 15, 1908, and this brought an end to the royal family's management of the DRC as a private entity (Léon de Saint Moulin 1992). When control of the EIC passed to the Belgian government, the administrative system immediately changed. The new government chose to implement a direct administrative system in the colony, but this was centralized in Brussels. According to Delvaux (1945) that system suited the new government perfectly in its continued exploitation of the colony. The colonial charter (which left a great deal of room for maneuverability) remained the only administrative document the Belgian government used in its governance of the Belgian Congo.

Functioning of the Colonial Government in Brussels

As indicated above, Act 7 of the colonial charter gave King Leopold II legislative power by decree once the measure was proposed by the relevant minister in Brussels. The king also had executive power, which was recognized by Act 8 of the charter. But as stipulated in Act 9, the decision of the king could only be implemented if it was countersigned by a minister. This meant, in effect, that all the decisions the king took in the Belgian Congo had to be countersigned by the minister in Brussels. However, although executive power was the prerogative of King Leopold II, there was an official in the colony (the governor general) who had administrative authority. He played a liaison role between Brussels and the colony and took charge of the general administration in the colony. He planned and took legislative decisions, handled the budget, managed public debts, and all such matters (Delvaux 1945).

Colonial Governance in the Colony

The highest rank in the Belgian Congo in terms of public administration was the governor general, who was appointed by King Leopold II and was his representative in the colony. He was assisted by many deputy governor generals in accordance with Act 21 of the colonial charter. The governor general had limited executive power in the colony, which was specified by the king's decree (Vunduawe 1982).

Within the colony he was the highest authority in the entire public administration, including the military services. The following administrative functions were undertaken in the Belgian Congo.

- The secretary general was in charge of coordination and centralization of administrative affairs.
- The provincial government was headed by a provincial commissioner who represented the governor general.
- Different services within the colony were coordinated by a provincial secretary, including agriculture and forestry, finance, customer services, economic affairs, public works, land affairs, and hygiene.

Most of these administrative services were provided in the various districts where the Belgians worked, and these services were primarily for the benefit of the white minority (the Europeans) rather than for the indigenous (Congolese) people. Indeed, the level of services available for the Congolese was extremely limited.

Until 1933, the colonial government introduced some administrative reform, but in most cases, if this benefited the Congolese, it was specifically adapted to the local culture and usually took the form of finding a traditional chief who was prepared to be a collaborator with the colonial government. In other words, the traditional chief was seen as a local official working hand in glove with the colonial government and implementation tended to be both centralized and authoritarian. In the colonial period, three stages of administrative reform took place. These are discussed below.

First Reform Measures in 1914

One of the first priorities for the colonial government was to implement an administrative demarcation of the country. At the time, the colony was divided into 22 districts with the capital based in Boma. These 22 districts and their capital towns were as follows, respectively: Aruwimi (Basoko), Bangala (Lisala), Bas-Congo (Boma), Bas-Uele (Buta), Equateur (Coquilhatville), Haut-Luapula (Kambove), Haut-Uele (Bambili), Ituri (no capital), Kasai (Luebo), Kivu (no capital), Kwango (Bandundu), Lac Leopold II (Inongo), Lomami (Kabinda), Lowa (no capital), Lulonga (Basankusu), Lulua (Kafukumbu), Maniema (no capital), Moyen-Congo (Leopoldville), Sankuru (Lusambo), Stanleyville (Stanleyville), Tanganyika-Moero (Kongolo), and Oubangui (Libenge).

Second Reform Measures in 1924

The second administrative reform measures were introduced in 1924, when the colonial government decided to transform the 22 districts into 4 provinces: Congo-Kasai, Equateur, Katanga, and Oriental Province. These four provinces were divided into districts and local municipalities. Administratively, as explained above, the country was managed by a governor general with a deputy governor general. In addition, in each province there was a deputy governor general who acted on behalf of the governor general and reported to him in the capital, keeping him abreast of administrative matters in the particular province (Kadima 2009).

Third Reform Measures in 1933

The third phase of reform was the most wide-reaching transformation undertaken by the colonial government. The demarcation of the province changed from four to six provinces. The names of the new provinces were Katanga, Equateur, Kasai, Oriental Province, Kivu, and Leopoldville. Each was managed by a provincial commissioner. In addition, in 1951 the provincial commissioner's job title changed;

he became the governor of the province. In terms of administrative reform, other measures were taken in 1957 and again in 1959.

Public Administration after Independence

One of the critical markers in the history of public administration in the DRC is that colonial rulers did not prepare the Congolese adequately to run the public service; they had not been trained to manage public affairs effectively. From the declaration of independence on June 30, 1960, they simply had to assume control. From that day forward, countless problems arose in terms of service delivery.

Most of the senior positions had been held previously by Belgians who soon fled the country because of the turmoil of the civil war. When this internal unrest finally ground to a halt in 1964, the DRC's public administration was barely functional.

The new government decided to adopt the same administrative structure it had inherited from the Belgian colonizers. This structure was reasonably sound, but the local people nevertheless struggled to maintain an adequate level of service delivery.

Looking back over the past 52 years since independence, there have been two phases of public administrative reform. Let us now examine these reforms and discuss what changes they brought to the country.

First Phase of Reform: 1960–1965

Under the first republic, the DRC adopted a political structure as laid down in the *Loi fondamentale* (fundamental law). The constitution adopted by the first republic was the Luluabourg constitution of August 1, 1964. Many of the clauses in that early constitution are still in use today.

The prime minister was elected to parliament and was appointed by the president of the republic. The first prime minister after independence was Patrice Emery Lumumba, who is now regarded as one of the country's national heroes. The president of the DRC at the time was Joseph Kasa Vubu, who rose to political leadership of the Bakongo people of the lower Congo, near Leopoldville.

Lumumba had emerged as a leader in Stanleyville and had high hopes that the DRC's newfound independence would be economically and politically viable, but his rule did not find favor with some of the Western countries because he approached the Soviet Union for assistance to improve the struggling economy. But within a few months of attaining its independence the country was riven by tribal quarrels and separatism. In July 1960 the province of Katanga (which was rich in minerals) in the south, broke away from Lumumba's government, led by Moise Tshombe.

The period from 1960 to 1964 is regarded as one of the most unstable in the DRC, both politically and administratively. Many civil wars between various factions raged across the provinces and the former prime minister, Moise Tshombe (elected in an earlier election and then ousted by his rivals), hired mercenaries from abroad to fight his adversaries. The Congolese army, led by General Joseph-Desire Mobutu, was also involved in the faction fighting.

Eventually, Tshombe won the civil war and peace returned to the country. Politically speaking, he became more popular than President Kasa Vubu, but this was unacceptable in the political forum in the capital. Kasa Vubu decided to replace Tshombe with one of his closest friends, Evarist Kimba, but that political honeymoon did not last long. In 1965, Mobutu staged a military coup and the first republic came to an end.

Mobutu's dictatorship began on a vicious note. He alleged that Evarist Kimba and several other military officials were implicated in a plot to seize control. Kimba, together with three cabinet ministers, Jerome Anany (the minister of defense), Emmanuel Bamba (the minister of finance), and Alexandre Mahamba (the minister of mines and energy), were tried in May 1966 and sent to the gallows on May 30. They were publicly hanged before an audience of 50,000 spectators (Young and Turner 1985).

After seizing control Mobutu immediately proclaimed a state of emergency. He remained in power until May 1997. Under the Mobutu regime there was what could be called a dictatorship bureaucracy, characterized by a single authoritative figure at the head of a bureaucratic governmental structure. This bureaucracy was manned by a diverse social group that had emerged since independence. As William (1972, p. 130) puts it:

> Since Mobutu took over power in 1965, his administration has been marked by several bureaucratic elements. These are the pursuit of an a political economic rationality, an emphasis on expertise in governmental function, centralization of power, an attempt to minimize uncertainty caused by tribal or personal loyalties, and an emphasis on secrecy.

The public service in Zaire had its own image, very different from other types of bureaucracies in modern states; it was managed by an authoritarian political system. The military regime changed the administrative culture and gave the Congolese bureaucracy a specific character. President Mobutu himself held a heavy concentration of power. He appointed senior military officers in most of the government positions and also in the provinces. Those who did not respond efficiently were rapidly removed. William (1972, p. 140) explains:

> The secrecy surrounding public affairs in Zaire was justified by a complex and elitist conception of political authority. The most significant official document in this respect is an essay entitled "From Legality to Legitimacy," published by the Zairian information minister and by Mobutu himself.

In this essay it was pointed out that all decision processes should involve two judgments—one should be value oriented and the other technical.

The bureaucratic system under Mobutu was based on the centralization of power. This is illustrated by the political and administrative reorganization that led to the reduction of the number of provinces from 21 to 11. The restructuring of the provinces in Mobutu's regime attempted to assume control of all the provinces. Another of the administrative changes made during that period was that most of the provinces were elevated to federal states.

When Mobutu seized power, he was not particularly concerned about provincial administration. Under the previous regime, the provinces were seen as the geographical basis for national unity (Lukamba 1999). In most of the key positions in the provinces, the president appointed military officers in the position of governor of the province. At the local level too, the central government reduced the power of local authorities and gave them less autonomy in decision making.

In addition, Mobutu implemented a system whereby the president held the ultimate authority over provincial and local administration. Before making a decision on how to proceed, the local authorities and provinces had to contact the central authority in the capital (Kinshasa). Thus all major decisions were made in the capital. The bureaucratic system under the Mobutu regime was an absolutist administrative system, and there was centralization of power along the lines of the colonial state. In other words, the political regime at the time was an authoritarian system.

The reforms in the civil service at this time were declared by government ordinance law 67/177 in 1974, and brought two major changes. They created a unitary, centralized state along the lines of the colonial structure, and reestablished the principle of unity of command in the administrative hierarchy. Most of the provinces lost their autonomy and became administrative units of the state. Furthermore, the provincial governments were abolished, and the premier and the deputy premier of the province became state officials appointed by the president of the republic.

The implementation of this system consolidated the power and effectiveness of the central government. This policy also applied in the military during the Mobutu regime. Every senior official for each department in the administrative hierarchy had limited authority over all civil servants working under his supervision.

A government report (DRC 1974) states:

> This important principle was reinforced in a circular from the ministry of interior in August 1974. Confronted with the refusal of certain state agents to comply with the orders of their superior, the council has decided that, except for the chief of state who alone directs the country and before whom everyone is responsible, the regional commissions who are his representatives must henceforth control the activities of the party, the army, the police and entire administration. Sub-regional and zone commissioners enjoy the same prerogatives as the regional commissioners in their respective sectors of activity.

The control of the administrative authority by the central government was laid down in the constitution of 1967. This progressively narrowed the authority of the provinces (Young and Turner 1985).

Second Phase of Reform: 1965–1997

Politically speaking, during this period the government of the second republic was still under the iron control of a military man, General Mobutu, with very few civilian officials. The government decided to once again reduce the number of provinces from 21 to 8: Katanga, Equateur, Kasai-Oriental, Kasai-Occidental, Congo-Central, Province-Oriental, Kivu, and Kinshasa. Furthermore, in 1971, the president decided to change the name of the country, calling it Zaire. Other provinces also had a name change, such as Katanga (which became Shaba); Central-Province was changed to Bas-Zaire and Oriental-Province became Haut-Zaire.

Shortly after the demarcation of provinces, the government decided in 1973 to standardize the administrative structure across the provinces, and it implemented law 015/05/01/1973 to centralize the administration in Kinshasa. Henceforth, any appointment of administrative officials had to be made in Kinshasa. At the same time, the provinces became known as regions, districts were renamed sous-regions, a territory was called a rural zone, and a municipality was now called an urban zone.

It is widely accepted that the impact of this centralization of decision making in the capital was the origin of public service failure in the DRC. The administrative officials could no longer make a quick decision without referring the problem to the capital.

Currently, this system still applies in the DRC public service. The existing constitution highlights the decentralization of public administration, but the authorities in the central government still have great difficulty implementing that policy. Most decisions must first be discussed and resolutions taken in the capital. There is no improvement in terms of devolution of power to the provinces.

Furthermore, the administrative structure during the second republic (the Mobutu regime) used virtually the same system as the colonial government; there was very little difference between the two. In summary, reform in the Zairian public service moved to establish theoretical absolutism.

Structure of Congolese Public Administration in 1981

The structure of the Congolese public administration is enacted in two pieces of legislation:

1. Act 81-003/17/07/1981 established the status of a civil servant within the public service and was published in the *State Journal.*

2. Act 82-006/25/02/1982 proclaimed the demarcation of the territory and the political structure and administration of the country (DRC 1981).

Act 81-003/17/07/1981 ensured the centralization of the public service across the country, while Act 82-006/25/02/1982 focused on the implementation of the decentralization and administrative structure at the local level. Local administration now has independent jurisdiction and independent status in terms of management.

The centralization of public administration and the decentralization of local authorities across the country present a complex problem in the DRC. This structure has a negative impact on the organization of public administration. To make decentralization effective, the DRC government should delegate some power to local authorities. According to Rondinelline (1981):

> Decentralization will be understood as the devolution by central [national] government of specific functions, with all the administrative, political and economic attributes that these entail, to local [municipal] governments which are independent of the center and sovereign within a legally delimited geographic and functional domain.

The pros and cons of decentralization in the DRC are a matter of debate. In terms of political and administrative control the central government wants to continue making the final decisions on all matters of governance.

According to the World Bank and European Union (2008) the implementation of decentralization in the country would essentially be a political process and would bring an element of broader peace and stability. It would also be a reflection of the reconciliation process that has taken place in the last five years. In this perspective decentralization is part of the process of seeking a new equilibrium and national consensus that provides a wider acceptance of sharing resources while maintaining the national integrity of the country. This sets the procedure apart from the donor-driven decentralization process that has often been seen in other African states. It also requires from the international community a different, less technical, and more politically conscious approach.

The period of employment in the DRC public service is 30 years; however, when the age of 55 years is reached, retirement is compulsory. Nevertheless, many civil servants in the DRC are still working, although they are 60 years old. One of the main reasons is that the government does not have money to pay the elderly employees their retirement packages.

Table 2.1 reflects the hierarchal structure of the public service in a DRC government department. The secretaire general (director general) is based in the Ministry of Public Service in the capital. Other senior directors below the secretaire general are also based there. Employees who work in middle management (the second level) are based in the ministerial departments. This also applies to the third level, which covers the clerical posts.

Table 2.1 Structure of Public Service in a Government Department in the DRC

First-level leadership (senior officials)	1. Secrétaires general (director general)
	2. Directeur (director)
	3. Chef de division (division head)
	4. Chef de bureau (head of office/section)
Second-level leadership (middle management)	5. Attaché de bureau de première classe (office staff: first class)
	6. Attache de bureau de deuxième classe (office staff: second class)
	7. Attache de bureau troisième classe (office staff: third class)
Third-level management (including clerical posts)	8. Agent de bureau de premiere classe (office employee: first class)
	9. Agent de bureau de deuxieme classe (office employee: second class)
	10. Agent auxiliaire de deuxième classe (auxiliary employee: second class)
	11. Huissier (messenger)

Source: Act 82/006 du 25/02/1982.

The secretary general (DG) and the directors are senior public servants in the DRC. Officials who provide administrative services at the provincial level are called *les administrateurs de territoires et les bourgmestres*. The structure of the Ministry of Public Service in the DRC is similar to that of other ministries.

In terms of recruitment in the DRC, public servants are required to pass a written examination. In some cases, appointments are made subject to being in possession of the required qualifications. However, in many instances, there is nepotism and corruption when the recruitment and selection of new civil servants is made.

As far as gender selection in the DRC public service is concerned, this remains a highly contentious issue. In the past years, the number of females employed in the lowest level of civil service was estimated at a mere 10% of all officials. In addition, the DRC law stipulates that a married woman has to produce evidence that she has the permission of her husband before accepting such employment (Shikha and Lukamba 2011). It remains a serious challenge today for the DRC government to recruit an acceptable number of young Congolese women to work in the public service. For example, the number of women who are employed in the DRC courts of law is very low indeed.

Moreover, in 1982 the government introduced another structural reform in the public service. This was primarily a change in the territorial decentralization of responsibility and was a move to give regional and local entities a more meaningful role. The central government realized that to centralize all power in the capital was counterproductive and not conducive to efficiency in the public service.

One of the major problems faced in the Mobutu regime, which was highly centralized, was to try to eradicate tribalism in the civil service.

This argument was supported by Ballandier (1980), who pointed out that the centralization of recruitment, promotion, and transfers had limited the autonomy of regional authorities, which tended to exacerbate tribal rivalries. The DRC government did have a system in place to transfer public servants from one province to another.

This system of relocating public servants still applies today in the DRC public sector. The central government in Kinshasa controls the appointment and transfer of public servants countrywide, as is seen, for example, in the case of magistrates, medical doctors, etc. In the DRC a civil servant cannot apply for a position in another province unless this is approved by the central authority in Kinshasa. This is different from the situation in other countries where public officials are free to resign and apply for a more senior position in another province. The public service in the DRC is a centralized system based on a unitary model and is controlled in the capital Kinshasa.

Moreover, the system of transferring public servants from one province to another does have a negative impact on service delivery. The central government is aware of these problems but has done nothing to change this practice. It argues that public servants should have enough time to become known in the area and grow accustomed to its people, their problems, its economy, etc. A government report (DRC 1974) stated: "It is clear that frequent transfer of regional [provincial] agents and others had severe consequences both for the territorial service and the agents themselves and their families."

This situation developed because of the government's desire to wield more control over administrative organization in the central government and the provinces, and to prevent patron-client linkages between central government officials and civil servants in the provinces. The government argues that this has a negative impact on the effectiveness of the public service in the country. There are also other issues of concern, such as general problems of provincial administration, especially staff control.

Virtually all the power was centralized in Kinshasa, and decisions have to be reached there. In his state of the nation address in 1978, Mobutu underlined the fact that government decisions were "made here in the political bureau and the executive council." He delivered this address before he depoliticized the public service. According to *Journal Elima* (1986), "issues discussed included improving the operation of the administration, controlling the urban influx, the vast housing and squatter problems, managing health, water, and electricity which could lead to explosion of subversive protests." Civil servants in the DRC worked under extremely difficult conditions. The majority of them were poorly trained, and it was a difficult task for government to improve the quality of services rendered to the community. In addition, the central government was far more concerned about their own interests than those of the ordinary people.

The lack of motivation among Congolese public servants led to high levels of corruption in the DRC public administration. Furthermore, civil servants were so poorly paid that they could barely stretch their pay to the end of each month, and this was also a factor in the rising rate of corruption and the reality that in DRC society virtually everyone was corrupt and corrupting (Kabongo 1977). This can in some measure be attributed to the dictatorial leadership of President Mobutu. The Zairian (Congolese) public service certainly had its own image—very different from other bureaucracies in the modern world. The powers of the state were in the hands of one person—the president. He appointed and dismissed senior servants in government as he wished.

The public service under the Mobutu administration was also expected to disseminate political propaganda. The president insisted that the Zairian (Congolese) public be subjected to political indoctrination designed to curb politicization of the masses. This made it very difficult for the civil service to contribute constructively to the development of the DRC.

Transitional Period: 1990–2011

This period is one in which political transformation took place in the DRC government. The regime in place in 1990 wanted the country to transform into a democracy. This promised to be difficult to achieve because of the political selfishness of those in power at the time. During this particular period the DRC engaged in political negotiations to form a different type of government, but no solution could be reached until the beginning of the civil war in 1996.

The administration was operating in terms of the same legislation, for instance, No. 006 of February 25, 1982, as described above, which proscribed the organization of public administration and local authorities across the country. This particular law was also applied by the rebel national movement, the Alliance des Forces Democratiques pour la liberation du Congo (AFDL), when they took power on May 17, 1997.

In July 1998, the late president Laurent Kabila introduced a reform that changed the name of the regions to provinces; the sous-regions became districts; the urban zones became known as municipalities; and rural zones were henceforth called territories.

Administratively speaking, nothing was changed with the introduction of the new government that was put in place after the collapse of Mobutu's autocratic regime. Nor had the fate of public servants improved; they were still not paid a regular salary at the end of each month.

The civil war played a destabilizing role, and the new government was hard-pressed to resolve the political crisis in the country. Political negotiations took place in the southern African region (Zambia, Botswana, and South Africa) in an effort to solve the political crisis in the DRC. When a country is destabilized it takes time for the government to make the necessary adjustments to the existing system. In addition, the political stability (or lack thereof) plays a significant role in the stability of the public service within the country in question. Public administration can only be truly effective when there is political, economic, and social stability. With these three elements unstable, it was very difficult for the DRC public administration to function effectively.

Once the civil war was over, a democratic dispensation was established in 2006. The DRC government asked the South African government, the United Nations Development Program, the World Bank, and the European Union to assist in the process of transforming the Congolese public administration. The first necessity was to remove the large number of "ghost workers" from the list of civil servants, because this malicious practice was still rife among senior officials in the ministry.

Many training programs and other forms of assistance were provided by international organizations, but public administration in the DRC still remains ineffective across the country. The decentralization of public service is still not in place, and politicians are struggling to implement this legislation. The government is still lagging behind in the introduction of reforms that will improve the level of public administration.

The main problem facing the DRC government in this endeavor is that international donors and financial institutions have made extensive recommendations. The main aims are to improve the quality of the public administration, the payroll management, and the capacity of the public sector to render an efficient service to the public (International Monetary Fund 2005).

Conclusion

It is the prerogative of the current DRC government to change the image of the public administration and to make it more accountable to the public. There is a real need for the government to introduce new incentives so that public servants will be motivated to work efficiently. Currently, the DRC public service remains corrupt and ineffective.

The public servants who represent the state have to provide essential services because these services are vital for the well-being of the local, regional, and national communities. The public servants have an obligation and a responsibility to both the government of the day and the community at large.

The DRC government still has a high level of centralization of power. For it to become more efficient, it should devolve some of this power and responsibility to the provincial and local levels of government to avoid corruption and conflict of interest. Thereafter, the Congolese government should begin to reorganize its administrative system. In addition, the central government should decentralize some of the functions in the provincial and local government levels. This will improve the situation at the local level, especially in the rural areas, where there is a dire need for upgrading of service provision. At present, decentralization is written into the constitution but remains very difficult for the government to implement.

This study recommends that efficiency in the DRC government should constitute a major challenge for government in order to institutionalize meaningful change. Efficiency is an ideal in the public administration; each civil servant needs to improve his or her level of commitment to duty. This should also apply to the delivery of services. In simple terms, efficiency is doing a great deal at a minimum cost. It is further recognized that as a way of improving on the efficiency of the civil service, government emphasis should be on the training of its personnel. Another crucial point that will bring change in the DRC public service will be the institutionalization of a code of conduct. This will inspire in the public servants an ethos of professionalism and a commitment to the concept of serving the people of the DRC.

References

Ballandier, G. 1980. *La situation colonial. Approche théorique: Cahier international du sociology*, vol. 11. Les Presse Universitaie de France, Bruxelles.
Central Intelligence Agency (CIA). 2006. *Democratic Republic of the Congo: The world fact book*. Washington, DC.
Delvaux, R. 1945. *L'organisation administrative du Congo Belge*. Anvers, Edition Zaïre. Kinshasa.
Democratic Republic of Congo (DRC). 2006. *Constitution de la République Démocratique du Congo*. Kinshasa, Gombe.
DRC. 1974. *Government report on public service*. Kinshasa, Gombe: Ministry of Public Service.
DRC. 1981. *Journal official de la République du Zaïre*. No. 15. Kinshasa, Gombe.
DRC. 2008. *La population dans différent provinces*. Kinshasa, Gombe: Minister de l'intérieure.
Gourou, P. 2004. The Democratic Republic of the Congo: Physical and social geography. In *Africa south of the Sahara*. 33rd ed. London: Europa.
Independent National Electoral Commission (CENI). 2008. DRC presidential and parliamentarian election 2006. CENI, Kinshasa.
International Monetary Fund. 2005. *Democratic Republic of the Congo: Selected issues and statistical appendix*. IMF Country Report 05/573. Washington, DC.
Journal Elima. 1986. Le problème de fonctionnaire de l'état.
Kabongo, I. 1977. *Interdisciplinarité et politique: pour une science politique Africaine du temps present*, p. 4. Discussion paper, CIEDOP 1. Université de Kinshasa.

Kadima, C.M. 2009. *Incidences du decoupage territorial sur l'organisation administrative de la RDC: Cas des services exterieurs au Kasai Oriental*. Mémoire de fin d'etude. Mbuji-Mayi: Universite de Mbuji-Mayi.

Léon de Saint Moulin, S.J. 1992. L'histoire de l'organisation administrative du Zaire. Extrait de la Revue—*Zaire-Afrique*, 224, Avril, 197–222.

Lukamba, M.-T., 1999. The Mobutu era (1965–1997): An examination of the public service in the DRC. Honors dissertation, Department of Political Studies, University of Cape Town, Cape Town.

Lukamba, M.-T., Uken, U., and Ferreira, I.W. 2008. Mechanisms to prevent corruption and to promote good governance in the DRC. *Journal of Business and Management Dynamics* 1: 111–121.

Ndaywel, E., and Nzieme, I. 1997. *Histoire du Zaire, de l'heritage ancient a l'age contemporain*. Brussels: Duculot.

Rondinelline, D.A. 1981. Government decentralization in comparative perspective: Developing countries. *International Review of Administrative Science* 47(2).

Shikha, V.D., and Lukamba, T.M. 2011. The status and political participation of women in the DRC (1960–2010). New Contree. *Journal of Historical and Human Sciences for Southern Africa* 62.

Vengroff, R. 1983. *Development administration at local level: The case of Zaire*. Syracuse, NY: Maxwell School of Citizenship and Public Affairs, Syracuse University.

Vunduawe, T.P. 1982. La decentralisation des responsabilites au Zaire, Pourquio et comment ? L'administration locale du Zaire 1885 a 1982. *Journal Zaire-Afrique*, Aout, 165–261.

Young, C., and Turner, T. 1985. *The rise and decline of the Zairian state*. Madison: University of Wisconsin Press.

William, J.C. 1972. *Patrimonialism and political change in the Congo*. Stanford, CA: Stanford University Press.

World Bank and European Union. 2008. *Decentralization in the Democratic Republic of Congo: Opportunities and risks*. Washington, DC.

Chapter 3

Public Administration and Corruption in Uganda

Benon C. Basheka

Contents

Introduction 45
Context of Uganda's Administrative Systems 54
Concept of Corruption in Public Administration 59
Determinants of Corruption in Public Administrative Systems 60
Forms of Corruption in Uganda's Public Administration 68
Effects of Corruption in Uganda 75
Conclusion 77
References 78

Introduction

This chapter discusses public administration and corruption in Uganda, two subjects that I must admit are too broad to be easily given comprehensive coverage in the few pages of a book chapter. The two subjects strangely owe their origins to ancient traditions and philosophies and have historically walked side by side, nourishing each other. The latter has often turned out to be a hostile marriage partner seriously undermining the former's capacity to efficiently manage public affairs. Corruption continues to poison any effort to provide members of society with better public services. The marriage between public administration and corruption seems to be paradoxically a forced one at best and one of convenience at worst. In a speech, then-U.S. trade representative Mickey Kantor (1996) noted that "corruption has existed as long as there have been people in power and money to influence them." Though it is unlikely that the world will ever be corruption-free, he said, we have "a legal, moral, economic and political responsibility to pursue this problem in every possible forum and with every tool at our disposal." Africa was never known to be historically corrupt as it is today. In the precolonial period, rather than use of bribes, people made offerings to their gods, elders, and leaders in the hope of receiving favors. Such reciprocities, in a sense, provided the social glue that allowed cultures and civilizations to develop. With the advent of colonial rule, the new religious and civil institutions started to demand rules of fairness and good governance to ensure the loyalty and trust of the populace. This demonstrated that the rule of law was above the influence of greasy palms,* hence the distinction between gifts and bribes (Martin 2005).

While this chapter addresses the corruption malaise in Uganda's public administration, corruption is a universal problem that is noticeable in every society. Insights from Uganda's case study can apply in other African administrative systems. Certainly, some administrative systems are more prone to corruption than others. In public administration, corruption manifests itself at individual, group, or entire system levels, or even as a combination of the three. Whatever its form, the greatest charge against corruption remains its ability to benefit few individuals at the expense of the majority of citizens. Corruption is cancerous and the malaise, once allowed to thrive, becomes a society-wide problem. Once prevalent, it has the potential to negatively impact every member of the society whether that member engages in it or not. It touches every sector, and more dangerously so if it becomes a "combined theatre of games" by political and administrative staff who run society's organization. Corruption can affect the young and the old, the educated and the uneducated. It can affect those in the public, private, or nongovernmental organization (NGO) sectors. It can affect the present generation but also those yet to be born. It can affect both the rich and the poor, although its effects on the poor are much more devastating. Such is the complex and notorious nature of corruption that continues to affect humanity, and if one was to make an honest wish, corruption ought to be condemned to death.

Uganda, just like any other developing country, did not invent corruption, irrationality, or incompetence in its administrative systems. Yet the country continues to pay heavy costs in the short run and will continue to do so in the long term due to corruption. The abuse of public office for private gain is as old as the history of government. Thus, in 350 B.C., Aristotle suggested in *The Politics* that "to protect the treasury from being defrauded, let all money be issued openly in front of the whole city, and let copies of the accounts be deposited in various wards" (Thai

---

* A popular term that means "corruption."

2005). While attempting explanations on increased trends of corruption on the African continent, Collier (2000) supplies us with four routes why Africa slides into corruption: (1) overregulation of private activity, (2) expanded public sector employment, (3) expanded public procurement, and (4) weakened scrutiny. To further put this debate in perspective, Aristotle observed that "it is by no means easy for one man to superintend many things; and that he will have to appoint a number of subordinates," an observation that suggests one of the basic reasons why administration has always been a central concern in the social life of any period (Dimock, Dimock, and Koerug 1953).

Shafritz, Rusell, and Borick (2011) help us to understand that public administrators tend to the public's business like building bridges and highways, collecting garbage, putting out fires, plowing snow, spraying for mosquitoes, and providing essential social services for the less fortunate. Harris (2005) contends that civil servants, most of whom are corrupt and incompetent, administer government policies and programs. There is a general acknowledgment that many public servants take bribes, inflate contract prices, receive kickbacks, and the like, a claim that cuts across many African countries—Uganda inclusive. A public official's act of wrongdoing is destructive of the claim that in a democracy all individuals are equal (Shafritz, Rusell, and Borick 2011). Systemic, grand corruption, and more recently, silent corruption create misery to the citizenry. Corruption has very unpleasant, deadly, and debilitating effects on nations where it has been allowed by default to get out of hand—it enriches a few corrupt individuals; it enables those who pay bribes to obtain favors to which they are not entitled; it causes widespread bitterness in those who cannot pay for favors when they see those who do pay being favored; it distorts standards when it enables those less deserving to reach goals ahead of those of greater merit, and when bribes are paid to prevent enforcement of law, respect for the rule of law is lost (Frimpong and Jacques 1999). In systems where corruption is institutionalized, building a competent, efficient, and professional public service is seriously impaired. Recruitment into the public service will not be based on the principle of meritocracy but on patronage, social connections, or some other political policies of ethnic balancing. As a result, the public service can easily become bloated with mediocre talent (Uneke 2010). Corruption places unbearable burden on the most vulnerable people, and hinders development toward poverty reduction (Harris 2005).

Corruption poses a great threat to the democratic notions of rule of law. When public officials misuse their office for self-gain, then the rule of law no longer obtains, and there is in effect a return to tyranny. Rule of law, underpinned by an independent court system, implies a predictable legal framework that helps to ensure settlement of conflicts between the state and individuals, on the one hand, and among individuals or groups, on the other (Adamolekun 1982). By engaging in such self-aggrandizement, corrupt representatives of the people illegally put themselves above the law. Corruption is frequently fingered as being responsible for underdevelopment and other problems in many countries. The word itself is hydra-headed, and so is the phenomenon it represents (Njoku 2005). Corruption damages the economic life of a society. Although some argue that it can help grease the wheels of a slow-moving and overregulated economy, there is little doubt that corruption increases the cost of goods and services, promotes unproductive investments in projects that are not economically viable or sustainable, contributes to a decline in standards, and can even increase a country's indebtedness and impoverishment (Stapenhurst and Kpundeh 1999).

In governance terms, corruption threatens democratic public institutions by permitting the influence of few citizens in the legitimate activities of the state at the expense of the majority. Uganda has for long been swimming in the waters of corruption, and it is hardly an exaggeration to plainly say the country is bleeding profusely from the pain inflicted by corruption, and no doctor seems available to fix the problem. Corruption in Uganda has reached what the current speaker of parliament, Honorable Rebecca Kadaga, termed crisis levels. Six cabinet ministers have been forced by parliament to resign due to corruption scandals, and more are destined to face the same fate. Within the East African region, Uganda is the only country where corruption is perceived to be increasing. A December 2011 report on the Corruption Perception Index by Transparency International (TI), on a scale from zero for the most corrupt to 10 for the cleanest country, scored Uganda at 2.4, lower than the 2.5 score of 2010. Uganda, among the unclean countries, was joined by Burundi, whose score was reported to be 1.9, slightly higher than its 1.8 score for 2010. Kenya had a score of 2.2, from the 2.1 ranking of 2010. Rwanda, the cleanest country in the region, had a score of 5.0, up from 4.0 in 2010, while Tanzania was ranked with a score of 3.0 from the 2.7 of 2010.

From 1986, when the current government took power through a revolutionary struggle, anticorruption was considered a priority goal of the National Resistance Movement (NRM) and played a key role in the government's stated aim of achieving a "decent standard of living for all Ugandans" (Dicklich 1994). The current state of corruption in the country suggests that something has gone seriously wrong in our administrative systems. Uganda is now a country characterized by major corruption scandals that involve highly connected political and administrative staff. The number of stories reported in the media, the number of investigations conducted by the Inspectorate of Government (IG), the number of audit queries raised by the auditor general, and the debates that keep occupying the members of parliament in the Public Accounts Committee, the Local Government Committee, and other oversight committees of parliament are all indicative of a crisis amidst us. The anticorruption court recently established in the country continues to try many corruption cases. Various local and international investigative reports by government agencies, the civil society, the media, and independent research groups all converge with almost the same conclusions. While acknowledging the delicate situation in Uganda as it relates to the corruption problem, the head of the Inspectorate of Government recently openly remarked that the corruption syndicate in the country had taken new forms and actually had become more sophisticated.

In his New Year's address to the nation delivered on December 31, 2011, from his country home in Rwakitura, President Yoweri Museveni delivered a very important message pertinent to our subject here. He boldly acknowledged that despite the increased resources and progress so far registered, the road sector was still characterized by a number of challenges, which included "lack of value for money spent on numerous road projects, high unit costs and corruption by both political and technical officers within the sector who collude with the contractors to inflate the contracts and also carry out sub standard road works." Such statements from a head of state signify the epitome of a society gone wrong. He stated in his address that he had been informed of the unit cost of constructing a road that was more than double what was to be spent on the Rwandan side, even when the terrain in the two countries was almost similar, other factors notwithstanding. He cautioned all the engineers who were involved in what he termed outright theft of inflating bills of quantities that translate into high bid prices that the law would undoubtedly catch up with them sooner or later. He directed the auditor general to carry out a forensic value for money audit in the roads sector using a firm of international repute and urgently submit a comprehensive report. It is only God who surely knows whether anything will come out of such investigations as the taxpayer keeps footing bills for such wasteful investigations and no action is taken.

The president largely acknowledged lapse in the administrative systems of the government he heads. In his speech, he noted significant constraints that pertained to the quality of education where government has invested huge resources through the Universal Primary Education (UPE) and Universal Secondary Education (USE) programs. He pointed out that studies had persistently shown the UPE was characterized by high rates of absenteeism (a form of corruption that has recently been termed silent corruption, and which is more corrosive than the earlier known forms of corruption), high dropouts, and the inability of the children to gain an acceptable standard of reading and writing. He noted that he had also established that the education sector was still marred by "ghost" schools, teachers, and pupils, problems that he attributed largely to weak inspection, supervision, and monitoring. He openly acknowledged more weaknesses in his own administration where he stated that he had set up a commission of inquiry into UPE almost three years before, but by the time of his address he had not received a report. Such is only part of the extent to which public administration and corruption have been nourishing each other in Uganda's case.

The Corruption Perception Index (CPI) report for 2011 indicated that Uganda is the third most corrupt country in the East African region, having this time round been beaten by Burundi and Kenya, which took the first and second unenviable positions, respectively. In that report, Rwanda was the cleanest country, followed by Tanzania. The *Second Annual Report on Corruption Trends in Uganda: Using the Data Tracking Mechanism* that was conducted by the Economic Policy Research Center based at Makerere University was launched by the Inspector General of Government on November 15, 2011. It was reported that the corruption problem in the country was now entrenched. Transparency International launched its East African Bribery Index report of 2011, where it was indicated that 68% of the respondents interviewed felt the incidence of corruption in Uganda had increased in the last year. About the same number (65.6%) believed that the problem would increase in the new year. On this same subject, the archbishop of the church of Uganda, the Rt. Rev. Luke Orombi, during his 2012 New Year's message to thousands of Christians, noted that Uganda was "a sick country that needed spiritual healing in 2012," as corruption and greed were now embedded in the citizens' blood right from childhood. He wondered why someone should be corrupt to build a house with 12 bedrooms, yet it is only him and his wife staying in that house. Almost all religious leaders in the country, cutting across all denominations, had a similar message on corruption during the 2011 Christmas celebrations, as quoted extensively by the various print and other media.

According to the 2007 African Peer Review Mechanism report, Uganda was estimated to be losing USD 258.6 million annually through corruption and procurement malfeasance. It was argued that if the country could eliminate corruption in public procurement, it would save USD 15.2 million a year. In the assessment by the country's auditor general and the background to the budget of 2009, it was reported that procurement accounted for 70% of public spending, and of this, an estimated 20% was lost via corruption. Local governments are estimated to be spending about 34% of their budgets on procurement of goods, services, and works, and this figure can be computed upwards from different perspectives of what actually constitutes public procurement. In the revised National Anticorruption Strategy 2008–2013, an ambitious agenda seeking to achieve a public service that appreciates and embraces integrity, accepts the need for transparency and accountability, and ensures full compliance with regulatory and legal requirements was proposed. It seeks a well-informed public that demands high standards from public officials and a private sector that operates on a level playing field and acts as a partner in the fight against corruption. This, however, seeks the active support of the executive and legislature to set a national example, deliver legislation, and lead the fight against corruption. In December 2006, the National Anticorruption Strategy II was launched covering the period 2006–2010. This second phase focused more specifically on engaging local government authorities, civil society, and the private sector in the fight against corruption. These efforts seem to have flatly failed to tame the problem.

The examples that follow give a brief portrayal of the corruption environment in Uganda's various sectors. Corruption in state institutions has wider implications for all individuals within and outside a particular administrative system. In Uganda's administrative systems, corruption is easily noticeable and its effects are clear to the young and the old, and at all levels of government and in every sector of the economy.

Education: Children in schools lack essential facilities and are forced to study under difficult conditions, yet government budgets for these facilities keep on increasing. Teachers remain primitively underpaid, and even the little they expect is sometimes swindled or delayed by those running the bureaucratic system. The quality of education at all levels is seriously compromised.

Health care: The health sector only raises more worry on the future state of this important social sector. Health facilities are underutilized, doctors are not adequately paid, the little allowances are delayed, and the only language that seems to awaken government to pay them is the threat of violence or strike. Drugs are openly stolen by people working in hospitals, and poor citizens cannot get what they expect. Patients have been reported in the national referral hospital to be lying in corridors without space, and those who manage to get little space receive medication, even if it is a drip, while standing as the beds, or even the rooms are unavailable. In December 2011, it was reported to the parliamentary committee that visited the hospital that some patients are put on drip while standing or seated on the floor. The health care system of the country is now in total shambles due to corruption.

Roads and transport: Roads are either nonexistent where they ought to have been or, if in existence, are poorly constructed even after millions of taxpayers' money has been spent. A well-designed road is completed with serious negative alterations as contractors complain that those in the bureaucracy take a lot of bribes. Roads are full of potholes, and those in the rural areas are now impassable, such that farm produce cannot find its way to the market. Yet, this is the service that governments worthy of the name should be providing.

Water and electricity: Getting adequate water and electricity supplies in all parts of the country is a problem. Foreign private companies awarded electricity installation and supply contracts through faulty processes continue to do a very poor job, but government pays for these inefficiencies. This could be attributable to the private companies' "smartness" at the stage of signing contracts. One wonders whether they do so with stringent penalty clauses that seem not to be seen by government bureaucrats who sign such deals. As a consequence, most citizens see more hours of darkness than light in their homesteads, and small businesses and industries incur high production costs due to erratic electricity supply.

Minerals and resources: Oil contracts have been reportedly awarded in complete disregard of the existing procurement regulations, and only companies connected to powerful politicians seem to have the criteria for winning such huge contracts. Institutions created by government to provide services are the same institutions used to deny people the same services. Individuals who lack experience and sometimes adequate qualifications find their way on government payroll, and yet those with experience and qualifications remain walking aimlessly on streets. Economists would be in a better position to compute the economic losses due to such a trend. While universities continue to produce brilliant young graduates, few get employed due to the corrupt systems. Some employees are quickly confirmed or promoted in their jobs not because of competence and merit, but because of how strongly they are connected—shattering all efforts that Max Weber made in his conceptions of a well-functioning bureaucracy.

Governance: The corporations are poorly run by inefficient, but politically correct managers (Harris 2005). Well-connected business people continue to get high compensation from government, and top government officials openly and quickly approve such payments in complete disregard of the existing public finance management regulations. Parliamentarians pass resolutions or policies through a well-entrenched corrupt system. They are paid bribes in order to approve legislations, yet their election was premised on serving the people. Court decisions are also sometimes heavily influenced by who has the capacity to pay for justice.

These are only a few examples that could illustrate the contemporary public administration system in Uganda. Uganda has consistently maintained a top position among countries with corrupt systems. Countries at the Crossroads report is an annual analysis of government performance in 70 strategically important countries worldwide that are at a critical crossroads in determining their political future. Uganda emerged among the countries on this list, and the in-depth comparative assessments and quantitative ratings—examining government accountability, civil liberties, rule of law, and anticorruption and transparency efforts—are intended to help international policy makers identify areas of progress, as well as to highlight areas of concern that could be addressed in diplomatic efforts and reform assistance. Unfortunately, our systems seem to be poor students to learn any lesson. In a recent report (2010), corruption in Uganda was reported to be endemic, especially within the public sector, where the line between the official and private interests of government officers was blurred. Despite much political and economic progress over the last two decades, it was noted that the increasingly personal and patronage-based rule of President Yoweri Museveni remained the most significant obstacle to the expansion of democracy and rule of law in Uganda. The country's significant ethnic, regional, and religious divisions had also complicated efforts to protect basic freedoms and prevent corruption.

The Weberian image of the efficient, rational, functionally specialized, impersonal, and nonpolitical bureaucratic hierarchy is virtually all gone in Uganda's public administration. With the aforementioned, if Max Weber were to suddenly appear, he would most probably fail to comprehend what has gone wrong with his efficient bureaucracy. Weber believed a bureaucratic organization was the most efficient way in which to control a large number of people. A bureaucracy was "the expression of rational and efficient administration" (Breton and Wintrobe 1985; Denhardt and Denhardt 2000). However, most administrative systems modeled along the bureaucratic arrangements have witnessed the malaise of corruption eat away the normal functioning of these systems. The capability of any country's public sector to provide high-quality goods and services in a cost-effective way is crucial to foster long-term growth and development of that country. Politicians and bureaucrats often claim to set rules and practices intended to increase efficiency and reduce slack to enable the delivery of the highest possible value for money to the citizens. However, political economy and public choice literature now suggests that one cannot take it for granted that decision makers will always use public resources in the most appropriate way (Giordano, Tommasino, and Casiraghi 2008).

Opportunism, advanced by the transaction economists, often sets in the way of most rational decision-making efforts by both political and administrative officials. This position is alive in most African countries and has been at the core of the problems that affect this good continent. In this same regard, observations by the World Bank (1994) may be helpful. In its report, it was noted that the public sector was at the core of the stagnation and decline in growth in Africa. This scenario may possibly remain so in the majority of the African countries, save a few like Rwanda that have decided to attack the corruption nuisance. There is substantial evidence that citizens around the world have lost confidence and trust in the public sector (Peter 2004). Advocates of institutional theorizing insist that a crucial part in shaping the incentives for engaging in public administration reforms (Padovani and Scorsone 2009) was to create institutions and processes that promote accountability, efficiency, and effectiveness in the public sector. However, as Ani and Carmen (2009) suggest to us, although efficiency represents the main objective of any administrative reforms, the need to be responsive and accountable is equally significant. But evidence in Uganda's public administration suggests that the country is moving on a rough road, and the journey of addressing corruption seems to be taking long and is hurting poor citizens through denial of efficient services. Public administrators work at different levels and have different opportunities for amassing wealth. Some are closely associated with petty corruption, while others, especially those administrators working closely with high political leaders, deal in grand corruption involving huge amounts. Certain public administrators in particular sectors have better opportunities for corruption than those in other sectors of the economy. Some public administrators are highly educated and become sophisticated while stealing government resources, and yet others do so in an amateurish way, given how easy it is to net them. Recently, the degree of sophisticated corruption scandals has been acknowledged by the anticorruption court. Educated people now, through a network arrangement, tend to put their documentation in order as though there was no corruption. However, a disagreement among the network individuals reveals the strategies used.

As society has learned to tolerate the increasing share of public administrators in everyday life, and more particularly in a welfare state, as Jayapalan (2000) informs us, in countries like Uganda, society seems to have learned—albeit through a hard lesson—to accept corruption as a normal fact in the administration of state affairs. Those who seek services from government officials now give bribes as though it was a normal thing. Uganda is an excellent candidate of African administrative systems where corruption, a vice that impedes socioeconomic development and growth, has been flourishing. Corruption in Uganda has become a common talk at all fora, both local and international. It is a routine element of the functioning of the administrative and para-administrative apparatus, from top to bottom. For more than four decades, corruption has spread like a hurricane throughout post-independence Africa. No country or region of the continent has remained untainted, to a greater or lesser degree, by the corruption pestilence (Uneke 2010).

Like public administration, which is home to many disciplinary approaches, corruption research has been home to a number of social science disciplines. Political scientists have concerned themselves with small themes, like how political systems address corruption and whether corruption hampers or promotes development in a particular country. They also are concerned with how public organizations are formed in ways that can minimize the size of corruption if the center of research is on public sector corruption as opposed to private sector corruption. Economists would be interested in the problem of corruption at a much broader level. They study determinants and effects of corruption at a broader macro economic level in different countries. Sociologists would be interested in understanding the social structure and cultural beliefs that could explain the corruption problem and its effects on social organizations. Economic literature has documented the benefits of corruption, but moral scientists have a different stand altogether. From a moral philosophy perspective, corruption is bad and its effects are negative.

In the next part of the chapter, the context of Uganda's administrative system is briefly examined before a conceptual understanding of corruption and the determinants of this malaise are discussed. The third section then ventures into the various forms of corruption. In this effort, examples from various sectors of Uganda's administrative systems will be used. The chapter will then discuss the consequences of corruption on the delivery of public services, before turning to an evaluation of the anticorruption strategies from both the legal and institutional points of view. Finally, the chapter will make suggestions on possibly new efforts that are needed to sustain the fight against corruption, with emphasis placed on noise-based as opposed to alarm-based approaches. The chapter will then give concluding remarks.

Context of Uganda's Administrative Systems

Governments have historically had core functions. Gildenhuys (1997) reminds us, however, that due to technological developments, government functions have not only changed, but increased dramatically over the past decades. As a result, one finds government functions as including the order and protection functions, social welfare functions, economic welfare functions, and a host of staff functions, like financial, personnel, office and secretarial, legal advisory services, organization and work study services, resource supply services, and accounting and auditing services. On the same subject, Mbaku (2007) suggests that economists often assign the state two main functions: (1) to maintain law and order, including enforcement of contracts, and (2) to provide public goods. An effective and efficient state is one that provides a framework that enforces the law and maintains an appropriate institution and environment for the efficient and equitable allocation of resources. Unfortunately, during the last 50 years or so since most African countries attained their independence, the institution of the state has just done a poor job. One of the perennial problems that have characterized most of these countries has been corruption.

Since the 1960s, Africa's economic development has been characterized by negative trends, with almost all economies on the continent not performing as expected because of corruption tendencies. Africa has experienced a downward trend in development because corrupt government officials who care about their "own businesses" (Marthur 1986) have continued to occupy central positions in government. It is thus no longer a secret that in Uganda, like other African countries, people are poor, resources are underutilized, and administrative and political institutions are ineffective in facilitating the process of efficient service delivery. Services such as health, infrastructure, water, and education range from poor to nonexistent, and unfortunately, the majority of the people in government remain insensitive to the cries of the masses. The existing infrastructure cannot be maintained; a number of promising projects are affected by the corruption syndrome, and thus the majority of these projects remain uncompleted, and even when they are, "unexplained" poor quality characterizes the majority. Public universities are overcrowded, lack adequate infrastructure and textbook materials, and as a result, teaching quality not only at university level but at all levels of the education system is on the decline.

The last five decades of post-independence Africa has been marked by the prevalence of corruption that has spread like brush fire across the continent. Politics, political processes, economic exchange, and public service have become synonymous with corruption in most African countries. Systemic corruption, arising from the wrongful conduct of the political leadership and top-level echelons of government bureaucracy, engenders a collapse of institutions designed to contain the malfeasance (Uneke 2010). Uganda's administrative systems have a serious problem of moral deficits—which essentially is the problem of choice between good and bad, do's and don'ts, etc. The problem of corruption is part of the broader moral dilemma. Chabal and Daloz (1999) suggest that corruption is not just endemic but an integral part of the social fabric of life. For those at the bottom end of society, like lowly civil servants, the sale of the limited amount of power they possess is virtually their only means of survival. Higher up in the administrative or political hierarchy, extortion is one of the major avenues of enrichment, and more often it facilitates social advancement and the upholding of one's position. Such inducements enable the political elites to fulfill their duties, to meet the expectations of their clients, and hence to enhance their status.

Uganda's public administration originated from the British system that was bequeathed by the former colonial power. Precolonial systems had stringent systems of fighting transgression against community rules, and even if corruption existed then, it must have been practiced by the colonial masters who wished to bring the African administrators on their side. It is a well-known fact that few Ugandans had an opportunity of being in the colonial administrative systems. Uganda was a British protectorate from 1894 to 1962, and colonial rule affected the local economic and social systems of the country because the British were concerned with economic exploitation and domination. The new British commissioner of Uganda in 1900, Sir Harry H. Johnson, had orders to establish an efficient administration and to levy taxes as quickly as possible. To achieve this economic objective, he approached the chiefs of Buganda Kingdom with offers of jobs in the colonial administration in return for their collaboration—a form of corruption at that. Johnston's 1900 Buganda Agreement imposed a tax on huts and guns and chiefs were designated as tax collectors, who also had to testify to their continued allegiance to British and Buganda interests. The British signed much more generous treaties with other kingdoms of Toro (1900), Ankole (1901), and Bunyoro (1933), ignoring the smaller chiefdoms of Busoga. The Buganda offered their services to the British as administrators over the conquered neighbors, and they often extended the *ganda* dominion over other tribes exhibited in the forceful use of their local language—Luganda, the dress code, and dictation on the type of crops to be grown (they introduced banana growing in a number of other regions).

Uganda during that historical epoch did not have democratic institutions as we know of the concept in its contemporary usage. Quite often, the systems at the time relied on excessive use of force, and people did not have the slightest opportunity of demanding accountability. After the country got independence in 1962, not much change in terms of administrative systems emerged. In fact, the regimes that emerged were more preoccupied with state power and use of force, and democratic processes were overthrown in the country—a situation that created fertile ground for the corruption problem that we see today. This overthrow of the democratic order has had devastating effect not only on the economic systems of the country, but also on its political and social organizational arrangements. Dr. Apollo Milton Obote led Uganda to political independence and was the prime minister of Uganda between 1962 and 1966 and president of Uganda from 1966 to 1971 and 1980 to 1985. In 1966, there was the climax of political maneuvers when Obote suspended the constitution and assumed all government powers, removing the positions of president and vice president. In September 1967, a new constitution proclaimed Uganda a republic and gave the president (Obote) even greater powers and abolished the traditional kingdoms that had previously formed a key part of organizational society. He was overthrown by his erstwhile ally and army commander, Major General Idi Amin, in 1971, but regained power in 1980. His second rule was marred by repression and the death of many civilians during the ensuing civil war.

Idi Amin's rule of Uganda began in 1971 when he seized power in a coup. When Amin overthrew the first Obote government, he declared himself president, dissolved parliament, and amended the constitution to give himself absolute power.

His eight-year rule as a president resulted in economic decline, social disintegration, and massive human rights abuses. After he was overthrown by a combined force of the Tanzanian military and Ugandan exiles, his regime was replaced by an interim government with Yusuf Lule as president. The government adopted a ministerial system of administration and created a quasi-parliamentary organ known as the National Consultative Council (NCC). Following a dispute over the extent of the presidential powers, the NCC replaced Lule with Godfrey Binaisa, but this largely did not solve the power disputes. Indeed, because of the acrimonious situation, Binaisa was removed in May 1980. Thereafter, Uganda was ruled by a military commission (itself an organ of the NCC) chaired by Paulo Muwanga, an old Obote ally and key member of his Uganda People's Congress (UPC). In December 1980, Uganda held elections that saw the UPC, with Obote at the helm, back in power. There were disputed elections that resulted in a guerrilla war. The National Resistance Army (NRA)/National Resistance Movement (NRM) took power in 1986 on a platform promising a fundamental revolution and not a mere change of guard. Since then, the NRM has enjoyed a monopoly of political power in Uganda until the July 2005 referendum, which brought back multiparty politics. The year 2005 also saw a change of the constitution, which lifted the presidential term limits.

Post-independence public administration had many challenges, and this not only created opportunities for corruption, but also nurtured it with unmatched speed. During the bad economic and social times resulting from the political manipulations that had gone wrong, there was massive demand for services like schools, hospitals, roads, etc. To satisfy this demand, there was a rush to establish public corporations to deliver the required services. On this subject, Hughes (2003: 97) helps us to contextualize our debate when he suggests that public utilities provide services—water, sewage, electricity, gas, and telecommunications—considered essential for the economy as a whole. He goes on to remind us that "the essential nature of public utilities means the services they supply are politically sensitive, with great disruption to the private economy and households resulting if supplies are interrupted." To provide these services, government had to award contracts, and these often went to the politically connected as a way of extending the patronage machinery—a bad practice that characterizes the current regime. Politicians often promote this tactical economic strategy to win political support.

In 1972, Uganda experienced another major political development. There was forceful expulsion of the Asians out of the country on the orders of President Idi Amin, and the nationalization of their properties created more need for public administrators. Yet the number of indigenous people at the time qualified for this job was limited. With this expansionism, systems became too big and lack of control set in, accountability became a problem, management systems broke down, patronage increased, and anarchy and state-inspired violence became the order of the day. As one would expect, service delivery became poor, and naturally corruption positioned itself in almost all systems of government. It is often characterized by its ability to benefit few at the expense of the majority. As a result of the political and economic problems that characterized the country, corruption was accepted as part of the society. In 1986, corruption was considered to be one of the evils in the country, and its fight formed one of the 10-point programs of the NRM government. The NRM took power through a 5-year protracted guerilla war, and the current president has essentially ruled the country for 25 years uninterrupted. But the problem of corruption is back on our doorsteps of an efficient public administrative system.

Uganda is a parliamentary democracy with the head of state as the leader of government. The country adopted a decentralized system of administration in the early 1990s, but many powers were still retained at the center. Uganda is now divided into numerous administrative units (districts) that are demarcated based on tribe and ethnicity. Religion remains a hidden criterion in ascending to some political and administrative positions in the country. While the maturity of a country on a democratic ladder of participation and citizen involvement is said to determine the level of corruption, the administrative systems of the country are increasingly becoming dysfunctional and personalized—a situation that has become a breeding ground for corruption in both a grand form and bureaucratic nature. The executive branch has increasingly overdominated the remaining two other branches of government, although since May 2011 parliament has tried to reassert its democratic roles with the current speaker (the first female in the country's history to occupy that office) showing total zeal to regain the "lost glory" of that institution. The inactive role of parliament had largely rendered its accountability role equally inactive.

The judiciary has not been saved the intrusive nature of the executive, as it is openly attacked by the latter, which affects its independence. Decisions of judges have sometimes been questioned by the president himself. State institutions are used to repress opposing voices, and freedom of speech is sometimes under attack, especially where matters of corruption scandals involving high-ranking government officials are involved. Strong civil society voices are largely nonexistent and citizen pressure is not effective, or where it emerges, it is silenced with the repressive hand of the police force that has been accused by opposition elements to be an extended arm of the ruling government.

The military remains heavily entrenched in the administrative machinery of government. For example, recruitments or promotions to sensitive political and administrative positions are only possible after extensive intelligence vetting. Most sensitive parts of the administrative system are occupied by intelligence operatives in civilian clothing, and their work is clear. While their role in security is critical, their involvement in the government bureaucracy affects the fundamental principles of public service. Some of these operatives have been agents of corruption or have been used to cover up corruption cases that involve the politically connected officials. It is often claimed that countries with a well-functioning multiparty democracy, where elections are conducted in a free and fair mode, for example, are likely to have leaders who represent the genuine wishes of their people. A sham election will most probably produce sham leaders who may get their way through paying bribes to voters, and once in power, may entrench undemocratic systems, with corruption and patronage likely to be part of the methods of entrenching their incompetence. Uganda's judiciary has, on a number of instances, ruled that a number of elected members of parliament, especially those from the party with the majority in parliament, got elected through voter bribery. The most notable is the former vice president, Professor Gilbert Bukenya, who lost his parliamentary seat on this ground but has since regained his seat through a new election.

Concept of Corruption in Public Administration

Noonan (1984) makes us understand that corruption is traceable from four historical epochs. The first epoch was from 3000 BC to 1000 AD and was characterized by the idea of nonreciprocity struggles against the norms of reciprocation, which cemented societies whose rulers were both judges and recipients of "offerings." The second epoch was from 1000 to 1500 AD, where "the anti-bribery ideal was dominant in religious, legal and literal expressions." The third epoch was from the sixteenth century, where there was the domestication of bribes in English Bibles, English plays, and English law, and culminated in the eighteenth century with the proclamation as the norm for the English empire. Finally, the fourth epoch was termed the American era, where the heirs of the English tradition began to apply and expand its influence until it was asserted as an "American norm around the earth." Noonan observes that the expansion of bribes as the moral wrong to the rest of the world was not merely the result of the American influence, but because of the general expansion of Western moral tradition.

In the Old Testament of the Bible, God warned Moses, "Neither shall thou take bribe which blind the wise and prevent the word of just" (Deuteronomy 16:19). Psalm 26:10 is another Old Testament verse that reminds us of the effect of bribes to "make the sinners," a bribe "corrupts conscience" (Exodus 23:8), which "brings chaos" (Amos 5:12), and therefore "merits punishment" (Amos 2:6).

Corruption, though widely used in public administration discourse, resembles terms like *democracy* and *freedom*, whereby even in a purely descriptive sense, they mean different things to different people. As such, attempts at defining corruption have been persistently plagued with definitional and ontological problems. Most commentators view corruption to be a highly charged concept that often invokes negative emotions. This is possibly due to the pain it inflicts on its victims—through denial of good services. Paradoxically, some scholars regard corruption to be beneficial. Some economists have in fact computed, through modeling, what they have termed the economic benefits of corruption. Corruption, regardless of its forms, undermines the performance of the public services and decreases satisfaction with them. It thus becomes necessary to have some understanding of what corruption exactly entails within the context of public administration.

Barker and Carter (1994) broadly define corruption as acts containing three elements: violation of laws, rules, regulations, or ethical standards; misuse of an officer's position; and acceptance of some actual or expected material reward or gain. Within the context of public administration, violating the laws, rules, regulations, or ethical standards creates a degree of unfairness and denial in the efficient delivery of public services, which in a democracy ought to be enjoyed by all citizens. Such violations only favor those who have the capacity to bribe their way to get services at the expense of those who cannot avoid. On this same subject, Rose-Ackerman (1999) aptly contends that corruption is "a symptom that something has gone wrong in the management of the state." Perceived corruption erodes public respect for the government of the day as the service provider disappoints citizens, and eventually fosters cynicism about the government.

Public corruption involves the misuse of public office for private gain. Public administrative systems of the Weberian mode were based on a clear separation of public and private interest. It was believed that if efficiency was a primary goal of a bureaucracy, personal interests had to be subordinate to public interests. However, African administrative systems are often characterized by illegal sale of government property by public officials, receiving kickbacks in public procurements, bribery, and embezzlement of government funds as conceived from Svensson's (2005) understanding of corruption. African administrative systems also entail a high degree of cronyism, nepotism, graft, and indirectly, drug trafficking, human trafficking, and counterfeit goods. These problems are not limited to Africa. Njunwa (2008) reminds us that individual cases of corruption in both the public and private sectors have been reported in the United States, Asia, Europe, and several African countries.

Corruption occurs as the form of behavior violating the official ethics of the public service (Park and Blenkinsopp 2011). Quiet corruption is the failure of public servants to deliver goods or services of the government. According to a recent World Bank report, it appears to be just as corrosive as other forms of corruption, and has long-term consequences for development. Quiet corruption includes absenteeism, but it also involves lower levels of effort and deliberative bending of rules for personal advantage. The African Development Indicators 2010 report notes that quiet corruption is present in a large share of health provider-patient and teacher-pupil interactions affecting the poor, who are more vulnerable and more reliant on government services and public systems to satisfy their most basic needs.

Determinants of Corruption in Public Administrative Systems

Many factors have been offered to explain the apparent failure of the development enterprise in Africa: the colonial legal, social pluralism and its centrifugal tendencies, the corruption of leaders, poor labor discipline, the lack of entrepreneurial skills, poor planning and incompetent management, inappropriate policies, the stifling market mechanism, low levels of technical assistance, the limited inflow of foreign capital, falling commodity prices and unfavorable terms of trade, and low levels of saving and investment. Alone or in combination, they could be serious impediments to development (Ake 1996). However, as the Organization for Economic Cooperation and Development (OECD 1999) rightly observed, corruption in government and public administration is a complex and pervasive phenomenon that, among other things, distorts the operation of economic activity and weakens political stability. It has variously been identified with major negative effects that have had a hand in the underdevelopment of the continent. The determinants of this problem in Uganda may not be in a fundamental way different from what is the cause in other countries.

Corruption is an outcome or a reflection of a country's legal, economic, cultural, and political institutions. A number of parallels have been proposed for thinking about corruption, and although each can be illuminating in certain ways, none of them capture the phenomenon perfectly. Thus, a multiple set of factors usually work either singly or in unison to first create the opportunities and appropriate environment for corruption and second, facilitate the nurturing and maturity of the same problem within various areas of the administrative systems. Corruption, regarded as "a criminal process of diverting public resources from their intended use to private hands for private benefit and depriving the public the use of these resources" (Kariuki and Awasom 2008), is often a complex phenomenon. Its complexity results in the complexity of the corruption cases themselves, especially where complicated matters of fraud involving highly educated and professional people are involved. The corruption referred to here involves the intelligent use of the pen and computer terminals. Such cases are more difficult for the investigators, prosecutors, and magistrates than the capital cases of murder, rape, and robbery. The people who get involved in corruption are well educated, economically connected, socially connected, and politically have sophisticated connections. They are specialists in their areas of training and work. They use modern equipment, technology, and skills. Public agencies and all government departments in Uganda are now actually suffering from negative acts of these well-trained officials whose corruption can be difficult to detect and fight unless there are well-trained officials in anticorruption agencies.

Treisman (2000) suggests that very little is known for sure about what causes corruption to be higher in one place than another. Moreover, corruption occurs in every sector, although some sectors are more prone to this malaise than others. A lot of theories and numerous case studies have examined the details of corruption in particular countries or regions, cross-nationally, and some good suggestive determinants have been given. But still, the phenomenon keeps becoming more sophisticated, and so will be the determinants. Lawal (2007), on this same subject, contends that corrupt practices span a wide spectrum, ranging from petty corruption, whereby bribes are required before normal bureaucratic procedures are accomplished, to large-scale corruption. whereby considerable sums of money are paid in return for preferential treatment or access. Corruption occurs in the political, economic, and administrative spheres. He reminds us that corruption is worse in countries where institutions, such as the legislature and the judiciary, are weak, where rule of law and adherence to formal rules are not rigorously observed, where political patronage is standard practice, where the independence and professionalism of the public sector have been eroded, and where civil society lacks the means to bring public pressure to bear.

Governance has been Africa's perennial challenge (Rotberg and Gisselquist 2009), and it continues to be so to date. Examining the trends of most East African partner states confirms that problems of governance are only worsening. All countries of the region have some notable serious deficits not only in governance but on the democratic agenda as well (Bana and Basheka 2011). These sentiments are voiced by academia, media, civil society organizations, the church, political parties, development partners, and professional groups in society. Coupled with governance challenges, issues of democracy continue to pose unique challenges to most African countries. There are many persistent challenges—including corruption—that continue to plague the continent, and countries like Zimbabwe and Somalia have become internally and internationally dysfunctional (although for different reasons) (Gatune and Najam 2011). The prevailing situations in most African countries, and more so the East African partnering states, cannot be divorced from the governance and democratic debates.

The difficulty of understanding accurate determinants of corruption and the difficulties often presented in measuring levels of relative corruption in different countries have always presented a major obstacle. Economists and political scientists have analyzed indices of perceived corruption prepared by business risk analysts and polling organizations, based on survey responses of businessmen and local residents, in an attempt to understand the problem and its determinants, but more issues have remained. However, as Gildenhuys (1997) suggests, one of the traditional cornerstones of democracy is the fact that each political representative, as well as each public official, is subject to accountability. Accountability is fundamental to any society with pretensions to being democratic. Stated in reverse, being democratic requires a suitable system of accountability. Government organizations are created by the public, for the public, and need to be accountable to the public (Hughes 2003). There are certain areas of a nation's existence that are cornerstones of this accountability—judiciary, legislature, and its accountability committees, as well as the auditor general's office, as examples. If these cornerstones are allowed to weaken and crack under the weight of corruption, the national structure is in real danger of collapsing. Key areas of a nation's existence include law enforcement, the judicial system, the electoral process, the security of the nation, the economy, the general public service, and the education system (Frimpong and Jacques 1999).

Alam (1989) observes that in modern bureaucratic systems, corruption is "an attribute of all principal-agent relationships." In each state, the citizen or principal grants the government (or the designated agent) the authority, for example, to impose and collect taxes, and in exchange, the agent provides the principal with public goods and services, including health care, security, and crime control. Corruption occurs when the agent, in the performance of official duties, sacrifices the interests of the principal for those of the agent. For example, the agent can violate the stipulated procedures guiding the conduct of the agent, illegally appropriate public resources for his own use, or engage in illegal taxation of private economic activities in a bid to draw extra-legal income (Mbaku 1998). Recent studies and reports on Uganda's status have, however, given the green light on what determines corruption in Uganda. In his comparative study of the control of bureaucratic corruption in Hong Kong, India, and Indonesia, Palmier (1985) identified three factors as important causes of corruption: opportunities (which depended on the extent of involvement of civil servants in the administration or control of lucrative activities), salaries, and policing (the probability of detection and punishment). Without smart regulation, which requires a well-organized system of public governance, the market economy often brings too many costs for the environment, public health, social welfare, or the economy as a whole, and it hinders the uptake of innovative opportunities. As a result, the benefits go to the few, but the costs go to the many, creating inevitable social tension and instability. That is why it has been previously argued that there is no consensus about the market model (Dore, Lazonick, and O'Sullivan, 1999).

Citizens suffer most in circumstances where the few benefit and the costs are borne by the majority since it is the citizens who finance the activities of government through payment of taxes. Weak institutional checks on the private appropriation of public resources contribute to patronage networks permeating the state's administrative structures, compromising public service effectiveness, and fueling corruption (Bayart 1993; Chabal and Daloz 1999). This pattern so profoundly affects opportunities for social advancement that class formation comes to be determined by relationships more to political power than to economic resources (Diamond 1990). The TI Global Corruption Barometer (2010) reported that there were more reported bribes in the judiciary, the police, and registry and permit services in 2010 than in 2006. Registry and permit services in Uganda would include the land registry, driving permit sections of the ministry of transport, immigration department of the ministry of internal affairs, trading licensing offices in various departments of government at both central and local levels, the registrar of companies, and Uganda Investment Authority, among others. Different countries according to the TI have different reasons for paying bribes, as indicated in Table 3.1.

Our focus of analysis is on sub-Saharan Africa where Uganda, as the case study in this chapter, geographically falls. According to TI, 67% of the participants in sub-Saharan Africa indicated they are forced to pay bribes to avoid problems with authorities, 20% pay bribes to speed up service delivery, and 11% do so to receive a service that they are entitled to. These findings suggest that because of the likely problems in the administrative systems of countries, citizens have no choice but to

Table 3.1 Reason for Paying Bribes by Regions of the World

Reason	Asia Pacific	European Union	Latin America	Middle East and North Africa	NIS	North America	Sub-Saharan Africa	Western Balkans and Turkey	Total
Avoid a problem with authorities	12%	6%	10%	9%	12%	16%	67%	6%	44%
Speed things up	28%	15%	44%	48%	28%	9%	20%	21%	22%
Receive a service not entitled to	35%	8%	34%	14%	21%	6%	11%	15%	17%
Don't know									
Don't remember									

Source: Transparency International, *Global Corruption Barometer*, 2010. Percentages are weighted.

pay the bribes as they need the services. Corruption is often attributable to systemic weak points opened up by the structures and procedures of administrative organization and civil service systems. Quite often, the organizational structures themselves are a product of corrupt interests, and their corrupted process of creation creates multiplier effects of problems during implementation. Typical manifestations of corruption in most African civil service systems, Uganda inclusive, include nepotism in job appointments or promotions, politicization of the administration, susceptibility to influence in office, dishonest handling of salaries and pensions, absenteeism, abuse of well-stated procedures, alarming costs in services sought by government, etc. Possible weak points are to be found both at the fundamental, i.e., structural, level and at the level of the organizational structures of individual administrative units. The former would include an oversized or overcentralized state (measured in relation to the subsidiary principle), and opaque structures of decision making and responsibility at the policy-making level (Table 3.2).

Corruption within the judiciary in Uganda is rampant and widespread and damages its public perception. Most corruption cases occur among court staff and the police, as well as within the magistrates' courts and the registrars. Cases of corruption of judges are less common, but this does not mean they are nonexistent. Widespread corruption within magistrates' courts and court staff hampers access to justice. The complexity of language and of court procedures is another impediment to access to justice for the general population, as well as a source of public distrust in the judicial system. There is little doubt that the institutions charged with curbing corruption in districts have been ignored, while those at the national level have no requisite capacity to supervise the 1,200 lower local governments, over 70 urban councils, and more than 80 districts that constitute the local government system in Uganda currently (Ashaba-Aheebwa 2009). Corruption has often been reported to be in higher magnitudes within the judiciary. Such systems do not promote accountability and good governance.

Corrupt court officials sometimes extort bribes from defendants unjustly jailed through cases based on fictitious affidavits. By July 2009, the recently established anticorruption division of the high court had convicted four officials and sentenced them to prison. However, it had a backlog of 350 cases, but with only 2 judges. Due to budgetary problems, there are not enough judges to process civil and criminal cases. While the higher courts are generally independent and impartial, the judgments of lower-level magistrates are frequently distorted by political and economic influences. Judges face intense political pressure in cases that threaten actions the president considers critical to his state control. A serious corruption problem, due in part to inadequate salaries for magistrates, leads to prejudicial decisions. The IG declared in April 2008 that for the second consecutive year, the judiciary and the police were the most corrupt institutions of government in Uganda. Once corruption finds its way into the judiciary, the end result is a distortion of the rule of law, which in turn hinders development and proper administration of justice. According to a report of the Judicial Service Commission (2008), there was

Table 3.2 Author-Constructed List of Major Reported Determinants of Corruption in Uganda Selected Sectors

Sector/Area/Function	Major Determinants
Road construction	Inflated prices
	Shoddy standards
	Poor and late delivery of contractors
	Alarming disparities in costs
	Alarming disparities in procurement procedures
	Inadequate government planning
	Lack of integrity among government contractors and consultants
	Politicization of procurement regulations and award decisions
	Influence peddling
	Unethical members of the contracts committees
	Syndicate syndrome
Judiciary	Complex court procedures
	Difficult court language to the litigants
Health	Low salaries
	Emergence of private clinics owned by health officials
Education	Too much discretion of education officials
	Bureaucratic education procedures in appointment and promotion
Police	Poor welfare
	Inadequate and poor housing conditions
	Lack of medical schemes
	Lack of stationery, furniture, and even computers
Local governments	Poverty
	Peer group pressures
	Political turbulence
	Weak institutional controls and supervision
	Moral decay
	Greed and excessive ambitions
	Inadequate remuneration to public servants
	HIV/AIDS scourge

evidence of persistent corruption in the judiciary. This report defined corruption in the judiciary as "the use of adjudication authority for the private benefit of court personnel in particular and/or public officials in general." This report identified various forms of corruption in the judiciary, including bribery, nepotism, influence peddling, fraud, abuse of office, causing financial loss, forgery, and others. The effects of these acts of corruption on the administration of justice are not well documented.

Aidt et al. (2008) argued that "corruption, while being tied particularly to the act of bribery, is a general term covering misuse of authority as a result of considerations of personal gain, which need not be monetary" (p. 206). He stressed that corruption is "outright theft, embezzlement of funds or other appropriation of state property, nepotism and the granting of favours to personal acquaintances, and the abuse of public authority and position to exact payments and privileges." The Inspectorate of Government Act (1999) defined corruption as abuse of public office for private gain and includes, but is not limited to, embezzlement, bribery, nepotism, influence peddling, theft of public funds or assets, fraud, forgery, causing financial or property loss, and false accounting of public funds.

There are a number of other general causes of corruption in Uganda that have appeared in various reports by civil society organizations, the media, and other government investigative organs. For example, these reports have identified too much discretion of public officials while executing their public duties as a cause of corruption. Public officials are believed to have liberty to serve whoever they want to serve, and many times hide under bureaucracy to demand facilitation payments in exchange for the needed services. A patronage political system that breeds impunity as long as those accused of corruption are part of the same political family is another general determinant that has often appeared in various reports. Rules and regulations that are poorly defined and disseminated and keep changing rapidly without people being adequately informed are an additional problem. Moral problems due to reduced religious and ethical values in societies, inadequate implementation of criminal and anticorruption laws, and low salaries to civil servants have also been identified. Compared to civil servants, politicians are well paid. For example, the monthly salary of a member of parliament can pay 100 primary school teachers or 50 doctors working in the private sector.

Politicians and some high-ranking CEOs in executive agencies get a salary many times higher than that of a university professor and other civil servants. In Uganda, lack of political will to address corruption, the culture of being silent and being complacent in regard to use of public resources that is rooted in citizens viewing government as a virtual organization, and pressures from politicians to recoup election expenses and amass resources to prepare for subsequent elections have combined to create grounds for both grand and bureaucratic corruption. Lack of coordination among anticorruption agencies has also in some way previously contributed to increased corruption. There used to be serious anti-accusations among these bodies, a problem that has not yet died away. This was mainly due to lack of knowledge of the process, but also the fight for money and status. Further, most anticorruption agencies generally have insufficient capacity compared to the highly complex capacities by the corruption networks. Shortage of handwriting experts (document examiners) has often been a big problem when it comes to analysis of questioned documents. The available few experts lack modern equipment for their work.

Forms of Corruption in Uganda's Public Administration

Corruption's pervasiveness and increasing cross-border and sophisticated forms are now well recognized in the new millennium. Its corrosive effects were recognized in the transformation of the Ethics IASIA working group (Collins 2011). In terms of structure, corruption can be organized vertically (linking subordinates and superiors in a system of payoffs) and horizontally (linking several agencies or branches of government in a web of dishonesty and injustice) (Uneke 2010). Theoretically, corruption takes various forms depending on factors from the supply or demand side. By the supply side we mean the sources from which corruption emanates, while the demand side includes the beneficiary receivers of corruption. Mathematically, for corruption to exist there must be two categories of people. There must be the giver and taker (for each of these, it may be individuals or groups). There must be an issue upon which the transaction takes place—upon which the giver and the taker interact. In the public administration context, the giver must be in need of a certain service that is in the jurisdictional mandate of the giver. One party to this transaction must be placed in a position of responsibility and trust, and the other party must be in need of a service.

Corruption can be high (grand scale) or low (small scale). It can involve high-level or low-level officials of government. Corruption can be induced by those who are in charge of a service, or it can be self-initiated by those who need favors to get the service. Corruption can be at policy formulation, implementation, or evaluation stages at both central and local government levels. It can be in the public and private sectors and the actors can be educated or not. The young and the old, the male and female, can all engage in corruption. Corruption has effects that are direct and indirect, short term, medium, or long term in nature. In whatever form, corruption is bad. High-level or grand corruption, for example, takes place at the policy formulation end of politics. It is at the top levels of the public sphere, where policies and rules are formulated, and it is usually (but not always) synonymous with political corruption, as most people who are politically connected engage quite often in this form of corruption. Small-scale, bureaucratic, or petty corruption is the everyday corruption that takes place at the implementation end of politics, where public officials meet the public. This form of bribery is connected to the implementation of existing laws, rules, and regulations. Petty corruption refers to the modest sums of money usually involved, and has also been called low level and street level to name the kind of corruption that people can experience more or less daily, in their encounter with public administration and services like hospitals, schools, local licensing authorities, police, taxing authorities, and others.

Harris (2005) gives the operational dynamics of corruption, describing it as a business that operates quietly below the visible spectrum. More often than not, victims suffer from it long before they realize that they have been damaged and well before a perpetrator is held to account for his behavior. Corruption generally tends to occur in incremental steps. Most activity that reaches the status of corrupt behavior may begin as innocent endeavor. While corruption may manifest itself in a simple and straightforward manner, in many cases it is carried out through complex methods involving cross-border transactions. Delivery of justice and other services by government can be negatively affected by corruption. Its effects are more devastating to the poor, who are not capable of seeking private services such as medical care and legal aid. The Inspectorate of Government (2010) report on the analysis of the complaints received against government departments/institutions during the period January–June 2010 indicates that most complaints received by the Inspectorate of Government were those against district administrations, which were 207, accounting for 19.9% of the total complaints received.

The common nature of complaints against district administrators includes mismanagement and misappropriation of public funds/resources, abuse of office, embezzlement, mishandling of tenders and contracts, and property disputes. Complaints against individual public officials ranked the second highest category complained against, constituting 13.4% (139) of the total complaints received. These are officials who have individually continued to use their offices for private gain. The nature of cases mostly reported in this category include abuse of office, conflict of interest, forgery and uttering false documents, property disputes, and victimization/oppression of other staff. The third ranked category was that of municipal councils/town councils, accounting for 10.1% (105) of the total complaints received. The nature of complaints in this category included mishandling of tenders/contracts, conflict of interest, abuse of office, embezzlement, and property disputes. Most complaints in this category were registered at the regional offices (Table 3.3).

The IG report (2010) found that complaints against school authorities, of both primary and secondary schools, ranked fourth, accounting for 6.1% (63) of the total complaints received. The nature of complaints in this category remains mismanagement and misappropriation, abuse of office, forgery, and uttering of false documents. The majority of these complaints were registered at regional offices. Complaints against police were the fifth highest, accounting for 4.8% (50) of the total complaints received. Most complaints against the police involved mismanagement, bribery, delay of service delivery, victimization/oppression, conflict of interest, and general misconduct, among others. Local councils were the sixth ranked category most complained against, accounting for 3.7% (38) of the total complaints received. The complaints against the local councils include mainly abuse of office and mismanagement. Most of these cases were registered at regional offices.

Table 3.3 Author-Constructed Forms of Corruption in the Education Sector in Uganda at Different Levels Based on Reported Cases in the Local Media

Level	Forms
Ministry	Kickbacks on supply of educational materials
	Kickbacks on classroom and other construction
	Kickbacks on procurement of science equipment
	Kickbacks on promotion, transfers, and appointments of head teachers
	Favoritism in hiring, appointments, and promotions
	Diversion of funds
	Delayed and withholding approvals until payments are done
	Gifts from officers in lower ranks
	Mismanagement and abuse of office
	Conflict of interest
District	Lack of inspection and monitoring visits
	Collusion in inclusion of ghost schools, teachers, and pupils
	Diversion of school materials to private markets or personal schools
	Favoritism in promotions, transfers, and appointments of teachers and head teachers
	Forgery
	Uttering false documents
	Mishandling of tenders
School	Ghost teachers
	Ghost pupils
	Unfair removal of unwanted teachers from payroll
	Delayed release of funds
	Diversion of school funds and materials
	Unregulated hire of school facilities
	Abuse of procurement regulations
	Diversion of students' examination fees
	Unfair dismissals or failure to give recommendations

(continued)

Table 3.3 Author-Constructed Forms of Corruption in the Education Sector in Uganda at Different Levels Based on Reported Cases in the Local Media (continued)

Level	Forms
School	Absenteeism of both teachers and head teachers
	Kickbacks for award of vacancies for new entrants
	Diversion of school fees
	Inflation of school purchases
	Mishandling of tenders
Individual	Siphoning of school supplies for sale or private use
	Selling notes and grades
	Coaching during teaching hours
	Demand from parents for paid trips for pupils
	Compulsory demands to pay for certain services
	Absenteeism during class hours
	Conflict of interest
Society	Tolerance of the corrupt
	Exertion of demands on teachers and school authorities
	Offering of gifts

Harris (2005) has done a fine job describing three forms of corruption—institutional, bureaucratic, and political. Institutional corruption involves a syndicate by a group of officers in a particular institution in corrupt practices known and approved by all of them. The corruption may take the form of direct soliciting of bribes from the public and shared among them, or fraudulent deals in goods and services that they are supposed to offer to the public free and for which they are employed to do. Bureaucratic corruption is where individual public officers systematically and consistently solicit or receive money in return for services rendered, exclusively for their personal benefit with or without necessarily the knowledge of others in the establishment. The act involves all levels of officers. Political corruption is where politicians are involved in fraudulent or morally unacceptable financial and political deals intended to benefit them financially and politically. Some people have called political corruption grand corruption because of the magnitudes involved (Table 3.4).

Uganda's Anticorruption Act (2009) regards corruption to involve solicitation or acceptance, directly or indirectly by a public official, of any goods of monetary value or benefits, such as a gift, favor, promise, advantage, or any other form of gratification for himself or herself or for another person or entity, in exchange for

Table 3.4 Author-Constructed Forms of Corruption in the Justice and Law and Order Sector in Uganda

Level	Forms
Judiciary	Delayed justice through unnecessary postponements
	Misplacement and loss of court files
	Bribery
	Abuse of office
	Mismanagement of cases
	Reliance on court technicalities
	Nepotism
	Influence peddling
	Fraud
	Causing financial loss
	Forgery
Police	Mismanagement of cases
	Bribery
	Delayed delivery of services
	Victimization or oppression
	Conflict of interest
	General misconduct

any or omission of the performance of his or her public functions. This indicates the complexities of corruption not only in its definition, but also its understanding, and therefore consequences and effects. Corruption has seeped into most public offices, and whereas some gains have been realized to curb the spread of corruption, it still remains a major obstacle to development in Uganda today. According to Wagona (2005), administration of justice, with particular reference to corruption, is a compendious term that stands for all the complexes of activity that operate to bring the substantive law of crime to abide, or to keep it from coming to bear, on persons who are suspected of having committed crimes. It refers to the rules of law that govern the detection, investigation, apprehension, interviewing, and trial of persons suspected of crime, and those persons whose responsibility it is to work within these rules. The administration of justice is not confined to the courts; it encompasses officers of the law and others whose duties are necessary to ensure that the courts function effectively. The concern of the administration of justice is the fair, just, and impartial upholding of rights, and punishment of wrongs, according to the rule of law. It was therefore in the interest of the current study to examine effects of corruption on the administration of justice, which justice seems to be too wanting, due to lack of rule of law.

Uganda's first national integrity survey was carried out in 1998 by CIET International, on behalf of the Inspectorate of Government, and designed to collect and evaluate experiences and perceptions of corruption in public services provisions from people in all 45 districts of Uganda. The findings of the 1998 study reported wide-scale systematically orchestrated petty corruption in many areas of Uganda's key public services: primary education, health, police, local administration, judiciary, Uganda Revenue Authority (URA), Uganda's integrated customs and excise, and inland revenue services. Most significantly, the survey confirmed that service users who paid bribes did not obtain better services than people who did not (Inspectorate of Government 1998). These are all critical areas that facilitate the functioning of effective public administration machinery, and the presence of this cancer of corruption generates unexpected negative consequences to the citizens.

In the same year, a 1998 World Bank mission to Uganda identified a high prevalence of corruption in public revenue and expenditure management, public procurement systems, public enterprise reform and privatization programs, political financing, and the military. The mission concluded then that the country was experiencing significant corruption. Coping with its resultant heavy burden on economic growth and poverty alleviation, it was observed, called for a series of institutional changes to strengthen the systems of government procurement and revenue collection and the investigations, as well as prosecution of all those engaged in corruption. The report highlighted publicly reported incidents of grand corruption and ended with a plea for a strong signal from top leadership that corruption of public officials needed to be punished.

In 2003, a case study on the prevalence of corruption in the country, specifically in the local government, education, justice, law and order, and procurement sectors, was commissioned by the Royal Netherlands Embassy in Uganda (2003). Findings of the study confirmed that while corruption was present in every sector, a recurrent issue, the so-called cross-cutting issue was procurement. It was reported that 90% of all corruption cases were procurement related, and 65% of this percentage, according to the Inspectorate of Government (IG) report, were related to procurement of government services and works. Procurement of supplies, another third category of any government procurement, though not mentioned, cannot be an exception as a breeding ground for corruption. However, public monies involved in this category are small compared to monies in the procurement of works and services. The U.S. Department of State Investment Climate Statements for 2009 noted that government procurement was not transparent, particularly for defense items. In previous years, several high-profile government tenders for infrastructure projects were suspended due to allegations of corruption. Petty corruption is likely to be dominant in the procurement of supplies, while grand corruption and state capture are likely to be dominant in the procurement of works and services because of the amounts involved, but also the complexity and number of players interested in these forms of procurements.

A baseline survey of national public procurement integrity conducted in 2006 by the Procurement and Disposal of Assets Authority (PPDA), the Inspectorate of Government (IG), and U.S. Agency for International Development (USAID) reported that illegal payments to secure government contracts at both the local and central levels were even higher, representing approximately 7% to 9% of the contract value. In 2007, the World Bank worldwide governance indicators noted that Uganda performed moderately in terms of regulatory quality (48.5) and government effectiveness (42.7), below average in terms of rule of law (37.6), and voice and accountability (33.2), and weakly in terms of control of corruption (24.6 compared to 26.2 in 2003) and political stability (13.9). Still in 2007, the government circumvented official procurement guidelines to contract an unknown company, Kenlloyd Logistics, to replenish Uganda's fuel reserves. Media reports said the company was being run by the son-in-law of the foreign minister, who is himself related to the president.

The Inspectorate of Government (IG) as a constitutional body is mandated under Chapter 13 of the 1995 Constitution of the Republic of Uganda to promote good governance, fight corruption, and enforce the leadership code of conduct. Specifically, Article 231 of the constitution requires the Inspectorate of Government to submit to parliament at least once every six months a report of the performance of its functions, making such recommendations as it considers necessary and containing such information as parliament may require. In its 23rd report (Inspectorate of Government, 2010) to the parliament of Uganda, the inspectorate reported as shown in Table 3.5.

Out of 4,089 complaints that were available for investigation, a total of 629 were investigated and completed, out of which 184 reports were issued, while 445

Table 3.5 Summary of the Number of Complaints Received by IG for 2009 and 2010

Number of Complaints	July–December 2009	January–June 2010	% Change
Complaints brought forward	2,572	2,938	
Audit reports	189	111	
New complaints received	827	1,040	
Investigated and completed	543	629	
Referred to other institutions	107	109	
Total complaints concluded	650	738	
Carried forward	2,938	3,351	

Source: Inspectorate of Government of Uganda, First Annual Report on Corruption Trends in Uganda: Using the Data Tracking Mechanism, Economic Policy Research Centre, 2009 and 2010. Available online at http://www.ansa-africa.net/uploads/documents/publications/EPRC_First_annual_report_November 2010.pdf.

complaints were handled, finalized, and results communicated without issuing reports. Preliminary inquiries were carried out for 109 complaints that were later referred to other institutions for appropriate action. During the previous period, a total of 543 complaints were investigated and completed compared to 629 complaints that were investigated during the current period, accounting for a 15% increment in the complaints investigated. The new complaints received increased from 827 (in the previous period) to 1,040 in the current period, accounting for a 25% increment. A total of 3,351 complaints were carried forward to the next period. Of the total number of new complaints received by the Inspectorate of Government, 487 (46.8%) were received at the headquarters in Kampala, while 553 (53.2%) were registered at the regional offices.

So far, evidence adduced suggests that in Uganda, there are certain administrative areas that are more prone to corruption than others. For example, the most corrupt sectors where grand-level corruption is likely to be pronounced or is pronounced include the oil and energy sector, road construction, education, health, local government, judiciary, the police, anticorruption agencies themselves, and public service. Within these sectors, certain professional functions are more corrupt than others. Evidence so far suggests that the public administration professions in Uganda more prone to corruption include those dealing with mainstream public finance, public procurement, internal audit, human resources management, law, and road construction professionals of all forms.

Effects of Corruption in Uganda

Lawal (2007) suggests that Africa presents a typical case of the countries in the world whose development has been undermined and retarded by the menace of corrupt practices. A series of reforms have been carried out in all the African countries so as to make the system (African states) efficient and results oriented. In the background to the 2010 corruption tracking report, the Inspectorate of Government (IG) observes: "Corruption remains an impediment to development and a barrier to poverty reduction in Uganda and in many other African countries. It is a problem, both at national and local government levels which manifest itself as bribery, financial leakages, conflict of interest, embezzlement, false accounting, fraud, influence peddling, nepotism, theft of public funds or theft of public assets. With the discovery of oil and the prospect of substantial windfall oil revenues coming on stream in the relatively near future, Uganda is bound to face major challenges with regard to the problem of corruption." Other international efforts to documenting the persistence of corruption in Uganda are evidently visible.

Measuring the costs of corruption is not an easy task. However, Stapenhurst and Kpundeh (1999: 4) have suggested that although the economic costs of corruption are difficult to measure, some studies suggest that they include the following: a 3 to 10% increase in the price of a given transaction to speed up the delivery of a government service, inflated prices of goods (as much as 15 to 20% higher) as a result of government-imposed monopolies, a loss of as much as 50% of government tax revenue because of graft and corruption, and excessive charges to government for goods and services because of overbilling on procurement contracts or the purchase of expensive and unnecessary items, with government paying 20% to 100% more than necessary.

The recently launched National Development Plan of the country (2010) singles out procurement corruption as one of the eight major factors likely to affect the implementation of the five-year development plan of the country. Other international efforts to documenting the persistence of corruption in Uganda have been made. According to Anticorruption Coalition Uganda (ACCU), a civil society organization formed to give more voice to anticorruption advocacy in the country, Uganda loses 200 billion shillings annually as a result of flaws in public procurement processes. On April 16, 2008, *The New Vision* newspaper reported that in 2007, the government of Uganda lost an estimated 148.5 billion shillings in procurement-related malpractices, and this position was confirmed by the Transparency International report (2009), which noted that public procurement was marred by high levels of corruption. Procurement officers and persons involved in procurement activities use wrong methods, leading to high procurement costs, poor quality purchases, late deliveries, or no deliveries at all. During preparations to host the Commonwealth Heads of Government Meeting (CHOGM) in 2007 in Uganda, there were many cases of impunity violations of existing procurement regulations involving high-ranking politicians and bureaucrats, and significant sums of taxpayers' money were lost. A report by the Public Accounts Committee of parliament, which implicated a number of top ministers and the vice president of the country, is now gathering dust in the good offices of the national parliament, as it was blocked by these powerful forces from being debated. In one case pointed out in this same inquiry, the value of the procurement to be made exceeded 100 million shillings, and the direct procurement method was used as opposed to the competitive procurement method that ought to have been used as required by the law.

Corruption seriously undermines democracy and good governance. Corruption in elections and legislative bodies reduces accountability and representation in policy making. Corruption in the judiciary has suspended the rule of law, and corruption in public administration has resulted in the unequal provision of services. Corruption has had devastating effects on governance and the electoral process. Corruption undermines fair pay, justice and equal opportunities, equality and nondiscrimination, which are underlying principles of human rights. Corruption has countless ways in which it negatively affects the economic and social rights, as well as the rights to education, health, adequate standard of living (including decent shelter, clean water, adequate food, and clothing), social security, employment, just and favorable conditions for work, etc. Corruption has also undermined economic development by increasing the cost of business through the price of bribes themselves, the management cost of negotiating with officials, and the risk of breached agreements or detection. In Uganda, corruption has generated economic distortions in the public sector by pulling public investments away from education, into projects where bribes and kickbacks are more plentiful. Corruption has lowered compliance with construction, environment, or other regulations, reduced the quality of government services, and increased the budgetary pressures on government.

By addressing corruption, local governments will enjoy substantial benefits. For example, Bitarabeho (2003) informs us that the fight against corruption in Bushenyi District in Uganda enhanced service delivery in that district through increased district revenues, which rose from Ushs 13.9 billion in 1998 to Ushs 26.4 billion. In the same period, water coverage increased from 51% to 62.5%, while feeder roads coverage increased from 670 km to 810 km in 2002. Out of these kilometers, 65% were eventually well maintained. Other benefits included: (1) recruitment and retention of qualified and competent personnel in public service, (2) selection of competent contractors, (3) increased public awareness on key issues of development and corruption, (4) adherence to financial regulations, as well as (5) apprehending, prosecuting, interdicting, and dismissing corrupt civil servants who violated the standing regulations. Experience shows that no single approach to curbing corruption is likely to be effective. Instead, success involves a wide range of strategies working together as much as possible in an integrated fashion. These must include strategies that reduce the opportunity and benefits of corruption (Stapenhurst and Kpundeh 1999).

Approaches in addressing corruption have often been of two forms. First, some approaches aim at restraining unethical or corrupt behavior through legal and regulatory sanctions, codes of conduct, independent watchdogs in the public sector, or in the private sector, the practice of whistle-blowing. Second has been the increased stress on the role of civic education to increase public awareness of their rights to standards from government, and innovative experiential learning and facilitated reflexivity aimed in public and private sectors alike at the rediscovery of the higher purpose (Collins 2011). Experience in all countries shows that no single approach can be effective in addressing the problem of corruption. The corruption problem can be addressed through a number of actions. It has been suggested, for example, that in Uganda it can be done through law reform, public sector pay reform, adequate resourcing of anticorruption agencies, commissions of inquiry, combating a culture of impunity, strengthening the accountability regime, court awards and compensation claims, addressing corruption in local governments, and semiannual anticorruption reviews.

Conclusion

Both the institutions of society and the organizations that we create to help us influence and navigate the world in which we live are significantly shaped by both the environment in which we operate and their immediate history (Rosenbaum 2011).

Such is true for a subject like corruption in public administration. Corruption keeps prevailing in new forms as public administration systems equally keep changing due to new developments. Uganda has made great efforts at establishing systems to fight corruption. By 1970, the Prevention of Corruption Act (1970) had been enacted; then the Inspector General of Government Statute (1988), the Anticorruption Act (2009), and the enforcement of the Leadership Code of Conduct Act (2002) were also put in place. However, the implementation of corruption prevention and detection and of anticorruption enforcement has been particularly weak. In a recent study of 114 countries, Uganda was found to have had the largest implementation gap, in which it was scored very highly (99%) on having a very good legal framework, but was awarded 45% for having a weak implementation record, giving an implementation gap of 54% (Global Integrity Report 2009).

There are seven government institutions that play a role in fighting corruption in Uganda, namely, the Inspectorate of Government, the Directorate of Ethics and Integrity, the Directorate of Public Prosecutions, the Criminal Investigations Department of the Police, the auditor general, the Public Procurement and Disposal of Public Assets Authority, and the Public Accounts Committee of parliament. It has to be kept in mind that even though these institutions are in place to curb corruption, sometimes they cannot execute their tasks properly, not only due to lack of capacity and infrastructure, but also due to corruption within some of the institutions. Currently, however, more collaboration and cooperation is taking place within the several institutions through, for example, the Interagency Forum, the Accountability Sector, and the African Parliamentarians Network against Corruption.

To tackle the challenge posed by anticorruption enforcement, the government of Uganda should consider the adoption and implementation of good enforcement practices similar to those of other countries that have made a serious commitment in this area; for example, Bangladesh has adopted a 60-day timeline for handling corruption prosecution in Bangladesh; Ghana has established a fast-track court for corruption cases in Ghana; and use of speedy and effective prosecutorial methods, including the protection of whistle-blowers in Singapore. We would recommend that government studies these examples and adopts at least one of the mechanisms as a way to accelerate prosecutions.

References

Adamolekun, L. 1982. *Public administration: A Nigerian and comparative perspective.* London: Longman.

Aidt, A., Dutta, J., and Sena, V. 2008. Government regimes, corruption, and growth: Theory and evidence. *Journal of Comparative Economics* 36: 195–220.

Ake, C. 1996. *Democracy and development in Africa.* Ibadan, Nigeria: Spectrum Books.

Alam, M.S. 1989. Anatomy of corruption: An approach to the political economy of underdevelopment. *American Journal of Economics and Sociology* 48(4): 441–456.

Ani, M., and Carmen, S. 2009. *The impact of reducing the administrative costs on the efficiency in the public sector.* MPRA Paper 19018. http://mpra.ub.uni-muenchen.de/19018/ MPRA (accessed on January 1, 2011).
Ashaba-Aheebwa, J. 2009. Ethics and integrity in local governments in Uganda. Paper prepared for the Africa Local Government Action Forum (ALGAF IX, Session I).
Bana, B., and Basheka, B.C. 2011. Governance and democracy as critical pillars for successful East African regional integration. Paper presented at the East African Conference, Dar e salaam, December 19–21.
Barker, T., and Carter, D.L. 1994. *Police deviance.* 3rd ed. Cincinnati, OH: Anderson.
Bayart, J.F. 1993. *The state in Africa: The politics of the belly.* London: Longman.
Bhatta, G. 2006. *International dictionary of public management and governance.* London: M.E. Sharpe.
Bitarabeho, J. 2003. *Curbing corruption and promoting transparency in local governments: The experience of Bushenyi District, Uganda.* Paper presented as part of the World Bank's open and participatory government program at the local level. Washington, DC: World Bank Institute. http://info.worldbank.org/etools/docs/library/94857/gapglobal/pdf/bushenyi_background.pdf (accessed on January 21, 2011).
Breton, A., and Wintrobe, R. 1985. *The logic of bureaucratic conduct: An economic analysis of competition, exchange, and efficiency in private and public organizations.* New York: Cambridge University Press.
Chabal, P., and Daloz, J.-P. 1999. *Africa works: Disorder as political instrument.* London: James Currey.
Collier, P. 2000. How to reduce corruption. *African Development Review* 12(2): 191–205.
Collins, P. 2011. The vicissitudes of change: Public policy sidelines. In *Public Administration in a Global Context: IASIA AT 50,* ed. O.P. Dwivedi. Bruylant, Brussels.
Courts of Judicature. 2008. *Anti-corruption division of the high court: Strategy and plan.* Kampala, Uganda.
Denhardt, R.B., and Denhardt, J.V. 2000. The new public service: Serving rather than steering. *Public Administration Review* 60(6).
Diamond, L.J. 1990. Three paradoxes of democracy. *Journal of Democracy* 1(3): 48–60.
Dicklich, S. 1994. The democratization of Uganda under the NRM regime. Paper prepared for presentation at the XVIth World Congress of the International Political Science Association, August 21–25.
Dimock, M.E., Dimock, G.O., and Koerug, L.W. 1953. *Public administration.* Rev. ed. New York: Rinehart and Company.
Dore, R., Lazonick, W., and O'Sullivan, M. 1999. Varieties of capitalism in the 20th century. http://oxrep.oxfordjournals.org/content/15/4/102.short.
Dutta, A., Toke, J., and Sena, V. 2008. Governance regimes, corruption and growth: Theory and evidence. *Journal of Comparative Economics* 36: 195–220.
Freedom House. 2010. Countries at the cross roads report. http://www.freedomhouse.org/report/countries-crossroads/countries-crossroads-2010.
Frimpong, K., and Jacques, G., eds. 1999. *Corruption, democracy and good governance in Africa. Essays on accountability and ethical behavior.* Botswana: Lightbooks.
Gatune, J., and Najam, A. 2011. Africa 2060: What could be driving the good news from Africa? *Foresight* 13(3): 100–110.
Gildenhuys, J.S.H. 1997. *Public financial management.* Pretoria: J.L. Van Schaik.
Giordano, R., Tommasino, P., and Casiraghi, M. 2008. Behind public sector efficiency: The role of culture and institutions. http://www.3.unipv.it/websiep/2009/200990.pdf.

Global Integrity Report. 2009. *Global integrity report by global integrity organization.* Washington, DC.
Harris, G. 2005. *Corruption: How to deal with its impact on business and society.* California: American Group.
Hughes, O.E. 2003. *Public management and administration: An introduction.* 3rd ed. New York: Palgrave-Macmillan.
Inspectorate of Government (IG). 1999. *Building integrity to fight corruption to improve service delivery.* Kampala, Uganda.
Inspectorate of Government (IG). 2008a. *National integrity baseline survey report.* Kampala, Uganda.
Inspectorate of Government (IG). 2008b. *Third national integrity survey: Final report.* Kampala.
Inspectorate of Government (IG). 2009. *Annual reports to parliament of Uganda.* Kampala, Uganda.
Inspectorate of Government (IG). 2010. *Annual reports to parliament of Uganda.* Kampala, Uganda.
Inspectorate of Government (IG). 2010. First annual report on corruption trends in Uganda: Using the data tracking mechanism. Economic Policy Research Center. http://www.ansa-africa.net/uploads/documents/publications/EPRC_First_annual_report_November2010.pdf (accessed January 22, 2011).
Jayapalan, N. 2000. *Public administration.* New Delhi: Atlantic Publishers and Distributors.
Kantor, M. (1996). Remarks prepared for delivery to the Emergency Committee for American Trade. March 6. http://www.clintonlibrary.com (accessed February 19, 2012).
Lawal, G. 2007. Corruption and development in Africa: Challenges for political and economic change. *Humanity and Social Sciences Journal* 2(1): 1–7.
Martin, S.B. 2005. The impact of crime on business: A model for prevention, detection and remedy. *Journal of Management and Marketing Research* 12, 23–36.
Mathur, M. 1986. *Administering development: Prospects and constraints.* London: Sage Publications.
Mbaku, J.M. 1998. Bureaucratic and political corruption in Africa. In *Corruption and the crisis of institutional reforms in Africa*, ed. J.M. Mbaku. African Studies 47. Lewiston, NY: Edwin Mellen Press.
Mbaku, J.M. 2007. *Corruption in Africa: Causes, consequences, and cleanups.* Toronto: Lexington Books.
Ngotho wa, K., and Awasom, S. 2008. Impact of corruption on women's economic empowerment in Africa. http://www.giz.de/Themen/de/dokumente/gtz2008-en-workshop-paper-ngotho-wa-kariuki.pdf.
Njoku, J.U. 2005. Colonial political re-engineering and the genesis of modern corruption in African public service: The issue of the warrant chiefs of south eastern Nigeria as a case in point. *Nordic Journal of African Studies* 14(1): 99–116.
Njunwa, M. 2008. Combating corruption in Tanzania's public service: Success and challenges. http://napsipag.org/PDF/MUJWAHUZI_NJUNWA.pdf.
Noonan, J., Jr. 1984. *Bribes.* New York: MacMillan.
OECD. 1999. Public sector corruption: An international survey of preventive measures. http://BOOKS.GOOGLE.CO.UG/Books.
Padovani, E., and Scorsone, E. 2009. Comparing local governments' performance internationally: A mission impossible? *International Review of Administrative Sciences* 75(2).
Palmier, L. 1985. *The control of bureaucratic corruption: Case studies in Asia.* New Delhi: Allied Publishers.

Park, H., and Blenkinsopp, J. 2011. The roles of transparency and trust in the relationship between corruption and citizen satisfaction. *International Review of Administrative Science* 77(2): 254–274.

Peters, G.B. 2004. Governance and public bureaucracy: New forms of democracy or new forms of control? *Asia Pacific Journal of Public Administration* 26(1): 3–15.

Rose-Ackerman, S. 1999. *Corruption and government: Causes, consequences and reform.* Cambridge: Cambridge University Press.

Rosenbaum, A. 2011. The post-governance world: Continuing challenges, new opportunities. In *Public Administration in a Global Context: IASIA AT 50*, ed. O.P. Dwivedi. Bruylant, Brussels.

Rotberg, R.I., and Gisselquist, R.M. 2009. *Strengthening African governance: Index of African governance, results and rankings 2009.* Cambridge, MA: Kennedy School of Government, Harvard University, and World Peace Foundation.

Royal Netherlands Embassy Kampala, Uganda. 2003. Uganda: The fight against corruption: A case study on the prevalence of corruption in Uganda, specifically in local government, education, justice, law and order, and procurement. http://www.u4.no/document/showdoc.cfm?id=94 (accessed on January 21, 2011).

Shafritz, J.M., Rusell, E.W., and Borick, C.P. 2011. *Introducing public administration.* 7th ed. London: Pearson.

Stapenhurst, R., and Kpundeh, S. 1999. *Curbing corruption: Toward a model for building national integrity.* Washington, DC: World Bank Economic Development Institute.

Svensson, J. 2005. Eight questions about corruption. *Journal of Economic Perspectives* 19: 19–42.

Thai, K.V. et al. (Eds.). 2005. *Challenges in public procurement: An international perspective.* Boca Raton: PRAcademics Press.

Transparency International. 2009. *Global corruption barometer.* Berlin: International Secretariat.

Treisman, D. 2000. The causes of corruption: A cross-national study. *Journal of Public Economics* 76: 399–457.

Uneke, O. 2010. Corruption in Africa south of the Sahara: Bureaucratic facilitator or handicap to development? *Journal of Pan African Studies* 3,6: 111–128.

World Bank. 1994. *Adjustment in Africa: Reforms, results and the road ahead.* Oxford: Oxford University Press.

World Bank. 2010. African development report indicators 2010: Silent and lethal. How quiet corruption undermines Africa's development efforts. Washington, DC: The World Bank.

Chapter 4

Public Sector Reforms in Nigeria: 1999–2009

Adewale Banjo

Contents

Introduction and Conceptual Framework 83
Case of Nigeria 85
PSR in Nigeria: A Review of Studies 86
Millennium Reforms: Background 89
Public Sector Reforms 1999–2009: Overview 91
Conclusion and Recommendations 94
References 94

Introduction and Conceptual Framework

Generally, the primary role of the public servant is to implement policies made by the elected public officials. Cloete (2006) defined public service as that part of an economy whose activities are under state control. When the public service efficiently and effectively delivers to the customers, national development is promoted. However, in order to achieve this goal, public service must be regularly regulated, shaped, and reshaped for maximum positive results.

Notwithstanding that theory and practice are rarely congruent in the real world, it equally appears that public sector reforms have not really achieved their main objective in Nigeria. This is a result of the difference in both the value and orientation of the political class that articulates the will of the state and that of the bureaucracy, whose principal function is to execute the will of the state as articulated by the chief executive.

Many scholars and bureaucrats have expressed various views to the meaning and desirability of public sector reforms. As many as the views are, there is a consensus that public sector reforms are attempts to enhance the capability of the public service. The idea behind it is that the sector has some deficiencies, which must be rectified to make it more effective. Arguably, the essence of reform is to purify the public sector's blood and prevent stagnation. Indeed, public sector reform can be described as a deliberate attempt to use power, authority, and influence to change the goal, structure, or procedure of the public sector, and therefore alter the behavior of its personnel.

In the literature six main goals of public sector reform have been identified. These include (Alexandra 2007; Rundell 2010; Asiodu 1999; Yesufu 1996; Obadan 2003; Iyoha 1999; Oshinebo 2002; Mercellina 2007):

1. Traditional administrative efficiency in the sense of saving money through form simplification, procedure change, duplication reduction, and methods approach
2. Reduction of perceived weakness, such as corruption, favoritism, and political spoils
3. Changing a particular main component of the administration system so as to meet some local usage
4. Adjusting the administrative system to advance overriding societal objectives such as accelerated modernization
5. Changing the division of labor between the administrative system and the political system
6. Changing the relation between the administrative system and the population or selected population segments

Further, public sector reform refers to all the processes put in place to enhance the efficiency and effectiveness of public servants and their ability to respond in practical terms to the policy decision of the chief executive, that is, the administrative system with the in-built orientation for goal attainment and quick responses to demand on the system.

This, of course, is in line with the World Bank demand in its annual report of 1988, referring to the public sector reform as the process to keep the adjustment and institutional development that not only foster effective macro economic management, but also build an internal capacity for policy analysis and implementation.

As observed by the then Nigeria head of state, General Ibrahim Babangida, while inaugurating a seven-man panel under the chairmanship of Mr. Alison Ayida, in 1988, the idea of public sector reform was to bring all the lofty ideas of efficiency, professionalism, and accountability and address all the fundamental problems of the public service.

Obadan (2003) in his contribution identifies public sector reform as an ideological drive of globalization, as globalization in its present status is a process that is more embracing and manifesting with such a very strong face that countries are ready to pull down the barriers that stand between development and backwardness in her bureaucratic operation.

Obadan (2003) sees public sector reform as a worldwide phenomenon, which means different things to different people and different things to the same people across time and space. However, it is basically referred to as the growing interdependence of the national policy making as a result of liberalization of financial market development technology and institutions. Public service reform is defined as producing a measurable improvement in services or positive change in relationship between the state and citizens. Lienert and Modi (1998) found out that there is limited success of African states in public service reform. The reforms are most often embarked upon to reduce bureaucratic abnormality, pervasiveness in administration, and institutional corruption, and are ambivalent to effective performance on the part of public functionaries. It is therefore not surprising that public sector reform is regarded as an integral part of any developmental process designed to enhance efficiency of the public service. Agbakoba (2004) argued that the essence of reform is to align delivery to cultural dictates of a nation.

Case of Nigeria

From the foregoing, it can be further enunciated that public sector reform (PSR) is majorly concerned with strengthening the way in which the public sector is managed. The public sector may be overextended, attempting to do too much with too few resources. It may be poorly organized, its decision-making processes may be irrational, staff may be mismanaged, accountability may be weak, public programs may be poorly designed and public services poorly delivered. PSR is the attempt to fix these problems.

Since the 1980s, developed and developing countries have been embarking on public sector management reforms. The role and institutional character of the state has been questioned, and the public sector has been under pressure to adopt private sector orientations. The earlier reforms aimed at shaping a public administration that could lead national development, and were based on the same institutional peculiarities inherited from the colonial period. More recently, the World Bank and other donors in Africa have been concerned with finding alternative ways of organizing and managing the public services and redefining the role of the state to give more prominence to markets and competition, and to the private and voluntary sectors. The alternative vision, based on issues of efficiency, representation, participation, and accountability, has sought to create a market-friendly, liberalized, lean, decentralized, customer-oriented, managerial, and democratic state.

Table 4.1 Nigeria Reform Commissions

Reform Commissions	Date
Tudoe Davies Commission	1945
Sir Walter Harragin Commission	1946
Gorsuch Commission	1954
Mbanefo Commission	1959
Morgan Commission	1963
Simeon Adebo Commission	1971
Udoji Commission	1971–1974
Williams and Williams Commission	1975
Presidential Commission on Salaries and Conditions of Service of University Staff (Cookey Commission) Report	1981
Presidential Commission on Parastatals (Onosode Commission) Report	1981
Dotun Philip Panel	1985
Public service reforms in Nigeria	1988
Justice Atanda Fatai Williams Committee	1990
Longe Commission Report	1991
Allison Ayida Panel	1994
Report of the Vision 2010 Committee	1997
Committee on Harmonization of Remuneration in the Public Service	1998

During the last two decades, most African countries have embarked on comprehensive public sector reform programs, and in many cases have received assistance from international institutions. Nigeria can be described as the most reform driven on the continent. The Nigerian experience is graphically presented in Table 4.1.

PSR in Nigeria: A Review of Studies

Recent studies have presented three distinct reasons that scholars have identified as the basis/reasons for reforms in Nigeria. These are the corrective, compliance, and complementary reasons. Ogujiuba and Obiechina (2011) argued in line with the *corrective/remediation* basis for reforms. The study observed that evidence as to whether and how reforms are remedying the traditional weaknesses of the financial sector is so far limited in Nigeria. Ongoing reforms to improve banks' corporate governance and internal systems suggest that the prospects for the financial sector to perform profitably and prudently, while reducing volatility in the system, exist. The study adopts an empirical review approach for its analysis. He argues that the present reforms be reviewed and sustained in an orderly manner, for appropriate channeling of resources for investment and productoisie purposes. Efforts should be concentrated on the linkages of the sector with macro accounts and where financial development appears to have been the weakest. Furthermore, advancement of the financial sector vis-à-vis instruments should be the primary focus for the authorities. A counterfactual feedback mechanism should also be integrated within the financial sector for an appropriate signaling for the economic productive base.

The study further noted that the financial system in Nigeria still remains fragile and vulnerable to several external risks, including (1) the economy's high dependence on volatile oil proceeds; (2) economic mismanagement, in particular fiscal imprudence; and (3) political uncertainty. Given the large size and role of the government in economic activity and its virtual monopoly over the country's export earnings, fiscal indiscipline is the single most important threat to the economy and the financial sector today. Adopting a prudent, medium-term-oriented fiscal policy and introducing more market-based mechanisms in the foreign exchange market and the domestic money market would help to reduce vulnerabilities, remove distortions, and hence improve the efficiency of the financial system.

Habu (2009) belongs to the *compliance school*. He argued that the one major undercurrent in Nigeria's democratization process in post-military rule is the reform of the public sector, which is carried out in the face of the heightened drive for globalization, and the ascendancy of neoliberal measures that are promoted by the International Monetary Fund (IMF) and World Bank. The reform is by no means a new process in the country's agenda for development, as its main features were encapsulated in the Structural Adjustment Program (SAP) introduced in 1986. However, the dynamics of the economic policy reform measures and their attendant contradictions since the return to civilian rule in 1999 have further heightened debate and contestation, in addition to adding another dilemma to the realization of democratic dividends. This is more pronounced in the economic disempowerment of the majority population in the country.

Democratization in the face of neoliberal reforms since the return of democracy in Nigeria in 1999 is an archetypical manifestation of democracy without responsive and responsible leadership. At the heart of the crisis of the Nigerian state in post-military rule is the problem of good governance. This explains why the state considers the implementation of public sector reform through privatization without looking into the main reasons why public enterprises are inefficient, corrupt, and counterproductive. By embarking on privatization, the state has created a window of opportunity for the local and international bourgeoisie to use the exercise as a gold mine for accumulation, thereby disempowering the society benefiting from public facilities at affordable rates. Worse still, the enterprises that had been sold have not demonstrated any significant improvement in their services, as is the case with the Power Holding Company of Nigeria (PHCN) and Nigeria Telecommunications (NITEL).

In addition, the view that holds that the private sector is by far more efficient and enduring in comparison with public enterprises is not factually supported. The performance of the two sectors is determined by many variables, which include, inter alia, political, economic, sociocultural, and environmental factors. According to the Manufacturers Association of Nigeria (MAN), in an eight-year period (1999–2007) of the civilian administration in Nigeria, over 1,800 industries closed down due to unfavorable economic climate (*Daily Trust*, April 1, 2007).

In Nigeria, a reform in the public sector in general and public enterprises in particular is needed in order to correct the ailing enterprises and address the fundamental question of why they are inefficient and embroiled in corruption. But transferring ownership of these enterprises from the state to private individuals and groups on the basis of their affiliation with the state is a disservice to the people and negation of their democratic rights. Their labor and taxes were used to set up these enterprises, and without being consulted, their heritage of development and welfare enrichment has been sold to the capitalist class.

Barima and Farhad (2010) argue that President Obasanjo and the donor community pursued a mutually convenient close relationship that impacted the nature of reform implementation during his tenure in office. They identify the forces motivating these close relations and illustrate how they shaped Obasanjo's record of economic, governance, and political reform. Several specific instances—debt relief, oil sector transparency, and the third-term gambit—illustrate both the benefits and shortcomings of the donor community as a reform advocate in Nigeria. They further state that international actors can increase the incentives for reform. They can offer material gains, as demonstrated dramatically by the Paris Club debt relief. But they can also offer reputational gains, such as the favorable attention and prestige that Obasanjo has gained from his promotion of oil sector transparency.

Ijeoma (2006) is of the *complementary* school. He argues that public health and human rights are complementary approaches to promoting and protecting human dignity and well-being. The aim of his paper is to examine international provisions and national policies on health and human rights that regulate the health system in Nigeria, along with the institutional arrangements created for the design and implementation of health services. The paper reviews the framework for policy formulation and planning on health matters and emphasizes the responsibilities of the state to implement Millennium Development Goals and international obligations of human rights.

Several reasons have been proffered for the dismal situation in Nigeria's health sector, the most important being the country's political instability and poor governance, the weak political commitment to addressing the crisis in the health sector, inadequate budgetary allocations, institutionalized corruption and waste, overdependence on donors, fragmentation of the health system into a mass of poorly coordinated, parallel, vertical programs, and the failure to give real content to the declared aims of decentralization and community participation in management. Nigeria's return to a democracy in 1999 provided opportunities for a fresh approach to health sector reform. However, signs of greater political will to tackle the underlying problems affecting the health system are still lacking despite a renewed enthusiasm on the part of some development partners and donors to assist in national efforts. The poor record of the public health service over the past two decades, despite a policy framework emphasizing primary health care, is largely attributable to the broader crisis of governance and leadership. The decay of institutional capacity, resulting from the collapse in salaries, brain drain, staff demotivation, and the generalization of corrupt practices, has taken a heavy toll on the public health system. Other factors include weak accountability and the limited impact of investments in staff development. In conclusion, the relevance, appropriateness, and potential for positive impact of policies and initiatives require political, legal, and social commitments by government to ensure that reform strategies realize and implement measures that would improve health delivery in Nigeria.

The *compliance report* M2PressWire (2009) reported that the World Bank's Board of Executive Directors approved a US$500 million development policy credit to support Nigeria's economic reforms in the financial sector and public financial management. The credit is in response to the current global financial crisis. "The loan is intended to provide budgetary support to the Federal Government of Nigeria to partially off-set the fiscal impact of the crisis as well as maintain its current economic reform path in the financial sector, fiscal policy and financial management, and governance," said Michael Fuchs, lead financial economist and task team leader.

Lohor (2006) reported that President Olusegun Obasanjo promised that he would ensure that all public sector reforms embarked upon by his administration are not to be stopped by any incoming administration. The president who emphasized that the reforms would be implemented "to the point of irreversibility" added that "we do not want the reforms to be reversed." Such a move could promote growth and stability in a sociopolitical system that has a history of instability and a wide range of failed policies and reforms.

Millennium Reforms: Background

As alluded to above, public sector management reforms are a central feature of economic policy reform programs. However, the performance of such reforms in Africa remains hindered by myriad factors, including lack of efficiency, lack of accountability, ineffective management practices, and corruption. However, despite the tremendous efforts and resources that have been allocated to this endeavor, progress remains scant. This is problematic to this study, and the aim is to highlight and review further efforts made by the Nigerian state on reform toward development and progress in the first decades of the fourth republic, 1999–2009.

This is important because the pivotal role of a well-functioning public sector in Africa's development process is indisputable. The challenge, however, is finding ways to create effective public sector organizations capable of facilitating national development. Indeed, many African countries, with the support of the World Bank and other pro-reform international institutions, have since the 1980s experimented with various public sector reform strategies.

These policies include the World Bank's first- and second-generation public sector reform programs. The first-generation reforms were introduced in the 1980s and focused on reducing the explosive public sector wage bill. However, they led to the erosion of public sector wages vis-à-vis the private sector, and many skilled workers left public employment. The second-generation reforms were introduced in the 1990s to improve the quality of the public sector, but these too have so far produced disappointing results in many African countries.

The first- and second-generation policies have two important flaws. First, the underlying assumption of the policies is that all public organizations are ineffective. Clearly, this assumption is flawed because within each country there are public organizations that perform relatively well, given the constraints that they face (Grindle 1997; Owusu 2005). Second, policies were applied across the board, i.e., a one-size-fits-all solution, and therefore did not take into consideration the country-specific conditions under which organizations operate. Moreover, because the policies are not based on the experiences of organizations, they are seen as outside impositions.

Failed accountability is at the root of public sector dysfunction. A strong bond of accountability between citizens and the public sector generates demand for PSR. Public sector performance is determined to an important extent by the interplay between the public sector and the country's key institutions of accountability. Successful PSR strategies should therefore be adapted to and (where possible) address shortcomings in the accountability environment within which the public sector operates. Reformers must have an appreciation of factors such as Internal Auditors' access to information about public programs and public expenditure, their capacity to analyze information about the public sector and place demands on it for better performance, and the degree to which public agencies feel compelled to respond.

Although local political and bureaucratic leadership is an essential ingredient for PSR, it is not sufficient. The public administration cannot be relied upon to reform itself. Impetus for reform must come from local stakeholders who are outside as well as inside the public sector. Organized civil society (e.g., civic associations, users' groups, labor unions, nongovernmental organizations (NGOs)), the private sector, political parties, and other influential domestic institutions all have a critically important role to play in pressuring the public sector to do a better job of serving society.

Public sector reforms in Nigeria were introduced to drive the human resource development process and form an effective resource utilization policy. The main goal of the government was to set a proper man management system. The development of any country very much depends on the caliber and organization of the human resources. So, the government of Nigeria introduced public sector reform.

Nigeria was not able to move along with the worldwide development in public sector reform. Revenues were not coming smoothly, which increased the economic and financial pressure. Rate of unemployment was on the higher side. New and upcoming technical as well as social challenges were coming, and political situations were getting unstable. The government introduced a contractual system for the laborers. Moreover, a direct taxation system was started for collecting tax from the laborers. The focus of the government remained on the optimum utilization of the human resources. Therefore, several changes had been made in the recruitment policies. Stress had been given on the experience and qualification of the resources.

In the second stage of public sector reform, the Nigerian government paid attention to the training and development program of the human resources. Several private and foreign enterprises were encouraged to train the workers. The Center for Management Development (CMD), the Administrative Staff College of Nigeria (ASCON), and the Industrial Training Fund (ITF) had been managing the training programs from the early 1970s. The government announced several policies and programs to enhance the operation of those organizations.

The employment policies were made more transparent to overcome the socio-economic crisis. Several administrative review commissions had been formed to improve the management of the public as well as private enterprises. More stress had been given by the government to improve inter- and intradepartmental communication. Ministry headquarters were centralized to make controlling the system easy. Through this reform the government of Nigeria was able to improve the labor quality. Unemployment issues had been solved to some extent. And lastly, the public service capacity had been enhanced, through which the performance deficits were minimized within 2005.

Public Sector Reforms 1999–2009: Overview

The return of democracy to Nigeria in 1999 was seen as a step forward in the protracted fight against persistent public sector problems. Asiodu (1999) confirmed the determination of the new government to create an enabling environment for rapid social and economic development.

The economic policy thrust of the government then had an overriding objective of improving the well-being of the people by providing the basic needs of life. It equally envisaged a significant reduction in poverty by at least 50%, as food production was expected to increase, unemployment decrease, and rural infrastructure was boasted. At the very foundation of the above objective was the pursuit of a strong, virile, and broad-based economy with adequate capacity to absorb externally generated shock.

For instance, the public enterprises owned by the federal government continued to constitute a drain pipe on the national treasury. As of 1999, there were about 600 such enterprises in the various sectors of the economy, most of them in a deplorable and inefficient state, which led to the government decision to embark on a program of public sector reform. The program entails the full divestiture of federal government interest in oil marketing, banking, manufacturing, and other enterprising operations.

The infrastructural base of the Nigerian economy remained weak in the past decades and further characterized by uneven distribution, unreliability, and decay. Arising from several years of neglect, in 1999, the government responded to the problem by expressing determination to improve the basic infrastructure as a means of promoting economic development.

Power supply in the country, for example, has been grossly inadequate, as only 30% of the population had access to electricity in 1999 due to the fact that only 27.3% of installed capacity of the eight power stations was actually generated. To this extent, it was the intention of the government to address these problems, and provide Nigerians with regular and uninterrupted electricity supply. To this end, therefore, the existing eight power stations were rehabilitated and maintained to operate at full capacity of 5,400 MW, while four additional stations were constructed and independent power production plants were encouraged to operate for power supply for domestic and even commercial use.

The health sector had deteriorated to such an extent that the experienced Nigerian health experts migrated to other countries in search of better conditions of service. Consequently, there was a high infant and maternal mortality rate as well as the prevalence of diseases in epidemic proportion. Therefore the government in 1999 decided to address the situation by massive immunization against all vaccine-preventable diseases, ensuring universal access to primary health care and eradication and prevention of epidemic diseases, resuscitating the secondary health care system, and stepping up the enlightenment campaign on the HIV/AIDs epidemic. The specific targets for the health care system by 2003 included 80% immunization coverage for all vaccine antigens, 80% essential drugs available in all health care establishments, reduction of infant and material mortality by 50%, reduction in the epidemic of malaria by 80%, and increase in primary health care services from 40% to 70%.

The state of transport infrastructure has been generally poor, as road, rail, air, and water transport systems have for several years been characterized by deplorable conditions. The federal government has therefore decided to establish a network of roads that would make a larger part of the country accessible. This was checked by rehabilitating 20,000 km of roads, dual using 1,230 km of roads, and constructing

1,300 km of new road before the end of 2003. This gesture was equally extended to all other aspects of transportation in Nigeria.

The communication infrastructure had remained government monopoly, and the cost of providing services was one of the highest in the world due to inefficiency. In 1999, out of the 400,000 telephone lines constructed, only 50% were functioning and tele-diversity was 4 per 1,000 persons, which is a far cry from the International Telecommunication Union (ITU) recommended density of 1 per 100 persons. The government aim of installing an efficient and effective communication system that was affordable to many Nigerians, more specifically, the ITU-recommended minimum tele-density of 1 telephone per 100 people, was accomplished by 2003. This was achieved by breaking the monopoly of Nigerian Telecommunication Ltd. (NITEL) and Mobile Telecommunication Ltd. (M-TEL). They were subsequently restructured and privatized to enhance their efficiency and performance.

The Nigerian financial sector recorded tremendous growth in the last two decades, especially in the number of banks and other financial institutions. In order to reposition the sector for better performance, the Central Bank of Nigeria (CBN) was granted more autonomy to regulate and facilitate efficiency and growth of the money market. In addition, more financial institutions have been brought under the control and supervision of the CBN, and their capital requirement rose to ensure more sanity in the system. The education system, which also experienced deep crises for several years, fell into a deplorable condition in the last two decades.

Government recognized the danger posed by this trend and packaged a set of objectives for the education system, which included eradication of illiteracy by 2010, an increase in the adult literacy rate from 57% to 70% by 2003, and more importantly, the acquisition of science and technology education and its effective application. The measures designed to achieve the objectives include

- Implementation of a Universal Basic Education (UBE) scheme
- Encouraging private sector participation in education
- Supporting research efforts in education
- Monitoring and evaluation of the entire system of education
- Institutional rationalization
- Emphasis on practical skills development
- Providing an enabling environment for teaching/learning comparable to that of developed countries

These measures are expected to reposition the education system to adequately play its role as a fundamental instrument for accelerating national development.

Conclusion and Recommendations

The public sector in Nigeria since independence in 1960 has experienced a steady decline in performance, a transformation that had a precarious level of dependence on the oil sector. Since 1999, Nigeria has therefore witnessed determined efforts by policy makers in the country to reverse deterioration of the public sector, which yielded some positive results that can be improved upon. It is thus necessary to invigorate the implementation of such policies that brought such results and to design more policies with high potential for facilitating public sector development.

To achieve efficiency, productivity, and reduction of waste in the public sector, there should be a deliberate arrangement to create a new orientation in the sector that will produce a quick response and be proactive to issues. The new orientation should emphasize urgency, exigencies, and time as facilitators of efficiency in the public sector.

The issue of redundancy should be well managed, and the government should put in place the zero-growth strategy and financial capping, by which the government, after every five years, focuses on what is to be done and not what has been done. This gives clarity of purpose and helps to avoid reluctance, as the defined purpose helps to determine the requirements for achieving it. Need and competence should determine recruitment into the public service.

The training organized by the public service should be tailored to individual needs on the job, while performance appraisal techniques should identify individual strengths and weakness, contributions, etc. Nigeria should follow countries like Singapore, Ghana, Australia, and Trinidad and Tobago, which have instituted customized training for their staff in the public sector.

Corruption should not be accommodated in the public sector. The federal government of Nigeria should seriously canvass the desirability of the Independent Corrupt Practices Commission of Nigeria (ICPC) and Economic and Financial Crimes Commission of Nigeria (EFCC) and give the commissions the necessary support and encouragement they deserve. Due advantage should be taken of the growing communication and information technology (CIT) for efficient revenue collection and financial management and accounting.

It is therefore necessary to recognize personal achievements, and those distinguished should be rewarded immensely. The present arrangement by the federal government of Nigeria for honoring those who are said to have distinguished themselves is to enlist rather than isolate. Achievement and hard work should be recognized and honored at the various levels and by different government departments and agencies.

References

Agbakoba, J.C. 2004. Developing appropriate administrative instruments for African cultural environment. *Contemporary African Societies* 7: 137.

Ajakaye, D. 1997. Ensuring a sustainable development oriented relationship between Nigerians public and private sectors in the 21st century. Paper presented at Proceedings of Seminar on Managing the Economy. Ibadan, Nigeria: Nigeria Institute of Social and Economic Research.

Alexandra, G. 2007. Obasanjo, the donor community and reform implementation in Nigeria. *Round Table* 96(392): 569–586.

Asiodu, P. 1999. *National economic policy*. Paper delivered at the Command and Staff College, Jaji.

Barima, A., and Farhad, A. 2010. *Challenges of making donor-driven public sector reform in sub-Saharan Africa sustainable: Some experiences from Ghana*. London: Routledge.

Cloete, J.J. 2006. *South African public administration and management*. 9th ed. Pretoria: JL van Schaik Publishers.

Daily Trust Newspapers. April 1, 2007. p. 2.

Gowon, B. 2010. Health sector reforms in Nigeria: The need to integrate traditional medicine into the health care system. *African Journal for Physical, Health Education, Recreation and Dance* 16(3): 385.

Grindle, M.S. 1997. Divergent cultures? Public organisation's performance in developing countries. *World Development* 25: 4.

Habu, M. 2009. Democratization in the face of neo-liberal reforms in Nigeria's public enterprises: A disempowerment or fair dividend? *An Interdisciplinary Journal* 22(2): 78–103.

Ijeoma, N.A. 2006. Health sector reform in Nigeria: A perspective on human rights and gender issues. *Local Environment* 11(1): 127–140.

Iyoha, F. 1999. *Local government and rural development, a bottom-up perspective*. Benin City, Nigeria: Sylva Publications.

Lienert, I., and Modi, J. 1998. *A decade of civil service reform in sub-Sahara Africa*. Washington, DC: International Monetary Fund.

Lohor, J. 2006. Public sector reforms can't be reversed after 2007, says Obasanjo. *This Day (Nigeria)*, June 30, p. 2.

M2PressWire. 2009. World Bank supports Nigeria's home-grown reforms in the financial sector and public financial management. August 4, p. 12.

Mercellina, C., Olugboji, A., Akuto, E.E., Odebunmi, A., Ezeilo, E., and Ugbene, E. 2007. A baseline survey of the primary healthcare system in south eastern Nigeria. *In Health Policy*, pp. 182–201.

Obadan, M. 2003. Globalization and economic management in Africa. *Nigerian Tribune*, September 9, pp. 26–28.

Ogujiuba, K., and Obiechina, E.M. 2011. Financial sector reforms in Nigeria. *International Journal of Business and Management* 6(6): 222–233.

Oshionebo, B. 2002. Institutional administrative reform for effective public sector management in Nigeria. Presented at a workshop on public sector management strategies and polices, NCEMA, Ibadan.

Owusu, F. 2005. Livelihood strategies and performance of Ghana's Health and Education sectors: Explaining the connections. *Public Administration and Development* 25: 2.

Rundell, S. 2010. Nigeria's new battle cry: Reform, reform, reform. *African Business* 369: 23.

Yesufu, T. 1996. *The Nigerian economy growth without development*. Benin Social Science Series for Africa. University of Benin, Nigeria.

Chapter 5

Combating Poverty in South Africa: Understanding the Informal Sector in the Context of Scarce Opportunities

Loraine Boitumelo "Tumi" Mzini

Contents

Introduction	98
Research Objectives	99
Research Methodology	99
Background of Poverty Dilemmas in South Africa	100
Paradigms for Poverty Alleviation	101
Provider Model	101
Support Model	102
Framework of the Informal Sector	102
Characteristics of the Informal Sector	103

Categories in the Informal Sector: Informal Activities and Informal
Employment 104
    Products of the Informal Sector Categories 105
    Locality of the Informal Sector 106
Research Results..107
    Demographic Profile of the Respondents 107
    Skills Development 109
    Informal Sector Operation 109
Findings of the Surveys Conducted 112
    Need for Employment 112
    Participants...112
    Innovative Skills in the Informal Sector 112
    Gender Dimensions 113
    Working Conditions...113
    Remuneration..113
    Infrastructure 113
    Benefits..113
Recommendations...114
Conclusion..114
References 115

Introduction

This study is contextualized in the arena of the informal sector. It is a form of economic activity but is by no means a new concept. The growth of the informal sector, particularly in developing countries, has been phenomenal, so much so that it has precipitated a rethinking of its role in the economy, notably by the International Labor Organization (ILO) in the early 1970s (Verick 2006). The concept of the informal sector is often used interchangeably with the concept informal economy or informal employment. For this study the term *informal sector* will be used.

The informal sector is defined as "an institution that comprises the informal workers who are not in regular employment" (Kingdon and Knight 2001, p. 5). This sector has traditionally been viewed as a temporary alternative to unemployment and poverty, which tends to disappear as an economy matures and becomes more developed (Badaoui, Strobl, and Walsh 2008). In this study, the practices of the informal sector are restricted to the urban context in the low-income households of the Sedibeng District Municipality (SDM) in Gauteng Province. The study also extends its concentration to three other provinces: the Free State, Limpopo, and KwaZulu-Natal.

In this chapter the research objectives and research methodology are discussed and the informal sector is defined as a working concept for this particular study. The paradigms for poverty alleviation are also discussed at some length, namely, the provider model, the support model, and the informal sector. These models reflect examples of the South African poverty alleviation initiatives. The contextual background and framework of the informal sector are also scrutinized, including the characteristics, the types of activity undertaken in the informal sector, and the locality of the informal sector. The categories of the informal sector, namely, informal activities and the issue of informal employment, are also included in this study. In addition, the results and the findings of the surveys conducted are analyzed. Every undertaking for improving one's livelihood has its own opportunities and challenges; therefore the advantages and disadvantages of the informal sector are debated at some length. The chapter concludes with a series of recommendations for making the informal sector more sustainable so that people who are active in this sector are able to support their families.

Research Objectives

This study stems from a doctoral thesis submitted by Mzini (2010) entitled "The Impact of Public Participation on Poverty Alleviation: A Case of Promoting Self-Reliance through Community Food Gardens." This follow-up study provides an evaluation of community participation in government-led poverty alleviation initiatives. It is based on research findings that indicate that there are unemployed households who do not participate in these government programs. Instead, many unemployed people are actively involved in the informal sector, which they regard as a survival strategy to support their households. The study thus provides an analysis of the informal sector in this context. The objectives of the study are to

- Explore the links between poverty alleviation and the informal sector
- Analyze the involvement and activities of the informal sector in combating poverty
- Look at the coping strategies of the unemployed households in times of scarce resources
- Understand the framework of the informal sector
- Examine the impact of the informal sector

The above-mentioned objectives were realized by means of the methods discussed in the section that follows.

Research Methodology

The researcher used the qualitative and quantitative approaches for this study. The units of analysis were the informal sector participants drawn from low-income households. Structured and unstructured questions formed part of the study. Structured questions serve to formalize the dialogue between the researcher and the participants. An interesting aspect of unstructured interviews is that they are stored in the scholar's long-term memory, and the visuals of the discussion are continuously reflected in his or her daily life. It is almost as if one is watching a video, and the voices of the participants are repeated when you think about them.

Data were gathered from a cross-sectional field survey involving 150 households who were active in the informal sector in the Sedibeng District Municipality (SDM) in Gauteng Province, South Africa. The areas visited included Evaton, Sebokeng, Sharpeville, Vanderbijlpark, and Vereeniging. Field trips and observations were also conducted in three other provinces in South Africa. In March 2012, the researcher visited Limpopo Province, conducting studies in Venda at Sibasa-Thohoyandou. In October 2011, another field trip was undertaken in KwaZulu-Natal, where a study took place at the Durban beachfront. The researcher frequently visits the Free State Province and she also observed the area of Qalabotjha in Villiers and Deneysville in Sasolburg.

Social science researchers are required to be sensitive toward the participants of their studies. In all cases the participants' informed consent to take part in this research was carefully confirmed. This involved confidentiality, fairness, and respect (Bless, Higson-Smith, and Kagee 2006). The names of the participants and their respective income brackets constitute confidential information and will not be revealed. The next section provides a brief background on poverty issues in South Africa and discusses the framework of the informal sector based on the findings discussed in subsequent sections.

Background of Poverty Dilemmas in South Africa

Africa has the highest poverty rate in the world. The South African unemployment rate was reported as 23.9% in the fourth quarter of 2011. From 2000 to 2008, South Africa's unemployment rate averaged 26.38%, reaching a historical high of 31.20% in March 2003 and a record low of 23% in September 2007 (Trading Economics 2012). These figures reflect the percentage of the labor force that is without jobs (Index Mundi 2012). Davies and Thurlow (2009) also maintain that unemployment is one of South Africa's most pressing socioeconomic challenges, affecting a quarter of the workforce.

Globally, governments are striving to eradicate poverty by the year 2015. Although some countries are on track to meet the Millennium Development Goal (MDG) of halving poverty by 2015, most are likely to fall well short of this target. Income inequality in Africa remains higher than in most other regions, while gender, ethnic, and regional inequalities persist (Bangura 2010). Since the dawn of a democratic South Africa in 1994, the government has encouraged community participation in activities that enhance economic development. For example, there is state support for small business development, especially among the previously disadvantaged communities. There was a measure of economic activity by members of these communities prior to democratization, but participation was skewed because of apartheid legislation and the lack of access to land and capital (Bangura 2010).

In 1994, after years of struggle for socioeconomic equality and political independence, South Africa became a true democracy. This transition gave rise to many opportunities for black South Africans, who were previously barred from participating in the formal economy (Von Broembsen 2007). In the same year, the government embarked on the Reconstruction and Development Program (RDP) as its socioeconomic policy framework and spelled out key pillars of delivery, including meeting basic needs and developing human resources (Krugell, Otto, and Van der Merwe 2009). Subsequently, macro economic policy frameworks such as Growth, Employment, and Redistribution (GEAR) (1996) and the Accelerated and Shared Growth Initiative for South Africa (ASGI-SA) (2006) were put in place to meet the RDP commitment (Krugell et al. 2009). The next section discusses the paradigms for poverty alleviation.

Paradigms for Poverty Alleviation

Reduction of urban poverty is central to a sustainable urban development strategy (Sethuraman 1997). Ackelman and Andersson (2008) identify two models that are used for alleviating poverty. These models were used for addressing housing problems in Sweden during the 1960s.

Provider Model

The provider model is a modernist model, whereby the government of a country is required to provide the basic needs (such as shelter, food, and electricity) for the poor sector of its population (Ackelman and Andersson 2008). In other words, the role of the authorities is to provide basic services and nonmonetary assistance to residents. This may also extend to monthly social security schemes provided by government to vulnerable communities in South Africa, such as monetary grants for child-headed households, disability grants, foster care grants, old-age pensions, and child support grants (participant observation). Some scholars do not acknowledge this model because they think that community members are encouraged to rely too heavily on handouts rather than making the effort to improve their lives without full support from government. The next model to be discussed is the support model.

Support Model

Vestbro (in Ackelman and Anderson 2008) indicates that the support model is similar to the enabling strategy. In this model, the state supports the people who embark on efforts to alleviating poverty (building their own homes or starting up a small business), rather than simply providing them with handouts in the form of homes or capital. The South African government had indeed embarked on a variety of such programs to alleviate poverty. For example, the South African government provides training opportunities, including small business, urban agriculture, food management, trade and artisan skills (bricklaying and paving), information technology development, and dressmaking. This model has a distinct possibility for community members to improve their living conditions and encourage lifelong sustainability. Trained individuals are then able to pursue a business with the skills acquired. Afterwards, the government provides the beneficiaries with start-up resources toward earning a living.

The effects of these models relate to the study conducted by Mzini (2010), which investigates whether low-income households participate in government-led projects such as backyard food gardens and community food gardens. Mzini found that such households were not inclined to participate in government projects aimed at alleviating poverty in the SDM. The reality is that in most cases, such projects fail because the community wants quick cash for instant relief of their impoverished situation. Although the researcher is of the opinion that these initiatives are introduced with good intentions, unless there is public participation, sustainable development will not be achieved. The section below discusses the framework of the informal sector.

Framework of the Informal Sector

The informal sector is another means of combating poverty in South Africa. As indicated above, the concept *informal sector* is sometimes used interchangeably with the term *informal activities* or *informal employment*. Kingdon and Knight (2001) describe the informal sector as an "institution that comprises the informal workers who are not in regular employment" (p. 5). Such workers are involved in casual wage employment, domestic service, or agricultural/nonagricultural self-employment (Kingdon and Knight 2001). Von Broembsen (2007) indicates that the activities performed by the informal sector include street trading, home-based businesses, casual and contract workers, domestic workers, and farm workers.

The growth of the informal sector is overwhelming in nature. When one travels in the streets of South Africa features of the informal sector are showcased that tell the story of the employment gap in the formal sector. Verick (2006) indicates that the informal sector growth has occurred in conjunction with increasing globalization and opening up of economies, which has provoked a debate about the impact of these processes on the formal sector. The nature of the informal sector is characterized by a number of traits and is both diverse and complex (Davies and Thurlow 2009). These characteristics have been reviewed by scholars in their studies of the informal sector and discussed below.

Characteristics of the Informal Sector

The sector is also typified by two operational strategies of survival: coping strategies (survival activities) and unofficial earnings (i.e., illegal earnings in the business setting). These two strategies are the driving force behind the survival of vulnerable households. The typical characteristics of the informal sector are in turn listed below.

- Ease of entry
- Unstructured and unofficial and operates on a small scale
- Reliance on indigenous resources
- Family ownership of enterprises
- Small scale of operation
- Skills acquired outside the formal school system
- Labor-intensive and adapted technology
- Unregulated and competitive markets
- Insecure working conditions (Davies and Thurlow 2009; Devey, Skinner, and Valodia 2003; Kingdon and Knight 2001; Verick 2006; UNECA 2010)

Participation in the informal sector arises from poverty and unemployment caused by the employment gaps in the formal sector. The informal sector comprises a continuum of survivalist and enterprise activities (Davies and Thurlow 2009). Survival depends on self-skills, self-knowledge, and the flexibility of an individual. Such businesses are not overseen by the state, and markets are not regulated or monitored. Such markets are based purely on competition. The sector does not have any written rules, and any agreements are based on verbal understanding (Fundsforngos 2009). Furthermore, there are no labor representatives for groups of workers, and there are few opportunities for skill enhancement (UNECA 2010) because the individuals cannot afford to enroll for formal training. The next section discusses the categories of the informal sector with reference to informal activities and informal employment.

Categories in the Informal Sector: Informal Activities and Informal Employment

Davies and Thurlow (2009) identify four types of informal activity and informal employment categories. These are presented in Table 5.1.

The informal producer may, for example, sell prepared food that is prepared on a daily basis or produce clothing such as traditional wear, formal wear, wedding gowns, and school uniforms. Such products are also offered in the formal sector, but if produced informally, will be priced somewhat lower because they have to compete with the large, established retail sector. On the other hand, the informal traders sell their products directly to their clients, so although they have a lower turnover, they have fewer overheads than the formal sector and the profit margin per unit sold is higher.

The informal service provider element creates employment, although the workers are employed informally and contribute to the success of the formal sector. In South Africa there are informal sector firms who supply the formal sector with products that are sold to the communities in different locations. In the media there

Table 5.1 The Four Informal Activities and Informal Employment Categories

Informal Activities	Informal Employment	Examples
Informal producers who compete with formal producers in product markets	Informal producers	Food, clothing, and transport (scholar transport or public transport)
Informal traders who sell formal sector products and charge a fixed transaction cost margin	Informal traders	Hairdresser, ice cream seller
Workers who are informally employed in producing formal sector products	Informal service providers	Dressmaker, domestic worker
Informally employed workers producing goods and services that are not produced by the formal sector	Informal day-laborers	Carpenter, painter, plumber, ceramicist

Source: Adapted from Davies, R., and Thurlow, J., (Eds.), Formal-Informal Economy Linkages and Unemployment in South Africa, 2009, http://www.ifpri.org (accessed February 10, 2012).

are reports on a daily basis that the police have confiscated illegal merchandise being sold informally on the streets. These episodes are increasing, and they are a very real threat to the economy of the country. As for informal day laborers, they produce the goods and services that are not offered by the formal sector, so they do not compete with the formal sector. However, the informal sector also employs day laborers to perform odd jobs and provide the goods and services for its intended customers. Day laborers are often seen on street corners in suburban areas. They usually have their working tools/equipment with them, so that if they are hired on the spot, they are able to perform the service requested. The researcher observed such casual laborers in Vanderbijlpark, Vereeniging, and Three Rivers in Gauteng, and in Sasolburg and Bloemfontein in the Free State. They practice self-advertising, often holding up informal billboards made of cardboard. Others attach metal advertising placards (written in long-lasting ink) to gates and walls or use signs in their motor vehicles to market their informal services.

The section that follows will discuss the types of activity undertaken in the informal sector.

Products of the Informal Sector Categories

The informal sector comprises various types of activity that are defined by the goods they provide. In the informal sector these activities are similar to those in the formal sector, but there is no formality or regulation that stipulates how or when such goods are produced. In Table 5.2 UNECA (2010) provides four types of activity in the informal sector: those that produce unprocessed products, artisanal products, products for re-export, and pharmaceutical products.

Table 5.2   The Products of the Informal Sector Categories

Products	Examples
Unprocessed products	Prepared meals: fat-cakes; homemade biscuits/scones, and food (meal).
Artisanal products	Steel products: household security gates; woodcarvings: decorated doors and sculptures; wire products: toy cars for children, earrings.
Products for re-export	Fabrics, second-hand clothing, automobiles, tires.
Pharmaceutical products	Pesticides, cosmetics, medicines, and herbs.

Source: United Nations Economic Commission for Africa (UNECA), in *Assessing Regional Integration in Africa*, 2010, 148–150.

The unprocessed products include most primary commodities, excluding agricultural seed and selected livestock breeds that are imported or developed in research laboratories (UNECA 2010). The products are prepared on a daily basis for a targeted market. The artisanal products are traded informally throughout Africa. Such products can be observed along the streets of the municipalities in South Africa. The researcher noted such informal traders and their wares at Bruma Lake in Germiston (in the Ekurhuleni Metro), near Vereeniging and Vanderbijlpark along the national road (N 14), in Muldersdrift (West Rand), at the Durban beachfront, and in Port Elizabeth (the Nelson Mandela Metro). Products for re-export originate from outside the continent. Pharmaceutical products are also sold in the informal sector (UNECA 2010). These may include industrial items and domestic items for killing household pests, such as bedbugs, cockroaches, ants, and rodents. We now turn to discussing where the informal sector operates.

Locality of the Informal Sector

The locality of the informal sector is influenced by varied factors, and is determined by the type of business conducted and the specific clientele involved. The informal sector operates in diversified locations; its aim is to earn a living in unemployed households, or to supplement the wages of low-income earners. The following are characteristics of the informal sector environment:

- Spaza shops
- Tuck shops
- Shebeens
- Street trading
- Transport hubs and mobile trading (Rolfe, Woodward, Ligthelm, and Guimarães 2010; Von Broembsen 2007)

The idea of running so-called spaza shops originated in black homes operation. Many spaza shops are run as family endeavors and may be operated in-house or separately from residences as tuck shops operated in schools, at street corners, and at transport hubs where there are many passersby. Shebeens are informal taverns, mostly located in black informal settlements, and are often driven by unemployment and seen as an opportunity to earn extra money. Street trading is another type of informal business in the retail sector and is operated from pavements or stalls in inner cities or town centers. Other informal sector initiatives are operated at transport hubs, including airport, train, bus, and taxi stations. The traders in these environments sell households items such as food, beverages, and nonfood items (clothes, socks for men, and stockings for ladies), whereas those at airports sell items such as souvenirs for international and domestic travelers. From the researcher's observations, the trading approaches that are practiced in South Africa are similar to those in other countries worldwide. It would seem that the informal sector functions in more or less the same way throughout the world. In 2010 and 2011, ample proof of this was evident to the researcher at airports in Malaysia, Indonesia, Moscow, and Dubai.

Research Results

The results that are presented here are based on surveys conducted in the Sedibeng District Municipality in Gauteng Province. However, information was also gleaned in studies undertaken in the Free State, KwaZulu-Natal, and Limpopo. The participants were drawn from unemployed communities, and they were selected based on their participation in the informal sector. Table 5.3 presents the demographic profile of the respondents.

Demographic Profile of the Respondents

The researcher interviewed 150 participants who expressed their willingness to participate in this study. The participants in this study are all South African citizens and were drawn from low-income households in the Sedibeng District Municipality (SDM) in Gauteng Province. The participants were unemployed at the time the interviews were conducted. South Africa has diversified racial groups, but this study was limited to the black community resident in the Sedibeng District. The reason for this is that the low-income households are occupied by black families. The researcher chose to have a proportional representation of 50% males and 50% females in the sample group.

The age groups represented in this study indicate that poverty and unemployment affect people of all ages. There is a wide range of age groups involved in the informal sector, but the researcher chose to exclude the youth below 25 years of age. Members of this age group are normally not active in the economic sector because some are busy with formal schooling, while others are studying at tertiary education institutions.

The participants interviewed appeared to be in stable households. Of them, 46% were unemployed, single, and had never married; others lived with their partners. All the participants had valid South African identity documents. Despite such academic achievements, these participants indicated that they live in poverty and are unemployed. Some had applied for government positions but had not received any response. Alleviation of poverty includes having access to adequate housing. As part of this study the researcher also assessed the residential profile of the respondents. The surveys indicate that the issue of human settlement in South Africa is an urgent one, and there is a real need for the provision of housing. The South African government strives to eradicate the unhygienic, congested, and poorly serviced informal settlements by 2015. However, the researcher found that 20% of the participants still live in these informal residential shacks. Many of those who live in shacks have survived in such conditions for as long as 20 years.

Table 5.3 Demographic Profile of the Respondents (N = 150)

Value Label	Frequency (v)	Percentage (%)
Gender		
Male	75	50
Female	75	50
Age Groups		
25–31	40	27
32–37	20	13
38–44	30	20
45–52	30	20
53–65	30	20
Marital Status		
Single	70	46
Married	60	40
Divorced	10	6
Widowed	11	8
Category		
Youth	40	27
Economically active	90	60
Elderly	20	13
Possession of an Identity Document		
Participants (all South Africans)	150	100
Education		
Less than high school (primary)	60	40
High school	60	40
Higher education	30	20

(continued)

Table 5.3 Demographic Profile of the Respondents (*N* = 150) (continued)

Value Label	Frequency (v)	Percentage (%)
Residence		
House	60	40
Hostel	10	6
Low-cost housing	50	34
Informal residence (shack)	30	20
Missing cases	0	0

Skills Development

Skills development plays an important role in human survival. Most of the participants said they had acquired certain skills to hold down jobs as motor mechanics, plumbers, electricians, carpenters, steel workers, and to do ceramic tiling, for example, while employed in the formal sector (especially in industries), but that they had either been retrenched, resigned, or had to leave because of illness or disability. In the vicinity of the SDM and the Ekurhuleni Metropolitan Municipality there are industries that offer sustainable jobs. The necessary skills to fill these jobs are offered as a service to community members.

Informal Sector Operation

Operating in the informal sector may be initiated by a government start-up or when an individual launches out to start his or her own business venture. Here the survey conducted made an assessment of the businesses or services offered in the SDM in Gauteng, although similar ventures have been initiated in the other provinces.

As shown in Table 5.4, the goods and services offered in the informal sector vary considerably. Some traders provide goods/services in more than one category. Here the survey conducted made an assessment of the businesses or services offered in the SDM in Gauteng, although similar ventures have been initiated in the other provinces.

As indicated earlier, these informal operators were observed on street corners, in sports stadiums, and at transport hubs. Some were also seen in municipal offices when old-age and children grant payouts were being made. Some food sellers were operating at the venue when the researcher went to a music festival in December 2011 at Vaal Show Grounds in Verenniging. The concert is an annual charity event, and informal traders took the opportunity to earn some money. Food traders seemed to be the most numerous of the informal sector operators in the places where the researcher conducted her study. Dressmakers base the clothes they make on customer demand, i.e., for weddings and cultural events (for example, in May

Table 5.4 Urban Informal Sector Business Operations

Value Label	Items Sold	Frequency (V)	Percentage (%)
Pharmaceutical	Herbs, facial creams, and insecticides.	5	0.03
Information and communications technologies	Public phones, photocopying, and ID photos (service provided for those applying for birth certificates, visas, and identity documents).	5	0.03
Artisan/trade	Plumber, electrician, welder, painter.	10	0.06
Baking	Confectionery (cakes and biscuits for domestic consumption, weddings, funerals, and birthdays).	10	0.06
Cooking	These are healthy prepared meals mostly sold to other members of the community. They also sell fat-cakes in the morning for the public. Cooked mealie cobs are sold during the summer season.	27	0.18
Dressmaking	Wedding dresses, cultural wear (isiXhosa, isiZulu), and school uniforms.	10	0.06
Hairdressing	Haircuts, plaiting, braids, relaxer/human hair extension.	10	0.06
Waste management	Waste collection and recycling.	10	0.06
Agribusiness	Plant production, poultry selling, dairy products (such as ice cream).	10	0.06
Arts and crafts (beading, etc.)	Earrings, necklaces, etc., made from beads.	5	0.03
Photography	Social functions (music), photo and video production.	5	0.02

(continued)

Table 5.4 Urban Informal Sector Business Operations (continued)

Value Label	Items Sold	Frequency (V)	Percentage (%)
Transport	Learner transport, transporting goods for informal sector.	7	0.05
Cigarettes	Although illegal, selling at transport hubs and to households.	5	0.03
Cosmetics	Makeup products (nail polish, eye shadow, lipstick).	7	0.05
Shebeens	Alcoholic and nonalcoholic beverages, snacks, cow and sheep heads and feet.	4	0.02
Car wash	Valet, dry wash and vacuuming, polishing.	5	0.03
Shoemaker	Replacing of shoe heels and soles; sewing shoe stitches and shoe dye.	5	0.03
Umbrellas	For all seasons, active during summer and spring.	4	0.02
Homeware	Kitchen utensils, bedding, mechanical tools, and construction tools.	6	0.04
Total		150	100

there is an Africa Day and September is a heritage month in South Africa). Their businesses operate throughout the year, although they tend to fluctuate and quiet periods are experienced. The homeware traders are also busy all year round; they sell their goods on credit and collect the money owed at month's end. The hair salon and car wash industries have mushroomed in urban areas. The researcher observed that on every street there were three to five car washers, people who were obviously unemployed and living in poverty. The hair salon and car wash enterprises operate illegally in the sense that the municipality provides domestic water for household use, and because of poverty, residents use the water for their business operations. This causes water shortages in the households. The car wash enterprises also pollute the environment; they do not have the necessary drainage systems to dispose of the grey water.

Waste management is another widely practiced informal business operation. The unemployed residents collect waste materials and then sell them to recycling enterprises, which are themselves part of the informal sector. The employees in these recycling businesses are unregistered, and they work in unhygienic conditions, but they are able to earn an income for their families.

Findings of the Surveys Conducted

This section presents the findings of the research project, based on the theoretical and empirical surveys conducted.

Need for Employment

Largely because of the high levels of poverty and escalating unemployment (currently measured at 23%), the informal sector is growing rapidly. South Africans participate in the informal sector because the state and the private sector seem unable to address the issue of unemployment and making jobs available for the poor. Participation in the informal sector is voluntary but carries many risks. This study found that some of the unemployed people have lost all hope of getting jobs. They are not bothered to look for work and instead resort to informal trading or illegal activities.

Participants

The informal sector comprises both employed and unemployed community members, although the unemployed are by far the most numerous. Those who are employed buy goods from either the formal or informal sector and then resell them to the public, with the aim of earning an extra income.

Innovative Skills in the Informal Sector

The work performed in this sector is labor-intensive and requires low-level skills. The participants operate without basic business and people skills; they eventually develop these while working in their informal jobs. It was amazing and yet heartbreaking to observe that poverty-stricken people are still able to support their families despite having such limited resources. Examples of innovation were seen in abundance and took many interesting forms. There was the woman with her catchphrases to sell insecticides, and makeshift advertisement boards to attract customers.

Gender Dimensions

Participation in the sector is dominated by females, who are often the breadwinners and have become the pillar of the household. The study showed that in most of the places visited it was women (single, widowed, or divorced) who were most active in the informal sector. However, women tend to sell their wares on the streets of the city centers, whereas men resort to day labor or artisanal labor, which is less obvious to the casual observer (and to the researcher in her surveys) compared to their female counterparts.

Working Conditions

Those working in the informal sector seem to enjoy their working conditions. The hours worked by those employed in the sector range from one to two hours per day to as much as nine hours per day. The most convenient trading is perhaps that performed in the household, as there is no transport necessary and trading is not affected by weather conditions.

Remuneration

The earnings of those employed in the sector vary considerably, depending on the size of the clientele and the products sold. Most informal sector participants have bank accounts and have learned how to save their profits and budget how these will be used to provide for their families. Some have even become affiliated with the stokvel (an informal group savings scheme), where the payouts are made on a weekly, fortnightly, or monthly basis.

Infrastructure

The work environment for this sector is congested and unhygienic. Although in certain areas the state has built trading zones for the informal sector, the researcher noticed that in some cases these were unoccupied, had been vandalized, and that some of the facilities provided had been stolen. According to respondents these zones are unused because they were constructed too far from their customer base and lack access to electricity, water, sanitation, and security.

Benefits

Participation in this sector can be reasonably profitable, although it can be risky. The sector does not receive much support from government because the operators do not want to be regulated. On the other hand, participation in the informal sector is less rigid. If a venture fails or is going through a seasonal lull, the operator can make a temporary (or permanent) change of direction to ensure a better living. In other words, there is more room for adaptability and innovation. In the next section, based on the findings observed in this study, the researcher offers some recommendations on ways to promote the informal sector in South Africa.

Recommendations

The researcher offers the following recommendations toward a more sustainable informal sector and its adherence to the letter of the law:

- Governments should develop policies that promote job creation.
- Strengthening of the regulations (by-laws) for the informal sector is a necessity, especially for the informal traders. The operators tend to make public streets unsightly in urban areas, although in some municipalities the natural beauty of parks and pavements has been preserved because by-laws are effective and well implemented.
- There must be continuous awareness of environmental and hygienic standards. There is illegal dumping in the city centers caused by informal traders.
- Assistance should be provided for the informal sector to participate in a global economy.
- The informal sector lives in a period where there are scarce resources. There should be access to credit and insurance for businesses.

The researcher's remarks are summarized in the following section.

Conclusion

There is an extensive literature on the informal sector that is indicative of its significance. Studies on poverty and strategies to alleviate poverty in the world are crucial if this issue is to be addressed. Poverty alleviation is of concern to everyone, be they policy makers, private or public officials, or scholars in their various fields of study. All strive to develop strategies, models, and approaches to eradicate poverty in the world. The literature reviewed indicates that the state is on a mission to alleviate poverty by 2015. The question posed by the researcher is whether the suggested time frame is realistic; perhaps another four years should be added.

The objective of this study was to assess how unemployed community members manage to survive in an era of scarce resources. The informal sector was found to be a powerful business activity, especially in vulnerable communities. It is impressive to see that community members can adapt to their circumstances and devise innovative ways of earning a living. Globally, governments are calling for community members to lead socioeconomic initiatives because the state cannot provide adequately for all members of society across the board. This study has shown that poverty and unemployment is particularly high in Africa. It also indicates that underdevelopment per se is not a threat to the unemployed; it tends to motivate poverty-stricken people to increase their efforts in order to support their families. The researcher observed that the unemployed are both innovative and skillful despite (in many cases) lacking in formal education. It has been shown that some have been afforded the opportunity to acquire skills by working (albeit, in some cases, temporarily) in the formal sector. However, the working environment in the case of informal workers is often far from ideal, which calls for intervention by the state.

This study concludes by suggesting that the informal sector is capable of combating poverty in South Africa; the same applies elsewhere in the world. The sector has proved that it is able to create jobs and reduce unemployment where productive resources are lacking. Furthermore, the informal sector is sustainable because it encourages entrepreneurial activity and puts bread on the table. The researcher pronounces that together we can make it happen. Vulnerable communities should not lose hope, because there is light at the end of the tunnel.

References

Ackelman, H., and Andersson, M. 2008. Methods to solve the problem of informal settlements: The case of Hangberg, South Africa. MSc thesis, Kungliga Tekniska Högskolan, Stockholm.

Badaoui, E., Strobl, E., and Walsh, F. 2008. *Is there an informal sector wage penalty? Evidence from South Africa*. Chicago: University of Chicago Press. From http://www.jstor.org (accessed September 15, 2012).

Bangura, Y. 2010. Jobs and equity the key to Africa's poverty fight: Progress on MDGs requires more than social safety nets. *Africa Renewal*, December 2010. From http://www.un.org (accessed January 20, 2012).

Bless, C., Higson-Smith, G., and Kagee, A. 2006. *Fundamentals of social research methods. An African perspective*. 4th ed. Cape Town: Juta.

Davies, R., and Thurlow, J., eds. 2009. *Formal-informal economy linkages and unemployment in South Africa*. From http://www.ifpri.org (accessed February 10, 2012).

Devey, R., Skinner, C., and Valodia, I. 2003. Informal economy employment data in South Africa: A critical analysis. In *Formal-informal economy linkages and unemployment in South Africa*, ed. R. Davies and J. Thurlow. From http://www.ifpri.org (accessed February 10, 2012).

Fundsforngos. 2009. Specific characteristics of the formal economy and informal economy. December 9. From http://www.fundsforngos.org (accessed December 12, 2012).

Index Mundi. 2012. South Africa. Unemployment rate: Historical data graphs per year. From http://www.indexmundi.com (accessed March 9, 2012).

Kingdon, G.G., and Knight, J. 2001. *Why high open unemployment and small informal sector in South Africa?* University of Oxford, Center for the Study of African Economies.

Krugell, W., Otto, H., and Van der Merwe, J. 2009. *Local municipalities and progress with the delivery of basic services in South Africa*. Working Paper 116. Potchefstroom: North-West University.

Mzini, L.B. 2010. The impact of public participation on poverty alleviation: A case of promoting self-reliance through community food gardens. PhD thesis, North-West University.

Rolfe, R., Woodward, D., Ligthelm, A., and Guimarães, P. 2010. The viability of informal micro-enterprise in South Africa. Paper presented at a conference on entrepreneurship in Africa, New York, April 1–3. http://whitman.syr.edu/ABP/Conference (accessed January 25, 2012).

Sethuraman, S.V. 1997. *Urban poverty and the informal sector: A critical assessment of current strategies*. New York: United Nations Development Program.

Trading Economics. 2012. *South African unemployment rate*. New York: Trading Economics. http://tradingeconomics.com (accessed February 24, 2012).

United Nations Economic Commission for Africa (UNECA). 2010. Informal trade in Africa. In *Assessing regional integration in Africa*, chap. 5. Addis Ababa.

Verick, S. 2006. *The impact of globalization on the informal sector in Africa*. Addis Ababa: Economic and Social Policy Division, UN Economic Commission for Africa (ECA) and Institute for the Study of Labor (IZA).

Von Broembsen, M. 2007. The legal empowerment of the poor: Informal business. Draft report. Prepared for the Commission for the Legal Empowerment of the Poor, Washington, DC, October.

Chapter 6

Media as a Catalyst for Good Governance in South Africa: An Expanded Vision of Public Administration

Shikha Vyas-Doorgapersad

Contents

Introduction	118
Media and Good Governance: Conceptual Framework	119
Meaning of Media	119
Meaning of Good Governance	119
Media for Good Governance	120
Media–Government–Society: A Nexus	121
Media, Government, and Society	121
Theories of Media Support the Nexus	122
Media and Society	124
Role of Media in South Africa	125
Constitutional Mandates	125
Status of Media in South Africa	126
The Media–Government–Society Nexus in South Africa	127

Emerging Challenges 129
Conclusion 129
References 130

Introduction

> The media have become such an indispensable part of modern democratic life that they often seem to dominate the political processes.
> —Koch-Baumgarten and Voltmer (2010, p. 1)

Many countries in the world are facing challenges associated with dictatorial regimes, corrupt politicians, and personal power games, supplemented by the elimination of public voices, needs, and demands for responsible governance. For democracy not only to exist but to be sustained, the media is required to play a catalyst role between the government and the masses, enhancing open communication channels. The title of a book by Iyengar and Reeves (1997) asks the question "Do the media govern?"—and many commentators might well reply in the positive, "pointing to numerous instances where media campaigns have put pressure on policy-makers to revise their decisions" (Koch-Baumgarten and Voltmer 2010, p. 1).

The media is regarded as a watchdog contrivance that can assist in exposing and controlling maladministration to promote good governance. Moreover, it plays a critical role in improving the quality of governance through distribution and transmission of information; it can be considered a catalyst to expand informed liaison between the government and the governed. It thus has considerable responsibility in maintaining the notion of democracy through diverse means, viz., transforming information for social-political reforms, sharing knowledge for civic empowerment, catalyzing between the government and the governed for evolutionary change, and escalating transformation for good governance. The author aims to explore the role of media in promoting efficient governance with special reference to South Africa. The chapter argues that the media has the power to break the barriers of information and can initiate a conduit relationship with society to improve the efficacy of administration and the status of government. There are challenges associated with the investigative powers of press and press freedom that raise concerns about the extent of exposition of information. Concerted attempts were (and still are) being made to manipulate the media, reduce or minimize the role of the free press, and curb the powers of the media for political and personal benefit.

Media and Good Governance: Conceptual Framework

Meaning of Media

Media is a medium of communication whereby information, stories, and messages can be transmitted to the public. There are varied forms of media available to serve the purpose, viz., print media, audiovisual media, broadcast media, interpersonal media, traditional media, electronic media, and mass communication media. The aim of the media is to bring awareness through the transfer of information to the targeted population. This transmission of information is an important ingredient of good governance, whereby the public is informed about the shifting or updated policies and programs of the government. It can therefore be substantiated that media can enhance the notion of good governance through improved transparency, strengthened accountability, enhanced freedom of expression, and expanded opportunity for citizen participation. Soola (2009, p. 25) emphasized this notion, maintaining that the

> hallmark of good democratic governance, to a varying extent, is its guarantee of citizen participation through politics of inclusiveness; freedom of association; freedom of expression.

Meaning of Good Governance

Good governance can be described as governance that operates in a multiparty democracy, abides to the rule of law, and has a free press to ensure that political leaders are held accountable for improved public administration (Wohlmuth, Bass, and Messner 1999 in Fourie 2006). Media is a pillar to strengthen the democracy and enhance sound governance through "surveillance of sociopolitical developments, identifying the most relevant issues, providing a platform for debate across a diverse range of views, holding officials to account for the way they exercise power, providing incentives for citizens to learn, choose and become involved in the political process" (Fog 2004, p. 2). The political process and "preferences are conceptualized as political values that are developed within the process of socialization in a political culture, the perception of political realities in modern democracies is mostly mediated through mass media" (Floss 2008, p. 2).

It is certainly true that the media is a strong pillar that upholds democracy. The concept of democracy has a "wide range of interpretations [including]: multipartyism, pluralism, political liberalism, etc. Whatever the definition, however, it is generally accepted that the hallmark of democracy is public accountability which is established through periodic elections. What happens between elections? How does government render account of its stewardship? … the obvious answer would be the mass media" (Cole 1995, p. 55). The media is able to subject the policies and actions of the government to close scrutiny on a regular basis to see whether they measure up to pre-election promises and to what extent programs and policies are being implemented.

It can nevertheless be argued that the diverse means of media are not fully available in emerging democracies; hence it is not feasible to evaluate the impact of media on governance as an absolute indicator of development or the sole assessment criteria for democratization. As Hansen (2002) puts it, "Development of free and independent media can itself take many forms and freedom and independence can have many gradations. It is important to know what kind of press in what kind of society will perform the functions necessary for the process of building democratic institutions" (p. 3) for good governance.

Media for Good Governance

In order to investigate the impact of the media as a tool for sound governance, the British Broadcasting Corporation (BBC) conducted a survey on governance and the media.* Responses were received from a number of diverse groups, including policy makers, academics, and practitioners from government and media sectors. The question put to them was along the lines of "How important do you consider the media to be as a watchdog of governance and is this issue receiving an appropriate measure of attention?" The responses were analyzed and the survey concluded that there was an "increasing recognition of media's role in governance in the development community and that there are some indicators that media are starting to be recognized at policy level" (Aveggio 2012, p. 1). The responsible media also assists "socialization of people into citizenship, democratization of the State and political society, institutionalization of civic culture through unfettered flow of information, and rationalized use of power in social relations … and any breakdown of the nerve may cause dysfunctional impact in the performance of the polity causing governance decay" (Yadav 2001, p. 1). As a metaphor, media is considered as the

> "Fourth Estate" which was coined by Lord Macaulay in 1832 … as "the emergence of the press to rival the power of the other three great estates; e.g. the Lords both temporal and spiritual and the commons." (Panday 2009, p. 4)

This metaphor was supported by Ambassador Ayodele Oke, the special adviser and head of the African section in the Political Affairs Division of the Commonwealth Secretariat in London, at the opening of the August 1–5, 2011, Commonwealth Media Development and Capacity Building Forum. The forum

---

* The full BBC Trust report is available at http://www.bbc.co.uk/worldservice/trust/pdf/governance_media_survey_April09.pdf.

was hosted by the government of Gambia in collaboration with the Commonwealth Secretariat. Ambassador Oke said:

> Governments are prime movers of development, and institution creation in social, economic and political spheres and often anticipate some degree of collaboration and partnership with the media who are, for this purpose, regarded as the constituents of the "Fourth Estate of the Realm." (Sillah 2011, p. 1)

Since then, in most countries of the world, the media is seen holistically as a parallel branch of government that serves as an instrument for checks and balances; it monitors and observes the activities of the public sector, acting as a watchdog and communicative catalyst for good governance. Ocitti (1999) also points out that "media mirrors the level of democratic maturity in a country, and is in turn affected by the maturity of that democracy. The media epitomize ... freedom of expression of ideas and opinions in a society ... democracy and media coexist ... [and are] aimed at developing a consensus about the public interest" (p. 6)

Media–Government–Society: A Nexus

Media, Government, and Society

According to Louw (2005) and Pearson and Patching (2008) there are "three distinct groups involved in the media-political process: political insiders, semi-insiders and outsiders" (pp. 17–18). The political office bearers are the political insiders responsible for policy formulation. The public office bearers, who are in direct contact with political insiders, but are not authorized to take absolute political decisions, are semi-insiders. The semi-insiders are responsible for implementing policies and are monitored by the political authorities. The end users of the policies are the public, that is, the outsiders of the political milieu. They are the "consumers of the political news disseminated by the media" (Pearson and Patching 2008, p. 34), and thus uphold the notion of democracy. The extent of dissemination of information to the public by the media; the scope of their reporting; the way the media records and interprets the official, governmental, and political events; and the magnitude of impact the media has over the political processes determine the power of the media to contour the public's viewpoint, and thus their ability to bring pressure to bear on the process of governance.

The relationship between the media and the government can be categorized as "space-binding and time-binding" (Kearl 2010). The space-binding media reports deal with information on wars and the development of decentralized governmental establishments that emerge after military regimes. The time-binding media reports disperse information about the historical evolution of governmental hierarchy in countries experiencing the growth of the state. The time-binding media may be responsible for developing the discipline of media studies that link its reportage to government (politics) and voters (citizens).

Theories of Media Support the Nexus

The media-government-society nexus can be supported by the evolution of media influence theories, notably the hypodermic needle theory, the two-step flow of communication theory, the limited effects theory, and the spiral of silence theory.

The hypodermic needle theory, evolved during the 1940s, is known to have a powerful impact on people's behavior. In this decade, there was a sudden rise in the broadcasting industry whereby radio and television began to popularize products through advertising, linking commercial ties with industries. The theory explores the media when it acts as a needle, a means to pierce the audience (the public) with influential messages, expecting them to react accordingly. This nature of this model is best suited during election campaigns when political parties are able to utilize the media to popularize their manifesto and gather public support.[*]

The two-step flow of communication theory, a hypothesis coined in 1944 by Paul Lazarsfeld, Bernard Berelson, and Hazel Gaudet,[†] suggests that the information is first communicated to the "opinion leaders who filter the information they gather to their associates, with whom they are influential" (Griswold 2011, p. 1). This kind of media policy can be witnessed in countries where the newspapers are government owned. Paul Felix Lazarsfeld introduced the use of surveys, observations, and related social science experiments to broaden the scope of scientific investigations on the impact of media on society.

The limited effects theory initiated by Lazarsfeld in the 1940s claims that the media has little effect on people's behavior, attitudes, and manner of voting.[‡] In 1974, some three decades later, the theory on spiral of silence was proposed by Elisabeth Noelle-Neumann. This theory looks at the diverse perspectives of a spiral and posits that people who are disadvantaged are more likely to suppress their opinions. Those with strong viewpoints, typically those in the majority, who are thus relatively powerful, are expected to explore their opinions. The notion behind this theory is that people discuss and raise opinions that fit their perspectives and satisfy

---

[*] For detailed information on the hypodermic needle theory, refer to http://www.utwente.nl/cw/theorieenoverzicht/Theory%20clusters/Mass%20Media/Hypodermic_Needle_Theory.doc/.

[†] For an understanding of the two-step flow of communication theory, refer to E. Katz, "The Two-Step Flow of Communication: An Up-to-Date Report on an Hypothesis, *Public Opinion Quarterly* 21(1): 61–78, 1957.

[‡] For an analytical understanding of the little effects theory, read E. Katz, "Lazarsfeld's Map of Media Effects," World Association for Public Opinion Research, 2001, pracownik.kul.pl/.../Katz_20Lazarsfeld_C2_B4s_20Map_20of_20media.pdf.

their own perceptions. This theory also indicates that the media cannot regulate people's outlook on an absolute basis.[*]

Intellectuals and practitioners in the field of media, communication, public administration, and political science believe in the impact of media on governance, yet not many studies have been conducted that explore the interaction between media and the process of governance. According to Koch-Baumgarten and Voltmer (2010), the literature on the relationship between media and policy making is "patchy" and tends to be "rather incoherent." There are studies that suggest that those responsible for policy making do indeed respond to media coverage and its effects on public opinion (Page and Shapiro 1992), while others indicate that legislators resist external pressure from the media (Kleinnijenhuis and Rietberg 1995). Walgrave and van Aelst (2006) reviewed 19 studies undertaken since the late 1970s on the influence of media on policy making, of which 12 "indicate strong or considerable media effects on policy making, while seven find only weak or minimal impact. This meta-analysis thus indicates that the media can be a relevant force in the policy process" and calls for a systematic study "if we are to better understand the dynamics of public policy in modern democracies" (Koch-Baumgarten and Voltmer 2010, p. 2).

In order to build the relationship between the government and the media, it is imperative to gather public opinion on the government-media-society nexus. This approach was commenced in 2009 when the highly acclaimed British Broadcasting Corporation (BBC) conducted a significant survey.[†] Its purpose was to gather information to analyze public opinion on government, media, and the role of society. The question structured for the interview was "How important is support for a free and pluralistic media to governance?" (Lines 2009, p. 8). The responses indicated that the freedom of information and the free flow of communication by the media "between citizen and citizen and state ... plays a central role in accountability and participation" (Lines 2009, p. 8).

The association between the government and the media assists the society to participate in the affairs of governance with updated information. According to a statement made by William Orme, a UN policy advisor on independent media development, part of the United Nations Development Program (UNDP), in an interview by Kathy Lines for BBC World Service Trust (2009), this methodology was witnessed in practice when the significance of media was recorded in the Accra Agenda for Action. The role of media was also acknowledged in the strategic political documents of an African Union (AU) commission. In addition, the importance

---

[*] For detailed information on the spiral of silence theory (in a diverse perspective), refer to S.A. Neill, "The Alternate Channel: How Social Media Is Challenging the Spiral of Silence Theory in GLBT Communities of Color," American University, Washington, DC, 2009, http://www.american.edu/soc/communication/upload/09-neill.pdf.

[†] For complete report, consult BBC Service Trust, "Governance and the Media: A Survey of Public Opinion," http://www.bbc.co.uk/worldservice/trust/pdf/governance_media_survey_April09.pdf.

of a free press (media) during elections is used as a powerful tool for public awareness about political manifestos. Indeed, as Orme put it, African governments "have become very aware that an independent and professional, responsible and well trained media is a really critical institution."

Any study of democracy in contemporary conditions is therefore also a study of how the media reports and interprets political events and issues, and how it influences the political processes and shapes public opinion. Thus, media has become central to politics and public life in contemporary democracy (Sharma 2002).

Media and Society

The media, by its "etymological origins, holds the traditional logic of being the middleman between the feudal land owning class (bourgeoisie) and the proletariat (the proverbial 'common-man') ... media operates in a social context of two-way traffic by informing and receiving feedback, educating as well as entertaining its large and diverse audience" (Opuamie-Ngoa 2010, p. 137). In terms of classical theoretical expositions, the core task of media is to develop two-way communication between government and governed. The media therefore focuses on channeling information to the public and receiving feedback from the public for improved governance. The question arises: How do citizens reach their government? (Gistern and Volmer 2004 in Vyas-Doorgapersad and Ababio 2006), and again the answer is via the media. It disseminates information through varied means of communication, utilizing traditional methods such as radio and television broadcasting, billboard and newspaper publishing, or new-age channels like satellite transmitters, mobile telephones, videos, and Internet networks.

Through the media, grassroots participation in public discourse is encouraged. "The public sphere is integral to the constitution of civil society. Within the public realm, deliberation based on reason, logic and persuasive argumentation which can be described as rational-critical debate provides the basis for discussion, consensus formation and democratic decision making" (Howley in Devereux 2007, p. 344; Pillay, Subban, and Vyas-Doorgapersad 2009). It can be argued that media is not only a means to improve and facilitate communication, but can be utilized as a constructive tool to instill transparency and openness in the governance. The media in this scenario can play a role as a catalyst between government, public office bearers, and the public to seek accountability. In the words of Abdul Waheed Khan, UNESCO assistant director-general for communication and information:

> If the media are not supposed to increase their investigative capacity, expectations for good governance, transparency and efficiency for service deliveries will not be adequately met. (James 2005, p. 6)

According to Koichiro Matsuura, director-general of UNESCO, speaking on the occasion of World Freedom Day in Senegal on May 3, 2005, it is crucial that "the transparency and accountability in public administration ... be backed up with laws" (James 2005, p. 7). This will promote freedom of access to information for increased public participation, a key aspect of good governance.

Role of Media in South Africa
Constitutional Mandates

During the apartheid era, the media industry launched the South African Broadcasting Corporation (SABC) that was responsible for broadcasting the information and news for both public and commercial purposes.

In order to break through this previous blanket of official secrecy, the post-apartheid government in South Africa drew up a new constitution (constitution of the Republic of South Africa 1996). In the emerging democratic era the emphasis is on governance that is transparent, accountable, responsive, effective, efficient, and honest in conduct.

One of the many rights enshrined in the constitution (Section 16) is that the people have the right to freedom of expression, including freedom of the press and the media, and freedom of dissemination of information. Section 32 stipulates that everyone has the right of access to any information held by the state. Sections 59, 72, and 118, respectively, state that the public has the right to information discussed in the National Assembly, National Council of Provinces, and the various provincial legislatures. Furthermore, the bill of rights in the constitution stipulates that every citizen has basic rights pertaining to communication practices and activities. Moreover, the constitution stresses that "government should be open in discharging its responsibilities to the public [and that this] ... is a key element of democracy, therefore, communication and accessibility of information have become essential in ensuring that citizens are empowered" (Vyas-Doorgapersad and Ababio 2006, p. 378).

The supporting legislative mandates include the Competition Act, No. 89 of 1998, implemented to review matters of competition that might arise in the communications sector; the Postal Services Act, No. 124 of 1998, in terms of which the media authority is obliged to license the postal addresses of the end users; and the Promotion of Administration of Justice Act, No. 3 of 2000 (PAJA), which reviews and holds the Independent Communications Authority of South Africa (ICASA) accountable on the exercise of their delegated administrative and judicial functions. In addition, the Broadcasting Act, No. 64 of 2002 is an amended version of the Independent Broadcasting Authority (IBA) Act of 1993, implemented with the purpose of enhancing democracy, promoting societal development, and contributing toward nation building. To encourage transparency in the South African public administration, the Promotion of Access to Information Act, No. 2 of 2000 was promulgated. This advances the dissemination of information to the population at large, bridging the gap between the people and the administrative sector.

Advanced media are employed, including electronic government (e-government, utilizing the Internet) and ubiquitous government (u-government, utilizing wireless technologies). The digital means of communication are regulated by the Electronic Communications and Transactions Act, No. 68 of 2002, to ensure seamless services to end users. The Electronic Communications Act, No. 36 of 2005 (ECA) regulates the functions of ICASA, encompassing postal, broadcasting, and electronic communication services in the country. The Independent Communications Authority of South Africa Amendment Act, No. 3 of 2006 (ICASA Amendment Act) oversees telecommunications and has established the South African Communications Authority as an independent regulatory body that monitors financially feasible telecommunication services on offer to society.

Status of Media in South Africa

In Africa, some "48 of the continent's 53 countries have 'insult' and criminal defamation laws which criminalise critical reporting of the conduct of public servants.... These countries would not make the grade under 'good governance' if required to show that their media functioned freely" (Louw 2008, p. 9).

The historical legacy of dictatorships, apartheid governments, and authoritarian leadership in Africa has meant that in some African countries the media was/still is restricted and prevented from disseminating full details and accurate information to the public. The 1990s witnessed the disintegration of state socialism, and throughout the world there was a corresponding rise and consolidation of capitalism. There was also increased public awareness of the advantages of democratic governance, and many previously authoritarian African states adopted liberal forms of democracy. Hyden and Okigbo (2002 in Banda 2010, pp. 29–53) maintain: "This would seem to agree with those who placed the media in Africa in what they call 'the two waves of democracy.' The 'first wave' refers to the colonial period. In other words, it sees the African-nationalist struggles for independence, giving way to a 'second wave' of postcolonialism." According to Banda (2010) this implies that "the work practices of the media can be viewed in terms of their relationship to the wider societal processes and institutions of democratization" (p. 7).

African countries need effective media; otherwise, they cannot hope to democratize, prosper, or engage with the rest of the world as equals. Yet in Africa the development of a pluralistic print and broadcast media has been fitful (De Gouveia 2005). Moreover, in the view of some, the "'third wave' of democracy has blown across the continent of Africa [but] democratization has not produced the expected result. Rather than engender development and good governance, it has led to anarchy, civil wars, genocide and general political instabilities" (Ogundiya 2010, p. 205). Two examples are Rwanda and the Democratic Republic of Congo, both of whom have controlled media processes, and the flow of information to the masses is heavily restricted, hampering the spirit of democracy.

In South Africa, because of the fundamental political, economic, and social upheaval after the dismantling of the apartheid state, the media had to undergo dramatic change. Jacobs (1999, p. 1) claims that the "partisan press is declining, producing greater media independence, characterized by more critical coverage of the government." Indeed, some feel that South Africa has become a "one-eyed man among the blind (whereas tyranny and press censorship have become the default form of governance in Zimbabwe, for example)" (Ndlovu 2010, p. 2).

In order to create the environment of an informed society, in 1992 the African National Congress (ANC) produced the "Ready to Govern" document, which included a declaration on the role of the media in a democratic society. This states that at the "core of democracy lies the recognition of the right of all citizens to take part in society's decision-making process. This requires that individuals are armed with the necessary information and have access to the contesting options they require to make informed choices. An ignorant society cannot be democratic" (ANC 2007, p. 1). Furthermore, at its 51st conference held in 2002 at the University of Stellenbosch, the ANC reiterated the significance of the media, pointing out that it has a communication capacity that can enhance democracy, bring social and political awareness, promote political dialogue, and strengthen societal reform through information dissemination, freedom of speech, and freedom of expression.

Constitutional Court Judge Kate O'Regan highlighted the significance of freedom of expression when she said that it is "valuable for ... its facilitation of the search for truth by individuals and society generally" (quoted in Bronstein 2010, p. 1). Moreover, Judge Frans Malan of the Judicial Service Commission took a holistic view, emphasizing the importance of media as the "watchdog of society ... [that encourages the people] ... to make informed choices about government and democracy" (quoted in Mail and Guardian Online 2010).

According to Nationmaster.com (2012), in 2011 democratic South Africa had 1,118,000 newspapers and periodicals, 13,750,000 radio receivers, 5,200,000 television receivers, and 147 website defacements. In addition, the 2010 All Media Products Study (AMPS) by the South African Advertising Research Foundation (SAARF) found that of adults over 15 years of age (of all races), 64.6% had access to 168 AMPS newspapers and magazines. Furthermore, statistics provided by Koenderman (2011) show a significant growth in media opportunities available in the Southern African Development Community (SADC) region. In May 2011 there were 160 TV stations and 173 radio stations to transfer information to the public.

The Media–Government–Society Nexus in South Africa

To improve communication between the government and the public, the media plays a significant role. The South African government has therefore opened a portal called South Africa Online that serves as an e-government gateway that can be accessed via http://www.gov.za. The gateway incorporates an information portal to access information on government policies, programs, and updates at http://www.info.gov.za and a service portal where the public can pay bills, file tenders, disburse fines, etc., at http://www.services.gov.za. The gateway utilizes the tools of e-government to inform the public with updated policies and is receptive to feedback for improvement via these Internet facilities. Riley and Riley emphasized the significance of e-government as an advanced form of media, stating that e-government "presents a real transformation in democratic governance, including design, decision making and service delivery capabilities." They go on to explain that "e-government refers to an IT-led reconfiguration of public sector governance.... This gives some credence to the ongoing thinking that e-governance results in some form of e-democracy ... for the citizen to influence government policy, programs or policy evolution" (Riley and Riley 2003, p. 13).

The digital media has also been introduced at the grassroots level to advance the dialogue between municipal office bearers and community members. According to the 2001 census conducted by Statistics South Africa, there were 19 million people living in rural areas, comprising 42% of the total population of the country (RSA: Department of Communication 2010). The "metamorphosis of governance from the traditional to digital will only improve the service delivery through technological advances in the system" (Vyas-Doorgapersad 2009, p. 460). Citizens' access to Internet should also be complemented by appropriate training to enhance technological literacy as well as the necessary training (in their mother tongue) to promote participation in the e-government facilities (Vyas-Doorgapersad 2009). In order to assist the community members to understand the digital governance in their regional/local language(s), community development workers are deployed by government at various stations in rural areas. According to the Department of Communication (DoC) (RSA 2010), Thusong Service Centers, comprising telecenters and cyber-labs (a total of 100 such centers by 2007), have been set up to accommodate service delivery needs and demands. Public interest terminals and gateway access channels have also been established to educate community members regarding government and governance.

The DoC is striving to meet the goals of the World Summit on Information Society to connect geographically scattered villages and rural areas through technological devices. The DoC has prepared a framework with set objectives emphasizing the establishment of telecommunications infrastructure in rural areas, capacitating rural communities, improving broadcasting services, and enhancing the status of services through e-government approaches. Diverse network service providers are contributing to the achievement of these objectives. Corporations such as Seacom, Easy African Submarine Cable Systems, Telkom, Neotel, Universal Service Obligations, Universal Services Access Agency of South Africa, and Digital Terrestrial Television are offering their information technology (IT) expertise to establish post offices, digital hubs, cyber-laboratories, community radio stations, e-cadres, e-cooperatives, IT-led small-medium-micro enterprises, local content generation hubs, and Information and Communication Technology (ICT)-led health and education facilities. It is thus clear that the process of media-incorporated living is ongoing.

Reviewing the significance of the diverse forms of media in South Africa, it can justifiably be claimed (as Tettey does for the situation in the United States) that they are not merely a means of expression for the "government, political parties or citizens ..., but have emerged as autonomous power centers in competition with other power centers. This is widely illustrated by the significant influence that the media have had in relation to civic education, election monitoring, and results tallying" (Tettey 2008, pp. 2–3).

In South Africa, that is a developing country with an emerging democracy, the

> role of media has sometimes been articulated as that of "nation building," creating a common sense of identity, and contributing to a consensus on the type of nation that is being strived after. (Maina 2010, p. 9)

Emerging Challenges

In 2011, the ANC, as the government of the day, tabled the Protection of Public Information Act. Upon approval, this act will allow public office bearers to decide which information should be released to the media and what needs to be held back in terms of the national interest. The ANC also anticipated the establishment of a media tribunal, which, upon recognition, will deal with the complaints reported against the media. The relevant stakeholders are currently expressing concern about the establishment of the tribunal and legislation seeing them as jeopardizing the constitutional right to freedom of expression. The proposals still require approval through all the stages of policy making. The impact of these proposals can therefore only be investigated and evaluated in the coming years.

Conclusion

The changes in communication mechanisms for improved participation in the affairs of governance have advanced the role of media required for good governance. These transformations have witnessed paradigm shifts in the history of humankind. Alvin Toffler's theory holds that a few times during the history of the world, a new civilization has emerged, which brings about new family styles, new political conflicts, and an altered consciousness. "Toffler identified three such waves of change (or revolutions), namely, the first wave of change, the Agricultural Revolution, which took thousands of years to play itself out; the second wave, which brought about the rise of the industrial society and took a mere hundred years to conclude; and the third wave, which is the rise of the Information Age. This wave will in all probability play itself out within the scope of few decades" (Toffler 1980 in Minnaar and Bekker 2005, p. 24), diminishing the traditional forms of media and eventually replacing them with digitally advanced communication devices.

As Breen (2007) puts it, holistically, "new technologies have a profound impact on the manner in which media content is produced, communicated and consumed." Older forms of media are likely to become progressively eroded over time. "Despite the relative increase in which new technologies can be harnessed by consumers with a potentially significant increase in audience agency," old media conglomerates will inevitably be dominated by corporates in both the private and public sector that rely on new forms of media. It is also true that "just as old media rarely enter into an analysis of their role in political economy, nor in any invitation to audiences to engage in serious reflections on systematic social issues and contexts, so too new media and new technologies are even more focused on the immediacy of content, often in a triumph of style over substance" (pp. 54–77).

According to the chief executive officer of the South African Human Rights Commission (SAHRC), Tseliso Thipanyane,

> the media is an institution whose role is to deliver information fairly and without discrimination … media professionals receive training in order to understand the Constitution and human rights … media must be ethically empowered to exercise professionalism and fairness in order to report from a human rights perspective. (Quoted in Senderayi 2008, p. 1)

These sentiments are fully supported by Godi (2007), who asserts that "freedom of expression and freedom of media are amongst the most basic human rights and an essential component of any democratic society. A free, independent and pluralistic media is essential to a free and open society and to accountable systems of government" (p. 4).

References

African National Congress (ANC). 2007. *Transformation of the media*. Pretoria: ANC Office.
Aveggio, M.T. 2012. *Good governance and media: A development partnership?* Canada: The World Association for Christian Communication.
Banda, F. 2010. *Citizen journalism and democracy in Africa: An exploratory study*. Rhodes University, Highway Africa School of Journalism and Media Studies.
Breen, M.J. 2007. Mass media and new media technologies. In *Media studies: Key issues and debates*, ed. E. Devereux, pp. 54–77. London: Sage Publications.
Bronstein, V. 2010. *What you can and can't say in South Africa*. Cape Town: Parliamentary Offices of the Democratic Alliance.
Cole, B. 1995. *Mass media, freedom, and democracy in Sierra Leone*. Sierra Leone: Premier Publication House.

De Gouveia, P.F. 2005. *An African Al-Jazeera? Mass media and the African renaissance.* London: The Foreign Policy Center.

Devereux, E. 2007. *Media studies: Key issues and debates.* London: Sage Publications.

Floss, D. 2008. *Mass media's impact on confidence in political institutions; the moderating role of political preferences: A preferences-perceptions model of media effects.* Geneva: Swiss National Science Foundation, National Center of Competence in Research.

Fog, A. 2004. The supposed and the real role of mass media in modern democracy. Working Paper, Polity Press. From http://www.agner.orgcultsel/mediacrisis.pdf (accessed July 17, 2010).

Fourie, D. 2006. The application of good governance in public financial management. *Journal of Public Administration* 41(2.2): 434–443.

Gistern, R., and Volmer, F. 2004. Engaging citizens: Communication between government and citizens in Netherlands. From http://www. tappan.nl (accessed February 12 2006).

Godi, T. 2007. Fighting corruption: National integrity systems, good practice examples. Paper presented at the Global Forum V: Fighting Corruption and Safeguarding Integrity. Johannesburg, South Africa.

Griswold, S. 2011. The two-step flow of communication theory. From http://www.ojla.eu/pubfiles/TSCT.doc (accessed January 9 2012).

Hansen, G. 2002. *The enabling environment for free and independent media: Contribution to transparent and accountable governance.* Washington, DC: Office of Democracy and Governance.

Hyden, G., and Okigbo, C. 2002. The media and the two waves of democracy. In *Media and democracy in Africa,* ed. G. Hyden, M. Leslie, and F. Folu Ogundimu, pp. 29–53. London: Transaction Publishers.

Iyengar, S., and Reeves, R. 1997. *Do the media govern?: Politicians, voters, and reporters in America.* UK: Sage.

Jacobs, S. 1999. *Tensions of a free press: South Africa after apartheid.* Cambridge, MA: Harvard University Press.

James, B. 2005. *Media and good governance.* Paris: United Nations Educational, Scientific and Cultural Organization.

Katz, E. 1957. The two-step flow of communication: An up-to-date report on an hypothesis. *Public Opinion Quarterly* 21(1): 61–78.

Kearl, M.C. 2010. *A sociological tour through cyberspace: Communication studies.* San Antonio, TX: Trinity University (Department of Sociology and Anthropology).

Kleinnijenhuis, J., and Rietberg, E. 1995. Parties, media, the public and the economy: Patterns of societal agenda-setting. *European Journal of Political Research,* 28: 95–118.

Koch-Baumgarten, S., and Voltmer, K. 2010. *Public policy and mass media: The interplay of mass communication and political decision-making.* New York: Routledge.

Koenderman, T. 2011. *AdReview: South Africa and SADC media facts 2011.* Auckland Park, Johannesburg: OMD Media Direction South Africa.

Lines, K. 2009. *Governance and the media: A survey of policy opinion.* London: BBC World Service Trust.

Louw, E. 2005. *The media and political process.* London: Sage Publications.

Louw, R. 2008. *Media freedom, transparency and governance.* Johannesburg: South African Institute of International Affairs.

Mail and Guardian Online. 2010. Total onslaught on the pillars of democracy. From http://www.mg.co.za/2010-08-25-total-onslaught-on-the-pillars-of-democracy (accessed December 10, 2011).

Maina, H.O. 2010. The role of the media in promoting good governance in the region. Paper at 2nd EAC Conference on Good Governance, Nairobi, August 19–20, 2010. From http://www.eac.int/politicalfederation/index.php?option=com (accessed December 15, 2011).
Minnaar, F., and Bekker, K. 2005. *Public management in the information age*. Pretoria: Van Schaik.
NationMaster.com. 2012. South African media data, statistics, facts and figures. From http://www.nationmaster.com/country/sf-south-africa/med-media (accessed September 14, 2011).
Ndlovu, T. 2010. *ANC plans taint Southern Africa's press freedom leader*. New York: Committee to Protect Journalists.
Ocitti, J. 1999. *Media and democracy in Africa: Mutual political bedfellows or implacable archfoes*. Cambridge, MA: Harvard University Press.
Ogundiya, I.S. 2010. Democracy and good governance: Nigeria's dilemma. *African Journal of Political Science and International Relations* 4(6): 201–208.
Opuamie-Ngoa, S.N. 2010. Functional democracy and mass media: A critique. *Global Media Journal African Edition* 4(2): 132–150.
Page, B.I., and Shapiro, R.Y. 1992. *The rational public: Fifty years of trends in Americans' policy preferences*. Chicago: University of Chicago Press.
Panday, P.K. 2009. Does globalization affect media role in a democratic country? Bangladesh perspective. *Journal of Media and Communication Studies* 1(2): 033–042.
Pearson, M., and Patching, R. 2008. *Government media relations: A "spin" through the literature*, pp. 1–62. Humanities and Social Sciences Paper 228. Bond University, Faculty of Humanities and Social Sciences. http://epublications.bond.edu.au/hss_pubs/228 (accessed September 20, 2011).
Pillay, P., Subban, M., and Vyas-Doorgapersad, S. 2009. The media as a catalyst for local government: Challenges and opportunities for good governance. Paper presented at SAAPAM 10th Annual Conference, October 7–9, 2009 at Port Elizabeth. *Journal of Public Administration Conference Proceedings* 216–227.
Republic of South Africa. 1993. The Independent Broadcasting Authority Act, No.153 of 1993. Pretoria: Government Printer.
Republic of South Africa. 1996. The Constitution of the Republic of South Africa, 1996. Pretoria: Government Printer.
Republic of South Africa. 1998a. The Competition Act, No. 89 of 1998. Pretoria: Government Printer.
Republic of South Africa. 1998b. The Postal Services Act, No. 124 of 1998. Pretoria: Government Printer.
Republic of South Africa. 2000a. The Promotion of Administration of Justice Act, No. 3 of 2000. Pretoria: Government Printer.
Republic of South Africa. 2000b. The Promotion of Access to Information Act, No. 2 of 2000. Pretoria: Government Printer.
Republic of South Africa. 2002. The Broadcasting Act, No. 64 of 2002. Pretoria: Government Printer.
Republic of South Africa. 2002. The Electronic Communications and Transactions Act, No. 68 of 2002. Pretoria: Government Printer.
Republic of South Africa. 2005. The Electronic Communications Act, No. 36 of 2005. Pretoria: Government Printer.
Republic of South Africa. 2006. The Independent Communications Authority of South Africa, Act No. 3 of 2006 (ICASA Amendment Act). Pretoria: Government Printer.

Republic of South Africa: Department of Communication. 2010. *Towards an information and communications technologies (ICT) rural development strategic framework*. Pretoria: Government Printer.

Riley, T.B., and Riley, G.R. 2003. *E-governance to e-democracy: Examining the evolution*. Ottawa: Commonwealth Center for E-Governance.

Senderayi, N. 2008. *The media in democratic South Africa*. Johannesburg: SANGONeT.

Sharma, M. 2002. Media and governance. From http://india-seminar.com/2002/514/514%mukul%20sharma.htm (accessed July 30, 2010).

Sillah, O. 2011. *Gambia: Media has key role in democratization, good governance, says Ambassador Ayo Oke of the Commonwealth*. Gambia: FOROYAA Newspaper.

Soola, E.O. 2009. Media, democracy and misgovernance in Africa. *International Journal of African Studies* 1(June): 25–35.

South African Advertising Research Foundation (SAARF). 2010. *All media products study: Magazine and newspaper readership*. Johannesburg: SAARF.

Tettey, W.J. 2008. Media pluralism, democratic discourses and political accountability in Africa. Paper presented in a Harvard-World Bank Workshop, Harvard Kennedy School, Cambridge, MA, May 29–31. From http://www.hks.harvard.edu/fs/pnorris/Conference/Conference%20papers/Tettey%20Africa.pdf (accessed September 14, 2011).

Toffler, A. 1980. *The third wave*. New York: Morrow.

Vyas-Doorgapersad, S. 2009. The application of e-government for increased service delivery in South Africa. *International Journal of Interdisciplinary Social Sciences* 4: 455–466.

Vyas-Doorgapersad, S., and Ababio, E.P. 2006. Effective local government communication for efficient service delivery in South Africa. Joint SAAPAM and ASSADPAM Conference at the Sun Coast Conference Centre, Durban, from September 20–22. *Journal of Public Administration Conference Proceedings* 377–387.

Walgrave, S., and Van Aelst, P. 2006. The contingency of the mass media's political agenda setting power: Towards a preliminary theory. *Journal of Communication* 56: 88–109.

Wohlmuth, K., Bass, H.H., and Messner, F. 1999. *African development perspectives yearbook 1997/9*. Münster: Lit.

Yadav, L.B. 2001. *Role of media in promoting good governance*. Nepal: Friedrich Ebert Stiftung.

Chapter 7

Implementing Good Governance Reform in Ghana: Issues and Experiences with Local Governance[1]

Peter Fuseini Haruna and Lawrence Akanweke Kannae

Contents

Introduction	136
Good Governance Overview	137
Local Governance Experience	139
Poverty Reduction Experience	142
Poverty Reduction Performance Management	144
Final Reflections on Local Governance	147
Notes	149
References	149

Introduction

Ghana's good governance initiative has entered a critical phase after that country conducted an independent, nonpartisan, and professional self-assessment of political, economic, corporate, and procedural governance under the African Peer Review Mechanism process.[2] Both Country Review Report and National Program of Action required Ghana not only to build on its achievements, but also to address challenges to good governance. In its African Governance Report II the Economic Commission for Africa (ECA) concluded that Africa had made only marginal progress on governance and that "capacity deficits" remained.[3] The ECA identified several political, economic, corporate, and procedural governance challenges, including poverty and corruption reduction and the improvement of the quality of life. While most studies have focused on national-level performance, this chapter examines the governance project from the perspective of local as opposed to national governance. The question is: How well has Ghana done to make good governance promise and practice reflect in decentralized governance?

A broad political economy perspective is applied in the analysis, using national official documentary review interviews with key actors in the governing process to explore and evaluate experience with the devolution process and decentralized governance reform.

The chapter argues that Ghana is faced with an administrative dilemma: implementing good governance policies with a bureaucratic mindset and techniques that have tended to work against effective local governance. On one hand, Ghana is committed in principle to good governance as based in an open, delegated, shared, and collaborative governing arrangement (United Nations 2000; Abdellatif 2003). On the other hand, implementing good governance policies practically has followed a top-down bureaucratic approach that somehow has placed national or urban over and above local or rural governance. In fact, Ghana is executing its good governance project within a largely bureaucratic institutional framework that has not supported fully local governance in a decentralized development framework. The value conflict between governance principle and bureaucratic practice has short-changed local and rural governance.

As a result of such a value conflict, the central purpose of good governance, i.e., reducing poverty and improving the quality of life of the majority of people, mostly has lagged behind. Institutional capacity building and development, the idea of improving institutional capability in policy formulation and implementation, has focused more on national or urban rather than local or rural governance. Within local governance the purpose of good governance similarly has been stalled in the hustle of creating structures. The decentralized policy framework states clearly:

> The unfinished business in Ghana's decentralization efforts include composite budgeting, the activation of local government service, functioning works departments, satisfactory public relations and complaints

committees have come up for concern. Ghanaians also identify a range of services that could be competently decentralized to the local level so that they do not have to go to the national and regional capitals to get these—including processing pension benefits, business registration amongst others. (Ministry of Local Government and Rural Development [MLGRD] 2010)[4]

To be sure, much work has been done to devolve political power and administrative authority to subnational jurisdictions as part of the development management strategy. The 1992 Ghana constitution, along with several pieces of legislation, including Local Government Service Act (1993), Institute of Local Government Studies Act (2003), District Assemblies Common Fund Act (1993), and National Medium Term Development Policy Framework (2010–2013), has created the enabling context for executing local or rural governance. But as the Ghana 2008 Demographic and Health Survey has indicated, quality of life is by far lower in local or rural than national or urban areas on all health, education, and income indicators. From the foregoing then, Ghana is trapped in two divergent theoretical perspectives: bureaucracy and good governance. Like the rest of Africa then, economic growth could not logically have been expected to be even and inclusive. The next section provides an overview of Ghana's good governance project before discussing specific experiences with local governance within a decentralized policy framework. The final section summarizes and reflects on capacity deficits of local governance and the way forward.

Good Governance Overview

Good governance has been accepted by now as critical for development management since the UN Millennium Declaration envisioned a world of "peace and security, development and poverty reduction, human rights, democracy and good governance" (Abdellatif 2003, p. 2). Ghana was among the first of sub-Saharan African countries to pursue good governance policies as a way of improving its quality of life. From the perspective of the international development community, four broad conceptualizations of good governance have crystallized and been applied in policy development and implementation in Ghana: political, economic, procedural, and corporate good governance (World Bank 1992; World Bank 1997; World Bank 2004; UNDP 1997; UNCHR 2001; OECD 2005; Kim et al. 2005). The underlying and cross-cutting elements that ground Ghana's good governance project include ensuring political participation, providing effective and efficient public services, promoting social and economic well-being, protecting human rights, and creating a climate for sound fiscal management and economic growth.

On the other hand, good governance has also connoted the process of managing across jurisdictions as scholars have noted: state-civil society, public-private, central-local, national-regional, and executive-legislative, to mention but a few (Peters and Pierre 2000; Haque 2002; Rondinelli and Cheema 2003; Kettl 2002; Hyden and Court 2002). In this respect, Ghana's good governance project has recognized that public problems are too complex and the transactions too extensive for one sector alone to carry. Countless procedural and substantive issues crosscut and span boundaries in a manner that requires partnership, collaboration, and cooperation between and among jurisdictions (Rondinelli and Cheema 2003). In the context of development management and Ghana's unique circumstance, interorganizational and interjurisdictional networks, interactions, and relationships are essential for effective governing.

Ghana since has made much good progress in almost all four categories of the good governance paradigm, especially with respect to institutional capacity building and legislative framework. The 1992 constitution, which has created a democratic, representative, and republican governing system with separate legislative, executive, and judicial branches of government, provides the legal framework for pursuing good governance. Article 34 has required Ghana to "make democracy a reality … by affording all possible opportunities to the people to participate in decision-making at every level in national life and in government." It has also created, empowered, and elaborated on the roles of several independent oversight and regulatory institutions for controlling public conduct and protecting individual rights, most notably: Electoral Commission, National Commission on Civic Education, Commission on Human Rights and Administrative Justice, Media Commission, Office of Accountability, Securities Exchange Commission, and Organized and Economic Crimes Office, among others.

Consistent with its economic and corporate governance aspiration for promoting the values of sound fiscal management, transparency, legality, accountability, equity, efficiency, and economic growth, Ghana has passed several pieces of legislation to guide public management and government operations, including the Ghana Revenue Authority Act, Civil Service Reform Act, Financial Administration Act, Public Office Holder Act, and public procurement law. In addition, Ghana has been a party to the Charter for the Public Service in Africa (2001) and the African Union's Convention on Preventing and Combating Corruption. Programs such as the School Feeding Program, National Health Insurance Scheme, National Youth Employment Program, and Free Compulsory Basic Education have been expanded. Ghana not only was the first country to be peer reviewed in 2005 under the African Peer Review Mechanism, but also has since conformed to the process by annually conducting and reporting on its self-assessment.[3]

Over the last three years, Ghana has recorded relative macro economic stability and prudent management. With the gross domestic product (GDP) averaging 4.1% growth, inflation falling to 9.38%, and the fiscal deficit reduced to 9.7% of GDP, Ghana is in much better shape than most of sub-Saharan Africa (Duffour 2010). In 2006–2007, Ghana successfully demonetized and redenominated its currency, enabling it to regain value and credibility against major international currencies. The Ghana Shared Growth and Development Agenda (2010–2013), a medium-term development strategy, has aimed to sustain macro economic stability and growth, accelerate agricultural modernization, develop human settlement, enhance international competitiveness, and promote transparency and accountable governance. As a result, the 2011 national fiscal and budget outlook is optimistic: targeting a real GDP growth rate (including oil) of 12.3%, projecting a fiscal deficit of 7.5%, and pegging inflation at 8.8%.[5]

Likewise, civil society has gained considerable respectability over the last decade, creating social, political, and economic space for nongovernmental organizations (NGOs) to play an effective role in governance. In 2004, NGOs negotiated with the government to develop a National Policy for Strategic Partnership that would facilitate the formation of an independent national NGO commission, guarantee tax exemptions, and pave the way for collaboration with local authorities. While the legislation has not yet been passed, it holds a good prospect for strengthening civil society participation in good governance. Several NGOs are beginning to make an impact in the governing process: Women's Initiative for Self-Empowerment (WISE) collaborates with the police to provide counseling for victims of domestic violence, while the Federation of Women Lawyers (FIDA) provides *pro bono* legal advice. The Ghana Integrity Initiative (GII), local chapter of Transparency International, has conducted national corruption perception surveys annually as a part of the fight against corrupt practices in the public sector.

But issues remain with good governance. Conceptually, the strength of good governance as a broad-based, comprehensive approach also represents its Achilles' heel. It has contrasted with bureaucratic and managerial reforms that emphasized development management as a narrowly circumscribed technical activity. It draws intellectual, analytic, and practical tools informed by several disciplines: economics, politics, public administration, management, and institutionalism, among others. However, Ghana's experience shows that as an all-embracing concept, it is hard to separate policy formulation from its implementation and to assess quality. Inevitably, governance has focused on rules and how they structure policy results and outcomes. But while a rule-governed approach is necessary, it has resulted in rebureaucratizing the public sector in a manner that is counterproductive to effective local governance, as we argue below.

Local Governance Experience

Ghana has a checkered local governance history and experience. Long before the transition to political independence, and thereafter, it had pursued local governance policies in varying shapes and forms (Ayee 2004; Olowu and Wunsch 2004). Then and even now local governance has remained important in the national discourse primarily because that is where nearly 70% of Ghanaians live and work (World Development Indicators Database 2010). This section describes and analyzes local and rural governance change and experience with respect to the good governance initiative. Like the structural adjustment and managerial reforms before it, governance has been grafted on a deep-rooted national bureaucratic framework that tends to hurt rather than promote the transformation of local and rural life.

The perspective of local governance taken here is one that focuses on a rule-governed process for making decisions on "locally important matters," as well as "outputs and outcomes" associated with those decisions (Olowu and Wunsch 2004). The significance of local governance is overwhelmingly supported theoretically: all of public administration occurs in a locality or at least has some proximate consequences. Frederickson (2004) has argued that "there is little, maybe nothing, that is national, international, or global that does not now have some sort of local manifestation" (p. 11). In other words, all "significant distant events and issues" have local consequences that cannot be ignored. By the same token, all significant local events and issues have distant, national, and international consequences. Likewise, Ventriss (2002) has emphasized that the "global-local interplay has given the subnational level a pronounced (and new) role in international economic affairs" (p. 82). This kind of globalization makes subnational governments, especially local jurisdictions, important actors in effective public governance.

As is well known, the forces that have conditioned local governance in Ghana are both exogenous and endogenous—emanating from within and outside of the locality. To be sure, endogenous forces, i.e., local elites, political parties, civil society organizations, businesses, and nongovernment agencies, have played and continue to play important roles in determining whether and how localities are successful. That granted, we emphasize that one exogenous factor, national "political will," is a necessary condition for guaranteeing effective local governance. But building local governance in the sense of devolution or the complete transfer of responsibility, resources, and accountability from center to periphery is itself problematic in a unitary system such as Ghana's (Davidson 1992). This is complicated by the fragile nature of a state that is still struggling to glue fragments of society together. Thus the weak and ostensibly ambivalent commitment to devolution, though undesirable, is somewhat understandable.

Nonetheless, interest in local governance has not only witnessed change, but also gained much momentum since Ghana implemented good governance. One important change has been the formulation and legislation of a national decentralized policy framework through a broad-based consultative and participatory process during 2009–2010.[6] To a large extent, the decentralization process has been redesigned and reinvented, breathing fresh new life into local governance. The policy, "Accelerating Decentralization and Local Governance for National Development," has aimed to harmonize sector approaches, promote rights-based orientation, integrate decentralized departments, build and strengthen local substructures capacity, stimulate popular participation and civic engagement, and streamline relationships with traditional authorities, development partners, and nongovernmental organizations. Thus for the first time in its administrative history, Ghana has adopted a more experienced-based, focused, and comprehensive devolution policy along with an action plan that will give impetus to "local level democracy and development" (Decentralization Policy Framework 2010).

Of particular interest and significance is the decentralization 10-point action plan designed to give meaning and effect to the policy during the implementation period (2010–2014). It demarcates and describes priority action areas: political and administrative decentralization, social development and spatial planning, economic development and fiscal decentralization, citizens' participation, social agenda dimension, and development partnerships and collaboration. The detailed action-based matrices specify policy objectives and measures, time frames, and responsible organizations and agencies. An umbrella interministerial coordinating committee oversees the revitalized implementation process along with support from the Ministry of Local Government and Rural Development, Office of Head of Civil Service, Public Services Commission, and National Development Planning Commission, to mention but a few. A monitoring and evaluation framework is also provided, based on the Functional Organizational Assessment Tool (FOAT), District Governance Citizens' Report Checklist, as well as other assessment tools that civil society organizations have developed.

In addition to these national-level changes, several international agreements, regional protocols, and pieces of national legislation have either supported or required Ghana to effectively devolve power and administrative authority toward enhancing local or rural governance. The UN Millennium Declaration (2000), Paris Declaration on Development Effectiveness (2005), African Development Bank (1999, 2004), and New Partnership for Africa's Development (NEPAD) have provided incentive frameworks for devolution aimed at improving livelihoods through good governance. The Millennial Compact includes concrete measurable objectives and Millennium Development Goals (MDGs), specifically targeting poverty reduction, among others, while commitments to NEPAD emphasize efforts at socioeconomic development. Like several sub-Saharan African countries, Ghana recognizes that it cannot meet the MDGs without delivering public services effectively through decentralized local governance.

From outside looking in, the impression is that devolution has entered a new and more dynamic phase in Ghana. With support interventions from the international development community and a more galvanized national momentum, Ghana seems to be on course to address most of the problems associated with decentralized governance that the African Development Bank (2006) had identified: lack of sustained political support, poor design, inadequate resources, local incapacity, corruption, conflict, and poor coordination. In terms of design, the current policy as outlined above has emphasized a "long-term, complex and iterative process," in contrast to previous approaches that viewed decentralization as a narrow technical activity. In particular, the broad-based consultative process sought input from a wide spectrum of the political-administrative landscape, renewed public interest in decentralization, and afforded Ghanaians opportunities to participate and contribute in a national or civic spirit.

But questions remain in regard to resource inadequacy and local institutional capacity gaps, among others. Of concern to governance is a general perception of corruption and poor living conditions in the country. The results of the 2008 Afrobarometer survey suggested that only 12% of Ghanaians had running water in their homes, while 48% considered their living conditions to be "bad or fairly bad." Despite several anticorruption pieces of legislation and institutions, Ghana has not fared well over the last decade, scoring below average in Transparency International's Corruption Perception Index (1999–2010). In fact, only 58% of Ghanaians felt that governmental effort to fight corruption was effective: down from 67% in 2007 (Global Corruption Barometer 2009: http://www.ghanadot.com/news). Thus Ghana still has long tortuous ways to travel in its good governance project.

While it is unreasonable to expect decentralized governance to occur in short order, of particular concern to us is state recentralization and rebureaucratization of public services, a top-down service delivery mode along with all of its functions and dysfunctions. Much attention has been paid to institutional restructuring and reorganization involving ministries, departments, and agencies, but a functional top-down relationship has remained. Policy making, budgeting, and implementation processes remained essentially bureaucratic in nature. The decentralized policy framework discussed above has been controlled from the top. Ministries and central parastatal organizations retain control of the implementation process. Institutional capacity building has often begun from the center, but hardly from the periphery. In the next section we describe experience with poverty reduction programs and how they reflect and are reflected by state recentralization and rebureaucratization that are counterproductive to effective local governance.

Poverty Reduction Experience

Poverty is synonymous with local and rural life in Ghana. The highest hard-core poverty rates are linked with the most deprived rural regions and communities (National Development Planning Commission 2003, 2005). Of necessity then, poverty reduction programs must target and transform local and rural life through effective local governance. This section outlines and discusses poverty reduction programs under the three most recent medium-term development plans: Ghana Poverty Reduction Strategy (GPRS I: 2003–2006), Growth and Poverty Reduction Strategy (GPRS II: 2005–2009), and Ghana Shared Growth and Development Agenda (GSDA: 2010–2013). Together, they consist of comprehensive policies, strategies, programs, and projects aimed at promoting, accelerating, and sustaining growth, thereby substantially controlling poverty. Although Ghana has achieved a high level of poverty reduction, from 51.7% in 1991, 39.5% in 1999, and eventually to 28.5% in 2006, poverty continues to be high in certain regions, particularly in the northern regions. A key facet of poverty is social exclusion and a lack of participation in governance. Citizen participation is not only a fundamental right in of itself, but also ensures appropriate service delivery for poverty reduction. But as we argue below, much work has gone into designing antipoverty programs, but their implementation and mode of delivery has remained basically trickle-down and top-down.

Although Ghana has a long history of development policy initiatives, none had made the desirable impact of directly addressing, controlling, and substantially reducing the high incidence of poverty. Perhaps it is fair to say that the Ghana Poverty Reduction Strategy (GPRS I) was the first conscious attempt aimed at advancing the broad national development goal "to improve the quality of life of all Ghanaians by reducing poverty, raising living standards through a sustained increase in national wealth and a more equitable distribution of the benefits there from." GPRS I was explicitly more poverty focused and pro-poor, with the goal of ensuring "sustainable equitable growth, accelerated poverty reduction and the protection of the vulnerable and excluded within a decentralized, democratic environment."[7] Its subgoals included achieving economic stability, ensuring gender equity, increasing production, supporting equitable human resource development, supporting the vulnerable and excluded, and involving the private sector.

Some GPRS I features are worth commenting on in relation to the focus of this chapter. By adopting an extensive consultative and participatory process and tapping into past experience and empirical evidence, it laid a solid basis for formulating a nationally oriented antipoverty plan. Several international, national, and local stakeholders participated. On one hand, there were World Bank and IMF representatives and central government officials, including National Development Planning Commission and Ministry of Planning and Regional Cooperation. On the other hand, there were civil society organizations: media, trade unions, employer associations, professional associations, religious bodies, think tanks, private sector, and women groups. Local and rural governance representatives came from local government, traditional authorities, and community-based organizations. This not only generated public interest, but also enhanced credibility, legitimacy, and transparency (Integrated Social Development Centre 2003).

Because a significant proportion of the population depends mainly upon peasant farming for their livelihood, GPRS I focused on attacking poverty at the local and rural community level in several respects. By providing small-scale irrigation schemes to promote all-year farming, productivity would increase and thereby raise average real incomes for small-scale farmers, farm laborers, and their families. Along with this economic intervention were the allied strategies to develop rural road networks, facilitate acquiring farm equipment and materials, and ease access to market facilities for farm produce. Also noteworthy was the need to provide basic social interventions: providing potable water, improving access to education and health, closing the gender gap, and developing nonfarming alternative employment opportunities. From the vantage point of policy development GPRS I was comprehensive and focused, with a good chance of being both effective and equitable: meeting the UN MDGs by addressing poverty, improving the quality of life, and transforming the local and rural social and economic environment.

The Growth and Poverty Reduction Strategy (GPRS II) drew from and built on the lessons learned from GPRS I, but with the specific goal of accelerating growth and attaining a middle-income status in the medium term. Like its predecessor, GPRS II adopted extensive consultation and participation at international, national, and local levels. In terms of content, it was anchored on and by three strategic objectives: developing private sector competitiveness, human resources, and good governance and civic responsibility. The strategic focus was on human resource development, beginning from the provision of free compulsory basic education through junior high school to vocational and technical training. Modernizing agriculture, the other leg of the strategy, has aimed at strengthening the fight against poverty by applying research, scientific, and technological improvements to broaden employment opportunity, increase productivity, raise family earning levels, and thereby sustain livelihoods.

While aiming to consolidate achievements of the previous two plans, the Ghana Shared Growth and Development Agenda (GSGDA) has emphasized structural transformation of the national economy from mainly agriculture to industrialization through the exploitation of natural resources, especially minerals, oil, gas, and energy. By expanding and growing the economy through industrialization, the plan was expected to create employment and income-earning opportunities toward rapid and sustained poverty reduction. One key strategic objective was to enhance the competitiveness of the private sector by reducing costs and risks of doing business, developing modern infrastructure, and providing human resource requirements with the relevant knowledge, skills, abilities, and competencies. In terms of good governance, the plan aimed to strengthen institutional reform and democracy by creating space for improved and effective local governance. In particular, the plan aimed to institutionalize local- and rural-level planning through establishing a full-scale local government service independent of the main civil service.[8]

Poverty Reduction Performance Management

The comprehensive performance management model developed under GPRS I was maintained and reinforced under GPRS II and GSGDA to control the process, track progress, and assess inputs, outputs, and outcomes. This laid out elaborate institutional relationships, roles, and responsibilities, established performance targets and indicators, and instituted measures for communicating and sharing information with stakeholders. It specifically identified the annual progress report mechanism and poverty and social impact analyses as the main monitoring and evaluation tools for determining policy impact on targeted populations. As well, planned activities were prioritized and harmonized within the medium-term expenditure framework, while a national expenditure tracking system was adopted to monitor expenditure and inputs. From the good governance perspective, then, the performance management system demonstrated potential for achieving public interest values of transparency, accountability, effectiveness, and efficiency.

However, as we have argued, the performance management framework was unbalanced, top-heavy, and skewed more in favor of central than local and rural governance. The institutional roles and responsibilities, no matter how well intentioned, reflect and reinforce the mindset of bureaucratic control and compliance, with central ministries, departments, and agencies playing the most important roles in managing the process. In the larger scheme of performance monitoring and evaluation the ministerial bodies (e.g., finance, economic planning and regional cooperation, and local government and rural development) retained considerable power and influence. Likewise, super-agencies, including National Development Planning Commission (NDPC), National Interagency Monitoring Group, and GPRS Technical Advisory Committee, play important roles, while the least influential and yet closest to local and rural governance included the regional and district planning and coordinating units (Table 7.1). In fact, in terms of sequencing and phasing of monitoring and evaluation activities, the GPRS Technical Advisory Committee was placed first, followed by the National Interagency Monitoring Group, before regional and district planning units, in that order. There is no doubt that the actual routine conduct of performance monitoring and evaluation has been oriented more toward the center than the periphery with NDPC calling the shots.

This is not necessarily to denigrate the work of the NDPC. In fact, since 2002, it has played the leading role in preparing several annual progress reports that have helped to gauge progress toward achieving GPRS targets as well as outcomes and impacts of public policies. These composite reports systematically and authoritatively have pulled together in a single document nationwide experiential knowledge and understanding of Ghana's good governance initiative. The 2008 report indicated a broad range of coverage that drew from all sectors to assess performance of the GPRS II policy goals: economic expansion and growth, private sector competitiveness, human resource development, and good governance and civic responsibility. The overall assessment was that Ghana had made good progress in all four thematic areas, particularly with respect to good governance and human resource development targeting basic education, health care, and provision of safe drinking water. Also, good effort had been made to better align the 2008 budget statement and economic policy with GPRS II targets.

Of specific interest to this chapter was the question of how the implementation of GPRS II at regional, local, and community levels was conducted to advance the cause of decentralized governance. Both Local Government Act (1993) and National Development Planning Act (1994) had empowered local authorities to perform planning, programming, monitoring, evaluating, and coordinating

Table 7.1 Institutional Roles for Performance Management

No.	Institution	Role
1	Office of President	Ensuring resourcing of GPRS
2	Parliament	Disseminating GPRS results
3	GPRS Technical Advisory Committee	Provides data collection, analysis, and interpretation support for GPRS
4	Ministry of Finance	Monitors government expenditure and external funding
5	Ministry of Economic Planning and Regional Cooperation	Supervises and monitors Monitoring and Evaluation (M&E) plan
6	National Development Planning Commission	Coordinates M&E plan and subcontracts poverty and social impact analyses
7	National Interagency Monitoring Group	Reviews GPRS I performance on specific thematic areas
8	Regional Planning Coordinating Unit	Coordinates and reports on regional M&E activities
9	District Planning Coordinating Unit	Coordinates and reports on district M&E activities

Source: Adapted from GPRS I.

functions. They were required to develop and implement performance monitoring and evaluation plans, define indicators, and prepare and submit annual progress reports. The 2008 report showed that the majority of them had complied with the NDPC annual report submission deadline. Even though this was an increase of 10% over 2007, they did not meet internally generated or own-source revenue mobilization targets. As a result, they were unable to fund and fully implement all planned activities. There were achievements, though, in poverty reduction interventions with respect to health and education.

The key concern with the poverty performance management model was that it emphasized centralized direction and information extraction. Implementing GPRS II at the local level was characterized predominantly as a top-down process with NDPC preparing and delivering guidelines and training manuals to subnational jurisdictions. In other words, regional and local authorities needed only to comply with standardized instructions provided to them without much regard to initiative and creative input. Ironically, strengthening performance monitoring and evaluation tended more toward recentralization and rebureaucratization than decentralized governance. This could not be made clearer, as indicated by the quote below:

The key institutions need to be strengthened and empowered to lead the process and sustain the system with continuous flow of timely, reliable, accurate and relevant information that will be used to track progress. A common centrally located database will be established for the storage and retrieval of basic data for the country as a whole, and also for regions and districts, providing easy access to all stake-holders of which a national database in the form of GhanaInfo is the core. (GPRS II)

Most of the "key institutions" referenced above included Office of the President, parliament, NDPC, Ghana Statistical Service (GSS), Ministry of Finance and Economic Planning, and National Interagency Monitoring Group. Regional and district planning units along with civil society organizations, while required to participate, always came in at the tail end. The responsibility for coordinating the system rested mainly with the NDPC, consistent with Articles 86 and 87 of the 1992 constitution. Thus working directly with international development partners, the NDPC authorized and commissioned several impact assessments. Although the NDPC did well to collate and compile annual progress reports, its effort exposed some disconnections between centralized and decentralized governance need and capacity. Several localities not only failed to comply fully with the guidelines provided by the NDPC, but also did not meet the annual progress report submission deadline. The lack of alignment between NDPC and local annual progress report timing was one of those disconnections.

Final Reflections on Local Governance

Ghana's good governance initiative has come a long way since the UN Millennial Compact took effect, but it still has a much longer way to travel, particularly with respect to decentralized governance. Over the last decade, Ghana has laid, refined, and strengthened the necessary political, administrative, and legal frameworks for implementing devolution and decentralized governance. The ratification of international agreements, establishment of a local government service along with a full-scale local government studies institute, creation of 170 local authorities, and passage of several pieces of legislation might all testify to Ghana's commitment to decentralized governance. But the real test of this commitment lies in formulating and implementing GPRS I, GPRS II, and GSGDA, which aimed to substantially reduce and eventually eliminate poverty and improve the quality of life of the people. Given its historical and political legacy and deep-rooted social and cultural norms, Ghana has made a good-faith effort, but decentralized governance reform still remains a work in progress.

This chapter was based on the proposition that political will was a necessary, if not sufficient, condition for achieving decentralized governance. Ghana has so far failed to muster and appropriately invest the needed political will: commitment, courage, and confidence of the political leadership to move more "men, women, money, and materials" from center to periphery toward building stronger local institutional capacity for effective and efficient poverty program delivery. The evidence from the annual progress reports all boiled down to resource constraint, which cannot be resolved without putting sufficient political weight and momentum behind it. This will require a bottom-up paradigmatic change, an epiphany that will finally show that the fate of Ghana's socioeconomic transformation is inextricably linked to effective local and rural governance, where the majority of the people, families, and individuals live and work.

Given Ghana's experience so far, how feasible is a bottom-up approach to decentralized governance? What are the chances that a paradigmatic change will occur? From the perspective of political and administrative pessimists, there is little or no chance for paradigm change. For over two decades Ghana has engaged in devolution experimentation that has resulted mostly in what Ayee (2004: 153) describes as "supervised or centralized decentralization," in which the central government has been firmly in control. There is also lack of sustained and sustainable national elite support for decentralized governance and "local elite capture" manifested in and by corrupt practices at play (Olowu 2006). Corruption in particular has been the bane of Ghanaian public life. Ghana has recorded below-average scores on Transparency International's Corruption Perception Indices, and there is little chance that is about to change anytime soon.

The elaborate constitutional provisions, legal and policy regimes notwithstanding, issues of responsiveness, and accountability remain elusive in Ghana's administrative system. The deficits in accountability are pronounced in the local governance system, where successive district assembly elections have recorded low patronage, resulting from lack of public interest and detachment of the governance process from local communities. Studies on the allocation and disbursement of the district assembly common funds (Banful 2007) showed evidence of widespread patronage and ethnic cronyism in selection of projects and contract awards (SEND Foundation 2006). Even more worrying is the lack of an effective system of information regarding the operations of the assemblies. There seems to be a block of free flow of information on resource availability, distribution, and service delivery. The accountability gap at the district level is reflected in the audit reports, tender and procurement irregularities reported by the Public Procurement Agency (2008) and the Auditor-General's Department (2008), research reports, misapplication of funds, and abuse of office. Thus decentralized governance will continue to suffer if such negative forces persist, viewing decentralization as a zero-sum game rather than win-win and entrenching the status quo.

We do not subscribe to this pessimistic perspective. In contrast, we hold the view that a window of opportunity exists for Ghana. There is substantial momentum globally to sustain good governance, especially among the international development community, that will work in Ghana's favor. Of particular interest is the African Development Bank's portfolio of policy initiatives for supporting decentralized governance among regional member countries, which has been increasing (2006). These initiatives are aimed at confronting and addressing challenges of decentralized governance, which Ghana can take advantage of. Also, there are strong sub-Saharan African examples of decentralized governance that Ghana can learn from, e.g., Uganda, South Africa, and Namibia. But we recognize that decentralization is a long, complex, and tedious undertaking. Ghana's experience reinforces the view that change is always hard and often characterized by resistance. In this case, change toward achieving decentralized governance seems even harder and more frustrating.

Notes

1. This chapter was prepared as part of research that the authors conducted while the first coauthor was on a Fulbright Scholarship at the Ghana Institute of Management and Public Administration during 2010–2011. We hereby acknowledge with gratitude the assistance of the Fulbright Scholar Program toward the completion of this research work.
2. Ghana was the first of African countries to undergo the African Peer Review Mechanism in 2005–2006. The Ghana Program of Action outlined obligations for strengthening the pursuit of sustainable growth and development through good governance practices.
3. The Economic Commission for Africa's African Governance Report (AGR II 2009) is a follow-up to the first report issued in 2005. It outlined progress and challenges and proposed an action plan for improving good governance in Africa.
4. The decentralized policy framework was developed by the Ministry of Local Government and Rural Development under the theme "Accelerating Decentralization and Local Governance for National Development."
5. The minister for finance and economic planning, Dr. Kwabena Duffour, presented the government budget statement and economic policy to parliament in January 2011 under the theme "Stimulating Growth for Development and Job Creation."
6. The process for developing the national decentralized policy framework consisted of several activities, including regional-level forums, consultations with interest groups, submission of written position papers, and expert report reviews.
7. See *Ghana Poverty Reduction Strategy, 2003–2005: An Agenda for Growth and Prosperity*, Vol. 1, *Analysis and Policy Statement*, February 19, 2003.
8. The Ghana Local Government Service Act (2003), Act 656, created an autonomous service that has been hived off from the mainstream civil service system.

References

Abdellatif, A.M. 2003. Good governance and its relationship to democracy and economic development. Paper presented at the Global Forum III on fighting corruption and safeguarding integrity, Seoul, South Korea, May 20–31.
African Peer Review Mechanism. 2005. *Country Review Report and Program of Action of the Republic of Ghana*. Midrand, South Africa: APRM Secretariat.

Audit General's Department. 2008. Report of the auditor-general on the public accounts of the year ended 31 December 2008.
Ayee, J. 2004. A top-down initiative. In *Local governance in Africa: The challenges of democratic decentralization*, ed. D. Olowu and J. Wunsch, pp. 125–154. Boulder, CO: Lynne Rienner Publishers.
Banful, A. B. 2009. Do institutions limit clientelism?: A study of the district assembly common fund in Ghana. International Food Policy Research. *IFPRI Discussion Papers* 855.
Davidson, B. 1992. *The blackman's burden: Africa and the curse of the nation-state*. London: James Currey Publishers.
Duffour, K. 2010. *Ghana 2011 budget statement*. Accra: Ministry of Finance and Economic Planning.
Frederickson, G. 2004. All public administration is local. *PA Times* 27(11): 11–12.
Ghana Integrity Initiative. 2010. Press conference to launch TI's Corruption Perception Index (2010), Coconut Grove Regent Hotel, Accra, Ghana, October 26.
Global Corruption Barometer. 2009. From http://www.ghanadot.com/news.
Haque, M. S. 2002. Globalization, new political economy, and governance: A third world viewpoint. *Administrative Theory & Praxis* 24, 102–124.
Hyden, G., and Court, J. 2002. Comparing governance across countries over time: Conceptual challenges. In *Better governance and public policy: Capacity building and democratic renewal in Africa*, ed. D. Olowu and S. Sako, pp. 13–33. Bloomfield, CT: Kumarian Press.
Integrated Social Development Centre. http://www.isodec.org.gh/aboutus.php.
Iyengar, S., and Reeves, R. 1997. *Do the media govern?: Politicians, voters, and reporters in America*. UK: Sage.
Kettl, D. 2002. *The transformation of governance: Public administration for twenty-first century America*. Baltimore: John Hopkins University Press.
Kim, P., Halligan, J., Cho, N., Oh, C., and Aikenberry, A. 2005. Toward participatory and transparent governance: Report on the Sixth Global Forum on Reinventing Government. *Public Administration Review* 65:646–654.
Olowu, D. 2006. *Towards a local governance and poverty reduction program at the African Development Bank*. Paper on ADB policy initiatives for addressing challenges of decentralized governance and poverty reduction.
Olowu, D., and Wunsch, J. 2004. Introduction: Local governance, and democratic decentralization in Africa. In *Local governance in Africa: The challenges of democratic decentralization*, ed. D. Olowu and J. Wunsch, pp. 1–27. Boulder, CO: Lynne Rienner Publishers.
Organization for Economic Cooperation and Development (OECD). 2005. *Modernizing government: The way forward*. Paris: OECD.
Peters, G., and Pierre, J. 2000. *Governance, politics, and state*. London: Macmillan.
Public Procurement Agency. 2008. Annual report 2008.
Republic of Ghana. 1992. *Constitution of the Republic of Ghana*. Accra: Government of Ghana.
Republic of Ghana. 2003. *Ghana poverty reduction strategy*. Accra: National Development Planning Commission.
Republic of Ghana. 2008. *Ghana demographic and health survey*. Accra: Ghana Statistical Service.
Republic of Ghana. 2009. *Implementation of the growth and poverty reduction strategy 2006–2009: 2008 annual progress report*. Accra: National Development Planning Commission.
Republic of Ghana. 2010a. *Decentralization policy framework*. Accra: Ministry of Local Government and Rural Development.

Republic of Ghana. 2010b. *Ghana shared growth and development agenda (2010–2013)*. Accra: National Development Planning Commission.

Rondinelli, D.A., and Cheema, S., eds. 2003. *Reinventing government for the twenty-first century: State capacity in a globalizing society*. Bloomfield, CT: Kumarian Press.

SEND Foundation. 2006. *Where did the HIPC funds go? Assessing HIPC expenditures on poverty alleviation 2002–2004*.

United Nations Development Program (UNDP). 1997. *Governance for sustainable human development*. New York: United Nations.

United Nations Economic Commission for Africa (ECA). 2009. *The African governance report II*. Addis-Ababa, Ethiopia: African Development Forum, African Union.

United Nations General Assembly. 2000. *United Nations millennium declaration*. A/RES/55/2. 8th Plenary Meeting, September.

United Nations High Commissioner for Human Rights (UNHCR). http://www.unhchr.ch/development/governance-01.html.

Ventriss, C. 2002. The rise of the entrepreneurial state governments in United States: The dilemma of public governance in the era of globalization. *Administrative Theory and Praxis* 24(1): 81–102.

World Bank. 1992. *Governance and development*. Washington, DC: World Bank.

World Bank. 1997. *The state in a changing world: World development report 1997*. New York: Oxford University Press for the World Bank.

World Bank. 2004. *Making services work for poor people: World development report 2004*. Washington, DC: World Bank.

World Bank. 2010. World development indicators database. http//data.worldbank.org/data-catalog/world-development-indicators.

Chapter 8

Overview of the African Peer Review Mechanism in Selected African Countries

Ernest Peprah Ababio

Contents

Introduction 153
Democracy and Governance 155
Concept of Public Service Reform 156
African Peer Review Mechanism 156
Structural Functioning of the APRM 157
    Matrix for Promoting Public Service Reforms 158
Specific Public Service Reforms 159
Lapses and Benefits of the Peer Review Process 160
States without Review 161
Conclusion 163
References 164

Introduction

African states have, since independence from the 1960s, been confronted by crises on various fronts. Lapses such as corruption, civil wars, one-party dictatorships, and bloated public service structures have been coupled with military *coups d'etat* that have disrupted the development and functioning of state institutions. Prominent among the causes of the chaos has been bad governance, which results in decay of public service delivery. Nor was the political stagnation helped by a continental union, the erstwhile Organization of African Unity that focused largely on the political liberation of states and ignored socioeconomic development.

A revamped African Union rectified the situation with the innovation of the New Partnership for Africa's Development (NEPAD) and its offshoot, the African Peer Review Mechanism (APRM). This is a mutually agreed instrument that members of the African Union have voluntarily acceded to as part of an African self-monitoring mechanism. This chapter examines the operational concepts of governance and public service reform as conditional to political stability and societal well-being. It analyzes the *modus operandi* of the APRM, the approaches adopted, and the stages of reform. It also highlights the benefits of peer review in fostering adoption of policies, standards, and practices that promote political stability, high economic growth, sustainable development, and accelerated subregional and continental integration. Best practices and deficiencies in governance, as identified by the APRM in selected African states, are outlined. Promotion of good governance through public service reform is the ultimate goal of the APRM, and the less than satisfactory progress, is this regard, resulted in the Arab spring crises.

The emergence of independent African states by the 1970s brought new hope to nationals and heightened expectations that the winds of change could be equated with a better life for all and freedom from the constraints of colonialism. Yet, no sooner had political freedom been gained than these expectations proved elusive. The cause was poor political governance, and soon many states were saddled with military interventions, one-party states, rank abuse of the rule of law, and mass corruption. In a word, newly independent African nations were disintegrating. Nor was the cause for freedom and dignity helped by a continental union that focused exclusively on the political liberation of Africa and disregarded any concerted effort for integration and promotion of the socioeconomic livelihood of the people.

This chapter looks into the role of the innovative African Peer Review Mechanism in promoting good governance through public service reform. For analytical purposes, good governance, public service reform, peer review, and constructive engagement comprise the conceptual framework and interpretation. The chapter thus contributes to the body of knowledge in the limited area of information on regional integration by highlighting the best practices and deficiencies of governance in selected African states. It also explores the extent to which lack of good governance resulted in the Arab spring.

Democracy and Governance

Democracy as a concept appears elusive in definition, yet specific issues that the concept embodies can be identified. Tenets of a developed, democratic state involve, among others, the existence of a political system with freedom of speech, freedom of association and assembly, the right to stand for office, a free press, and a secret ballot. Further, these pillars of democracy are strengthened by the presence of a credible opposition, pluralism based on a strong civil society, a strong economy, and a clear distinction between the state and the ruling party (Thomson 2000). The democratic tenets outlined above are a function of *good governance*, which is also a multifaceted concept outlined by Maserumule (2005):

- The act or manner of governing, of exercising control or authority over the actions of subjects
- The use of political authority and exercise of control in society in relation to the management of resources for social and economic development
- The use of political, economic, and administrative authority and resources to manage the affairs of a nation
- The acquisition of and accountability for the application of political authority to the direction of public affairs and management of public resources

Currently, the concept of good governance has become very popular, and its definition varies from one organization (or group or individual) to another (Agere 2000). Good governance is a social management process that maximizes the public interest; it involves the implementation of policies that improve the lives of the majority of the people (Hanekom 1987). The substantive characteristic of good governance is that "it is a co-management of public life operated by both government and citizens, and establishes a relationship between government and civil society" (Yuanfang, Lei, and Ka 2009, p. 1). Kuye (2004, p. 467) sums it up thus:

> Governance is good when there is accountability and transparency, monitoring techniques, the development of successful communication strategies, the running of successful public awareness campaigns, [and] the development of efficient relations with the media and with the community.

For the purpose of this analysis, governance is seen as the acquisition of political power by a political party through a democratic process and the judicious allocation of resources for the improved well-being of a citizenry. It is the tenets of good governance that the African Union (AU) has struggled to promote and which have become the Achilles' heel of the African Peer Review Mechanism. Achieving good governance is a function that is closely linked with the concept of public service reform, which is discussed next.

Concept of Public Service Reform

The concept of public service reform may be seen as "a change in the direction of greater economic or political equality, a broadening of participation in society and policy," and as "the devolution of responsibilities away from centralized bureaucracy" (Huttington in Kuye 2006, p. 291). A common theme in these definitions is that a process of public service reform has as its objective the involvement of civil society in the art of government, and the enhancement of service delivery through devolution and decentralization. Such is the summary of the mission of the African Peer Review Mechanism. Broken into more convenient pieces, the concept of public service reform involves, among other functions, as Mutahaba (2006) puts it:

- Restructuring and rationalization of government operations
- Control of employment and size of the public service
- Good governance
- Decentralization and local government
- Privatization and private sector development
- Legal/judicial service reform
- Reforms related to improving performance of specific sectors

The evaluation and monitoring of the above indicators are the *modus operandi* of the APRM, which is discussed at some length in the sections that follow.

African Peer Review Mechanism

Peer review refers to the systematic examination and assessment of the performance of a state by other states (peers), by designated institutions, or by a combination of states and designated institutions. Thus a number of intergovernmental and international organizations, such as the European Union (EU), UN bodies, and the International Monetary Fund (IMF), use peer review to monitor and assess national policies and performance in several sectors (Hope 2005). In academia, peer review is undertaken when an editor of academic repute makes an initial assessment of the suitability of a paper submitted for a journal, and then sends it to several referees to adjudicate its suitability for publication (Kanbur, 2004). However, the peer review process of African states is largely political, in that it covers the entire fabric of the way governments are functioning.

The African Peer Review Mechanism (APRM) is an African-led innovation that represents a bold approach to reform for building capable states with enduring good governance and sustainable development. The APRM is designed to monitor and assess progress made by African countries in meeting their commitment toward achieving good governance, social reform, and sustainable development (Hope 2005). It is an instrument voluntarily acceded to by member states of the AU, and is an African self-monitoring mechanism. The mandate of the APRM is to ensure that the policies and practices of participating states conform to the agreed political, economic, and corporate governance values, codes, and standards laid down in the Declaration on Democracy, Political, Economic and Corporate Governance (Hope 2005).

Structural Functioning of the APRM

The overall responsibility for the APRM is vested in the Committee of Participating Heads of State and Government of the Member States of the APRM, known more simply as the APR forum. The mandate of the APR forum includes, among other directives (http://www.nepad.org):

- Appointing the APR Panel of Eminent Persons, considering the country review reports, making appropriate recommendations to the reviewed countries, and exercising constructive peer dialogue and persuasion
- Ensuring that the APR process is fully funded
- Persuading development partners to provide technical and financial assistance to support the implementation of the program of action of the reviewed countries

Another constructive process of engaging Africa is the composition of the review panel. The Panel of Eminent Persons (APR panel), reflecting regional and gender diversity, is appointed by the heads of state to oversee the conduct of the APRM process and ensure its integrity. The APR panel is assisted by the APR secretariat, which provides the secretarial, technical, coordinating, and administrative support services for the APRM. The secretariat is currently part of the NEPAD secretariat located in Midrand, South Africa. Candidature for membership of the APR panel is dependent on criteria such as Africans who have distinguished themselves in careers considered relevant to the work of the APRM, namely, expertise in the areas of political governance, macro economic management, public financial management, and corporate governance. Furthermore, appointees are required to be persons of high moral stature who have demonstrated their commitment to the ideals of Pan-Africanism. Candidates for possible appointment are nominated by participating countries, short listed by a committee of ministers, and appointed by heads of state and government of participating countries.

The APR panel exercises close oversight over the review process, in particular to ensure its integrity. The APR charter secures the independence, objectivity, and integrity of the panel. The panel is supported by a competent secretariat that has the technical capacity to undertake the analytical work that underpins the peer review process, and also conforms to the principles of the APRM. The functions of the secretariat include maintenance of extensive database information on political and economic developments in all participating countries, preparation of background documents for the peer review teams, proposing performance indicators, and tracking performance of individual countries (http://www.nepad.org).

Participation in the APRM is voluntary and is open to all member states of the African Union. As pointed out by Kuye (2006), voluntary participation upholds the principle of sovereignty of states and recognizes that a state cannot be compelled to follow any prescribed model of governance. Instead, the APRM seeks to help willing countries improve governance as a precondition for integration and development. It also acknowledges that each country is unique in terms of sociopolitical, economic, and cultural environment, and that these characteristics should inform recommendations for improvement. What makes engagement by APRM quite constructive is that the mechanism of peer review is a nonadversarial and nonpunitive process, in which trust among participating countries is crucial for its success.

The issue of voluntary participation is, however, an anomaly. Invariably the decision for nonmembership of the APRM is a prerogative of a small elite of the political bureau in states whose agenda is the continued maintenance of policies that oppress the wider masses. It is submitted that states that belong to a common union must be reviewed under a common denominator. Currently (2012), 31 countries have acceded by signing the memorandum of understanding. These are Algeria, Angola, Benin, Burkina Faso, Cameroon, Djibouti, Republic of Congo, Egypt, Ethiopia, Equatorial Guinea, Gabon, Mali, Mauritania, Mauritius, Senegal, Tanzania, Lesotho, Sierra Leone, Malawi, Ghana, Kenya, Liberia, Mozambique, Nigeria, Rwanda, São Tome and Principe, Togo, South Africa, Sudan, Uganda, and Zambia. Thus, as a clear departure of the mood and position of noninterference, by 2000, about half of African states have laid bare their governance systems in all sincerity, for constructive territorial review (http://www.nepad.org).

Matrix for Promoting Public Service Reforms

The APRM process involves scientifically devised objectives and stages. At the time of acceding to the peer review process, each state is required to define a clear, time-bound program of action for implementing the Declaration on Democracy, Political, Economic and Corporate Governance, including periodic reviews. To facilitate the process, it has become the norm for a reviewing state to designate or create an institution as a focal point for this review. Thus Ghana created a new Ministry of Regional Cooperation and NEPAD, and in South Africa, the then president allocated the Department of Public Service and Administration with the coordinating responsibility for the APRM process (http://www.aprm.org.za). In an attempt to facilitate public service reform, the APR process involves four types of reviews (http://www.nepad.org).

The first country review is the base review that is carried out within 18 months of a country becoming a member of the APRM process. Second, there is a periodic review that takes place every two to four years. Third, a member country can, for its own reasons, ask for a review that is not part of the periodically mandated reviews. Fourth, early signs of impending political or economic crisis in a member country may also be sufficient cause for instituting a review. Such a review can be called by participating heads of state and government "in a spirit of helpfulness" to the government concerned.

The APR process involves specific stages. Stage 1 entails a study of the political, economic, and corporate governance and development environment in the country under review. This study is based on current documentation prepared by the APRM secretariat and material provided by national and international institutions. In the second stage, the review team visits the country concerned to carry out the widest possible range of consultation with the government, officials, political parties, parliamentarians, and representatives of civil society organizations, including the media, academia, trade unions, and business and professional bodies. In stage 3, the review team prepares its report, which is based on information from the secretariat and the consultation briefings that were held. The report is initially handed to the government for comment, providing it with the opportunity to study how the identified shortcomings may be addressed. Stage 4 begins when the review team's report is submitted to the participating heads of state and government through the APRM secretariat. Thereafter, participating heads of state continue to engage the reviewed state on assistance in the form of dialogue, technical assistance, and a collective intention to proceed with appropriate measures by a given date. Six months after the report has been considered by participating heads of state and government, it is tabled in key regional structures such as the Pan-African Parliament and the Peace and Security Council. This constitutes the fifth and final stage of the process.

Specific Public Service Reforms

In engaging a process of public service reform in Africa, there are commonalities that exist in most states. Further, a primary element of good governance that needs reform in Africa is ensuring that citizens have a voice in how they are governed (Kuye 2006). Consequently, Mutahaba (2006) outlines the following commonalities for reform:

- Reexamination of the role of government, i.e., what government should do and not do
- Reexamination of the costs of running government business
- Decentralization and devolution of authority within government
- Consideration of more cost-effective ways of service delivery, including privatization or corporatization of activities
- Partnership between the government and the private sector in the provision of service

The specific reforms that mark the peer review agenda follow key objectives in each particular regard.

The primary objective of the APRM process is to identify the extent of development, or signs of weakness, in specific public service functions in the context of the four peer review areas. The key objectives for democracy and political governance, as correctly observed by Maloka (2004), draw strongly from the declaration on unconstitutional changes of government. The objectives are (http://www.aprm.org.za) to prevent and reduce intra- and intercountry conflict; the consolidation of constitutional democracy that includes periodic political competition; the rule of law and the supremacy of the firm establishment of the constitution; upholding tenets of separation of powers, including the protection of the independence of the judiciary and of an effective parliament; ensuring accountable, efficient, and effective public office holders and civil servants; fighting corruption in the political arena; and promotion and protection of the rights of vulnerable groups, including women, children, the disabled, and displaced persons.

The key objectives for economic governance and management include promoting macro economic policies that support sustainable development; implementing transparent, predictable, and credible government economic policies; promoting sound public finance management; fighting corruption and money laundering; and accelerating regional integration by participating in harmonization of monetary, trade, and investment policies among participating states. Equally laudable key objectives are outlined in the key areas of corporate governance, and for socioeconomic development.

Lapses and Benefits of the Peer Review Process

Notwithstanding its urgent need to promote good governance in Africa, the APRM does have some lapses that need to be examined. The issue of APRM membership stands tallest. Years after its inception, membership comprises a meager 55% of African states. Thus, while good governance is being relatively promoted in participating states, political and economic turmoil is a very real possibility in 45% of the states. Worse still is the reality that a number of nonmember states have authoritarian systems, such as was the case in Libya.

The process of engagement also requires further attention. Currently, engagement by the forum of participating heads of state with a reviewed state occurs only at the fourth stage of the process. Yet, political flashpoints abound in Africa, particularly in nonparticipating states. There is an urgent need to include a group of elder statesmen in the APRM process, whose function would be timely engagement with the potentially troubled states to ameliorate tension and incidents of underdevelopment. In Africa, elder statesmen of such reputable functional diplomatic experience include the former UN secretary general, Kofi Annan; South Africa's former president, Thabo Mbeki; former president of Nigeria, Olusegun Obasanjo; and former

Mozambican president, Joachim Chisano. Kuye and Kakumba (2008) call them political ombuds. It is therefore recommended that the current establishment of the APRM be restructured for purposes of promoting proactive political and economic intervention in potentially troubled African states. Such a restructured institution could be called the African Peer Review Ombuds (APRO).

Benefits accruing from the APRM process have certainly proved worthwhile. Given the international experience with peer reviews, the APRM has the potential to provide a number of benefits to reviewed states (Hope 2005). As African countries seek to improve their governance through public service reforms, the APRM provides the basis for policy changes to meet commitments and to observe the agreed standards and codes. The process facilitates the monitoring of compliance with agreements entered into, and participant states are thus far more inclined to comply with oversight functions of APRM. Given the history of the disastrous effects of bad governance in Africa, with a lack of openness and rampant corruption, the review process represents a sea change in the thinking of African leaders and a major milestone in the political development of the continent. The South African government, for example, has acknowledged that the APRM country review will enhance its efforts to meet challenges of the next decade; help build institutions involved in the promotion of democracy, and the relationships between these institutions and individuals; help address the challenges raised by the second economy; and assist South Africa's efforts in job creation and improved service areas, such as health, education, housing, and other basic services (http://www.aprm.org.za). In addition, the peer review process lends credibility to Africa at a time of growing donor fatigue and deep external cynicism. More crucially, the APRM represents a legitimization of the reform process that wards off the external pressure usually associated with imposed conditions from external lending institutions (Juma 2004). The measurement of these benefits will depend on assessment of effects of the work of the APR Group on countries reviewed. A random sample of selected reviewed states is shown in Table 8.1.

A positive outcome of the review process is that it creates an awareness in the reviewed state and a realization among civil society and government alike, especially with regard to the identified deficiencies. The redress of such deficiencies thus becomes a joint responsibility of government and civil society as partners, thereby promoting public participation in affairs of the state.

States without Review

Between December 2010 and September 2011, there were political tremors and upheavals in some African states that led to regime change. Such was the case in Tunisia, Cote d'Ivoire, Egypt, and Libya. The issue of bad governance was the root cause underlying these revolts and forcible overthrow of existing governments. Further, it may be noted that none of the affected states had been reviewed by the

Table 8.1 Overview of Governance in Selected Reviewed States

Country	Best Practice	Deficiencies
Algeria	Fifth reviewed country in 2008, Algeria has virtually eliminated political terrorism; has satisfactory systems of education, health, and housing; a steep reduction in extreme forms of poverty; and growing credibility in financial, political, and diplomatic levels.	Reforms and modernization of the state, corruption, gender equality, youth employment, and town planning.
Rwanda	Second reviewed country in 2006, Rwanda is a success story in gender equality with high female participation in politics, successful economic reform, provision of social services, implementation of compulsory primary education, fight against corruption, and ambitious ICT strategy.	Managing diversity; legitimacy of Gacaca courts; land constraints; human, financial, and institutional capacities; narrow tax base; inadequate corporate governance; high incidence of HIV/AIDS; obsolete laws on energy and markets; and heavy reliance on foreign aid.
Ghana	First reviewed country in 2005, Ghana has unique institutions for promoting dialogue, successful contribution to peacekeeping and regional integration, and a strong system of political competition based on people's assemblies.	Gender equity, corruption, land issues, chieftaincy, unemployment, and heavy external dependence.
South Africa	Fourth reviewed country in 2007, the report identified 18 best practices. Among these are keen political participation, decentralization, equity laws and practices, gender equity, excellent infrastructure, and strong private sector governance.	Eleven overaching deficiencies of unemployment, poor service delivery, poverty and inequality, land reform, violence against women and children, HIV/AIDS, corruption, crime, racism and xenophobia, and management of diversity.

Source: From http://www.nepad.org; http://www.aprmsa.org.

APRM, an exercise that may well have exposed the deficiencies and might possibly have helped preempt such crises (Ababio 2011).

The Tunisian revolution was an intensive campaign of civil resistance that began in December 2010 and led to the overthrow of long-standing president Zine El Abidine Ben Ali in January 2011. The demonstrations were precipitated by high unemployment, corruption, a lack of freedom of speech, and poor living conditions (Cole 2011). These social ills lend credence to the effectiveness of democratic values espoused earlier, which might have been averted had Tunisia gone through the APRM review process.

The Ivorian crisis began after incumbent president Laurent Gbagbo claimed he had won the election, the first to be held in 10 years—which in itself is contrary to the APRM principle of political competition. The opposition candidate, Alassane Ouattara, and a number of countries, organizations, and leaders worldwide, believed that Ouattara had won. Hectic violence and deaths ensued. On December 5, 2010, the African Union appointed the former president of South Africa, Thabo Mbeki, as mediator. However, Mbeki left Cote d'Ivoire the following day without brokering a deal. Several months later, on April 11, 2011, Gbagbo was captured by pro-Ouattara forces backed by French troops (Cohen 2011).

The Egyptian revolution began on January 25, 2011. Protesters' grievances focused on governance issues of a legal and political nature, including police brutality, state of emergency laws, lack of free elections and freedom of speech, uncontrollable corruption, high unemployment, food price inflation, and an end to the regime of Hosni Mubarak, who had ruled Egypt for no less than 30 years, since 1981 (Ashton 2011).

The Libyan civil war from February 15, 2011, was yet another example of the effects of bad governance and lack of APRM intervention. The irony here was that Libya had never acceded to membership of the APRM despite the Libyan leader, Muammar Gaddafi, being an influential and indeed regular chairperson of the AU. President Gaddafi had ruled Libya since 1969, seizing power when he overthrew King Idris I in a military takeover. The governance style of Gaddafi was blatant nepotism, placing relatives and loyal tribe members in central military and government positions. Despite an annual per capita income of $14,878 at the time of the civil war, an estimated 21% of Libyans were unemployed, and one-third lived below the poverty line. The popularity of the mass uprising was demonstrated by its composition, namely, teachers, students, lawyers, oil workers, and a contingent of professional soldiers who had defected from the Libyan army (Lamb 2011).

Conclusion

The concern in this chapter is the apparent denial of some African governments of the basic tenets of democracy and good governance that should lead to reform of public services. It is the lack of these that lies at the heart of popular uprisings and revolt in some states. The promotion of appropriate reforms, it is argued here, could stem these political upheavals and put African states on the road to development. The institution that promotes and monitors stability is the inspection agency of the African Union, the APRM.

The APRM has been widely welcomed by African states and leaders. The initiative holds much hope for the promotion of political stability, economic growth, and ultimate improved living standards. It is a worthwhile institution that can assist the continent to heed the admonishment expressed by U.S. President Barack Obama that "Africa does not need strong men, it needs strong institutions" (cited in Pelser 2009, p. 2).

References

Ababio, E.P. 2011. Reincarnation of winds of change in Africa: An African Union impotence? *Journal of Transdisciplinary Research in Southern Africa* 7(2).
African Union. 2004. African Union in a nutshell. From http://www.africanunion.org (accessed July 24, 2004).
Agere, S. 2000. *Promoting good government: Principles and perspectives.* London: Management and Training Service Division of the Commonwealth Secretariat.
APRM South Africa. 2007. African Peer Review Mechanism. From http://www.aprm.org.za (accessed May 4, 2007).
Ashton, C. 2011. International reaction to Egyptian protests. From http://www.reuters.com/article2011/01/29 (accessed August 18, 2011).
Cohen, M. 2011. Ivory Coast Ouattara presidency claim opposed by army. From http://www.businessweek.com/news/2010-12-11 (accessed August 18, 2011).
Cole, J. 2011. Tunisian uprising is a populist revolution. From http://www.democracynow.org/2011/01/18 (accessed August 18, 2011).
Hanekom, S.X. 1987. *Public policy: Framework and instrument for action.* Johannesburg: Macmillan.
Hope, K.R. 2005. Toward good governance and sustainable development: The African Peer Review Mechanism in governance. *An International Journal of Policy, Administration, and Institutions* 18(2).
Juma, M.K. 2004. Africa's governance audit: The African Peer Review Mechanism. *New Economy*, April.
Kanbur, R. 2004. The African Peer Review Mechanism (APRM): An assessment of concept and design. *Politikon* 31(2).
Kuye, J.O. 2004. Continental policy targeting and the Nepadisation process: Issues, trends and options. *Journal of Public Administration* 39(4): 1.
Kuye, J.O. 2006. Public sector reforms: The case of South Africa, 1994–2005. *Journal of Public Administration* 41(2).
Kuye, J.O., and Kakumba, U. 2008. Development initiatives and global governance: A continental perspective. *Journal of Public Administration* 43(4).
Lamb, K. 2011. Libya estimate at least 30,000 die in civil war. *San Francisco Chronicle*, 57–73.

Maloka, E. 2004. NEPAD and its critics. *Africa Insight* 34(4).
Maserumule, M.H. 2005. Good governance as a *sine qua non* for sustainable development in the New Partnership for Africa's Development (NEPAD): A conceptual perspective. *Journal of Public Administration* 40(3).
Mutahaba, G. 2006. African perspectives on public service reform: Issues and performance. *Journal of Public Administration* 41(2).
NEPAD. 2005. African Peer Review Mechanism. From http://www.nepad.org/documents/49.pdf (accessed March 9, 2007).
Pelser, W. 2009. Africa's future is up to Africans. *City Press*, September 25.
Thomson, A. 2000. *An introduction to African politics*. London: Routledge.
Yuanfang, P., Lei, X., and Ka, W. 2009. The conceptual transformation from government to governance and its representations: A case study on the innovations in city management of Ganzhou. From http://www.newurbanquestion.ifou.org/fullpapers/FO501 (accessed August 31, 2011).

Chapter 9

Lessons for Africa in Economic Policy Reform: The Mauritius Best Practice Case

Daniel Francois Meyer and Annelise Venter

Contents

Introduction 168
Socioeconomic Comparison 169
    Introduction 169
    Socioeconomic Key Indicators 169
    Human Development Index (HDI) 170
    Poverty and Inequality Index 170
    Population Analysis 171
    Unemployment 171
    Government 171
    Macro Economic Aspects 172
    Rural Development 173
    Infrastructure: Access to Sewer and Water 175
    Safety and Security 175
    Health Issues 175
    Education and Research 177

Economic Policy Reforms 178
    Background 178
    Historical Overview of Economic Policy Reforms 178
    Recent Economic Policy Reforms (2006–2012) 179
    Good Governance and Strong Institutions 181
Lessons Learned for Africa 181
    Good Governance and Strong Institutions 181
    Coherent Competitiveness Strategy 182
    Consolidation of Physical, Human, and Social Capital 182
    Diversification of the Economy 183
    Private Sector Involvement 183
    Fiscal Management Reforms 183
    Generous and Broad-Based Social Security Policies 183
    Foreign Direct Investment (FDI) 184
Conclusion 184
References 185

Introduction

The Republic of Mauritius is located in the Indian Ocean to the east of the African continent. The island has a total area of 2,040 km², making it the smallest country in the African group of countries. Mauritius is also the African country with the smallest population, with only approximately 1,300,000 people. Since independence in 1968, the country has developed from a poor, single economic sector-based economy to a modern diversified economy (U.S. Department of State 2012).

Mauritius has shown over the past few decades that small can be successful. Although Mauritius has a number of negative factors that impact on the development of the country, such as its isolated locality, lack of natural resources, a small local market, relatively limited infrastructure, and a shortage in skilled manpower, the country has managed to achieve high levels of economic development despite the above-listed constraints. The country has, however, maximized its limited resources and is seen as an example of what can be achieved through hard work and solid policy implementation (Peacock 2011).

As part of the maximization of limited resources concept, Mauritius has capitalized on its locality between Africa to the west and Asia and India to the east. Mauritius is seen as the gateway for China and India as a platform to enter and penetrate the growing African market. Mauritius will continue to experience the impact of China's trade presence in the country with its open, well-established economic and diplomatic ties (Ancharaz 2009; Zafar 2011).

Initial factors for the Mauritius success story include aspects such as trade-led diversification, effective economic policies, strong public sector and private sector coordination, and the use of its ethnic diversity to ensure national unity and consensus (Zafar 2011). Mauritius has excellent international relationships with all major economic regions. Due to this, the country has managed to attract large-scale foreign direct investment (FDI) over the past decade. FDI has increased on a year-to-year basis, and the country is an attractive destination for investors. It is especially in the export processing zone (EPZ) sector, the tourism sector, and the telecommunication sector, where the majority of FDI has been directed to. The United Kingdom, the United States, China, and France have been the main sources of FDI in recent years. To prove the country's excellent global relations, the Mauritian government has concluded 33 tax treaties with various countries, including India (OECD 2011).

In the rest of this chapter, Mauritius will first be compared on a socioeconomic basis with South Africa, the African continent, the BRIC countries (Brazil, Russia, India, and China), and developed countries. Second, the Mauritian government's economic policy reforms will be analyzed, and last, the lessons learned for Africa from the Mauritian successes will be listed and analyzed.

Socioeconomic Comparison

Introduction

The tiny island of Mauritius, with a total area of only 2,040 km^2, located to the east of the African continent, has been "boxing above its weight division" over the last few decades in terms of socioeconomic development. In this section, Mauritius will be compared to South Africa as the largest economy on the African continent, Africa as a whole, the BRIC countries, as well as developed countries. Specific key socioeconomic indicators have been selected from databases of various organizations, such as the United Nations (UN), International Monetary Fund (IMF), and World Bank (WB).

Socioeconomic Key Indicators

The following indicators have been selected for comparison:

- Human Development Index
- Poverty and Inequality Index
- Population analysis
- Unemployment
- Government
- Macro economic aspects
- Rural development and agriculture
- Infrastructure: access to sewer and water

- Safety and security
- Health issues
- Education and research

Human Development Index (HDI)

Refer to Table 9.1 for a summary of HDI indicators. In terms of human development, Mauritius has shown vast improvement over the last 20 years. HDI is a composite measurement of quality of life and development within a country. HDI measurements range between 0 and 1, with an index close to 1 as the highest measurement, indicating high levels of quality of life. Mauritius, with Libyia, Tunisia, and Algeria, is listed as a high human development country in Africa. South Africa, Gabon, Egypt, Botswana, and Namibia are listed as medium human development countries, while the Democratic Republic of Congo (DRC), Niger, Burundi, Mozambique, and Chad are listed as low human development countries (UN 2010).

Mauritius is ranked 72nd in the world and 2nd in Africa in terms of HDI, with Libya the highest ranked African country in 2010. The Mauritius HDI ranking has improved steadily since 1990, with an HDI of 0.618 to 0.672 in 2000. The current HDI for Mauritius is 0.726. This index is above the world average index of 0.682 (UN 2010).

Poverty and Inequality Index

Poverty levels in the country have improved as the country's economy has diversified over the last decade. The national poverty head count has improved from 5.8% of the population in 2001 to 4.1% in 2006. If compared to South Africa, poverty rates in Mauritius are relatively low. Poverty rates in South Africa have remained constant from 1995 to 2005 at approximately 41% of the population. In terms of

Table 9.1 HDI Level

Country/Region	HDI Level
Mauritius	0.726
South Africa	0.597
African countries average	0.480
BRIC countries average	0.650
Developed countries average	0.880

Source: United Nations (UN), Human Development Index (HDI): 2010 Rankings, 2010, http://hds.undp.org/en/statistics (accessed April 12, 2011).

inequality, Mauritius has a greater level of equality than most African countries with a Gini Index of 0.34 in 2006. South Africa, as one of the least equal countries in the world, has a Gini Index of 0.62 (Duclos and Verdier-Chouchane 2011).

Population Analysis

Mauritius has the smallest population of all the African countries, with only 1,281,214, with a population growth rate of 0.4% (World Bank 2010). The country with the largest population in Africa is Nigeria, with 150,000,000 people (IMF 2011). Population migration between rural and urban areas is also analyzed, listed as the level of urbanization. The rate of urbanization in Mauritius is only 43% compared to the same average rate of urbanization for the total African continent. Libya has the highest rate of urbanization of 78%, while the rate in South Africa is 60%. Malawi has the lowest rate of urbanization of only 19%. The average rate of urbanization for the BRIC countries is 58%, and the average for developed countries is 80% (World Bank 2010). Most African countries have a net loss regarding migration with an average net migration loss of 131,000 from 2006 to 2010. Mauritius had a net loss in migration of close to zero during this period. The global trend is for migration from developing countries to developed countries. Of the African countries, South Africa had the highest net gain of migrants of 700,000, and Zimbabwe the highest net loss of 700,000 people over the same period. The average net gain for developed countries equates to approximately 860,000 people during the same period (World Bank 2010).

Unemployment

Mauritius, with an unemployment rate of 7.8%, has one of the lowest unemployment rates in Africa, with the African continent average unemployment rate at 11.9%. South Africa (24.4%) and Swaziland (25%) have the highest unemployment rates of all the African countries with official unemployment statistics available. Mauritius compares favorably with the average for the developed countries, which have an average unemployment rate of 8.2% (IMF 2011). Refer to Table 9.2 for unemployment statistics.

Government

In terms of the 2011 Mo Ibrahim Index on governance performance in African countries, Mauritius was ranked the best with a score of 82.5 out of 100. South Africa scored 70.6 with the average score for African countries at 50%. Mauritius was also ranked the best in indicators such as personal safety, national security, business environment, and welfare (Ibrahim 2011). The Mauritius government's expenditure as percentage of the total GDP is only 25.7%, which is lower than the average for African countries, and relatively low if compared to developed countries

Table 9.2 Unemployment Rates

Country	Unemployment Rate as %	Employment-to-Population Ratio of People 15 Years and Older as % of Total Population
Mauritius	7.8%	54%
Swaziland	25.0%	50%
South Africa	24.4%	41%
Cameroon	3.2%	59%
African countries average	11.9%	61%
BRIC countries average	5.6%	62%
Developed countries average	8.2%	55%

Source: Table compiled by author from statistics obtained from IMF database per country (IMF 2011).

with an average of 45.5%. Government debt in Mauritius is relatively high at 51.4% of GDP if compared to South Africa, but not as high as the average debt for developed countries. Imports are still exceeding exports within the local economy of Mauritius, with a current account balance in 2011 of −11.6%. Mauritius has received much less aid than African countries on average (World Bank 2010). Refer to Table 9.3 for statistics on the above issues.

Macro Economic Aspects

In terms of total GDP figures, Mauritius has a small economy compared to Africa and the rest of the world. However, in terms of GDP per capita, it is in the top 5 in Africa, and even better than the average if compared to the BRIC countries. Mauritius and African countries, however, lag far behind the developed countries in terms of GDP per capita. Inflation is a rising problem in Mauritius and has increased from 2.9% in 2010 to 6.5% in 2011. The economic growth rate in Mauritius has been below the average for African countries at 4.0%, but exceeded the 2.8% growth rate in South Africa in 2010. Mauritius, with its exports as a percentage of GDP at 48%, is far above global averages for 2009 (IMF 2011). Table 9.4 provides a summary of some of the macro economic statistics listed above. Table 9.5 provides information on agricultural development. Mauritius, similar to South Africa, produces only limited final products from agriculture compared to the rest of Africa and BRIC countries. If seems that the higher the rate of development, the lower the focus on agriculture and final products and the level of employment in the sector. In terms of agriculture and

Table 9.3 Government Financial Control

Country	Government Expenditure as % of GDP (2011)	Debt as % of GDP (2011)	Current Account Balance as % of GDP (2011)	Net Official Aid and Assistance Received in US$ in Millions (2009)
Mauritius	25.7%	51.4%	−11.6%	155
South Africa	33.3%	39.5%	−4.3%	1,075
African countries average	29.9%	38.6%	−3.8%	1,138
BRIC countries average	31.4%	39.8%	1.2%	1,287
Developed countries average	45.5%	87.6%	0.7%	0

Source: International Monetary Fund (IMF), Data and Statistics, 2011, http://www.imf.org/external/data.htm (accessed March 20, 2012); World Bank, The World Bank Indicators, 2010, http://data.worldbank.org/indicator (accessed April 20, 2011).

employment, Mauritius has a relatively low average of people working in this sector compared to the rest of Africa (World Bank 2010).

In terms of the 2012 Global Competitiveness Report by the World Economic Forum, Tunisia was ranked the highest of the African countries, at 32nd in the world, followed by South Africa in 54th and Mauritius in 55th place. The major economic sectors in Mauritius are tourism, construction, agriculture (especially sugar), and the textile industry (World Economic Forum 2011a).

Rural Development

In terms of the World Bank (2010), up to 48% of all the land in Mauritius is potential agricultural land. However, agricultural arable land in hectares (ha) per person is relatively low, with only 0.1 ha or 1,000 m² per person available. In South Africa this figure is three times higher at 0.3 ha per person, with the African average at 0.21 ha per person. The ratio in the BRIC countries is 0.35 ha per person, and for developed countries the average is 0.4 ha per person of arable agricultural land. Production and export of final products in the agricultural sector are important for development in this sector (see Table 9.5).

Table 9.4 Macro Economic Aspects

Country	GDP in US$ in Billions (2011)	GDP per Capita in US$ (2011)	GDP Growth % (2010)	Exports as % of GDP (2009)
Mauritius	10.3	7,989	4.0%	48%
South Africa	383.1	7,584	2.8%	27%
African countries average	64.3	2,163	5.0%	34%
BRIC countries average	2,006.7	6,585	7.8%	22%
Developed countries average	2,630.6	47,700	1.8%	20%

Source: International Monetary Fund (IMF), Data and Statistics, 2011, http://www.imf.org/external/data.htm (accessed March 20, 2012); World Bank, The World Bank Indicators, 2010, http://data.worldbank.org/indicator (accessed April 20, 2011).

Table 9.5 Agriculture: Final Products and Employment

Country	Final Products in Agriculture as % of GDP (2009)	Employment in Agriculture as % of Total Employment (2008)
Mauritius	4%	9.1%
South Africa	3%	8.8%
African average	19.8%	30.6%
BRIC average	9.7%	14.1%
Developed countries average	2.1%	3.6%

Source: Table compiled by author from statistics obtained from the World Bank database per country (World Bank 2010).

Infrastructure: Access to Sewer and Water

In terms of provision of services, specifically access to water and sewer services, Mauritius compares on an equal basis with developed countries, and is on a much more advanced level than other African (including South Africa) and developing countries (World Bank 2010). Refer to Table 9.6 for statistics regarding infrastructure.

Safety and Security

The level of law and order in a country affects business development, the quality of life of people, and the marketability of the country. Mauritius has relatively low crime rates compared to South Africa and the average for African countries. Even if compared to the BRIC countries and developed countries, the law and order situation seems to be under control in Mauritius (UN 2010). Refer to Table 9.7 for more detail.

Health Issues

Table 9.8 provides for a summary of health issues. Life expectancy is an indicator of quality of life and equality in a country. Mauritius, with an average life expectancy of 72.1 years, compares well with South Africa (52 years) and the average for Africa (57.8). Mauritius has a life expectancy rate comparable with those of more developed countries (UN 2010). In terms of maternal mortality rates and child mortality rates, Mauritius compares to developed countries. The low level of mortality indicates high levels of health care in the country. The average for Africa in

Table 9.6 Access to Sewer and Water

Country	% of Rural Population with Access to Water (2008)	% of Population with Access to Sewer (2008)
Mauritius	99%	91%
South Africa	78%	77%
African countries average	61%	49.8%
BRIC countries average	84%	63%
Developed countries average	99%	99.8%

Source: Table compiled by author from statistics obtained from the World Bank database per country (World Bank 2010).

Table 9.7 Safety and Security

Country	Homicide Rate per 100,000 of Population (2010)	Robbery Rate per 100,000 of Population (2010)
Mauritius	3.8	98
South Africa	36.5	Very high; exact info not available
African countries average	6.4	42.6
BRIC countries average	10.0	87.5
Developed countries average	1.6	277

Source: United Nations (UN), Human Development Index (HDI): 2010 Rankings, 2010, http://hds.undp.org/en/statistics (accessed April 12, 2011).

Table 9.8 Health Indicators

Country	Life Expectancy (2010) in Years	Maternal Mortality Rate per 100,000 Births (2010)	Mortality Rate under 5 Years per 1,000 Births (2010)	Prevalence of HIV as % of Population (2009)	Health Expenditure as % of GDP (2010)
Mauritius	72.1	15	17	1%	2.0%
South Africa	52.0	400	67	18%	3.6%
African countries average	57.8	589	95	7.4%	2.8%
BRIC countries average	69.5	158	31	0.5%	2.5%
Developed countries average	80.8	6	5	0.1%	7.0%

Source: United Nations (UN), Human Development Index (HDI): 2010 Rankings, 2010, http://hds.undp.org/en/statistics (accessed April 12, 2011); World Bank, The World Bank Indicators, 2010, http://data.worldbank.org/indicator (accessed April 20, 2011).

terms of maternal and child mortality is in some cases up to 40 times worse than in Mauritius. Even South Africa, with its advanced infrastructure and health care, could not be compared with Mauritius in terms of health care.

Southern Africa (South Africa, Botswana, Swaziland, Zambia, and Zimbabwe) is the focus point in global terms regarding HIV/AIDS. Mauritius has only a 1% prevalence of HIV of the population (2009) compared to South Africa at 18% and Botswana at 25%. The average for Africa is estimated at 7.4%. The level of health expenditures by government is an indication of the level of health infrastructure and facilities and the level of health of the population. Developed countries spend an average of 7% of GDP on health. BRIC countries spend only 2.5% on health, and the average for Africa is 2.8%. Mauritius spends only 2.0% of GDP on health, while South Africa, at 3.6%, is spending above the average for Africa on health (UN 2010; World Bank 2010).

Education and Research

Table 9.9 is a summary of education and research statistics. The number of years at school for children in Mauritius is 7.2 years on average. This figure compares well with the BRIC countries, but South Africa and the developed world have much higher averages. The average for Mauritius is, however, much higher than for Africa, at 5.6 years. The literacy rate on a global scale ranges between 36%

Table 9.9   Education and Research

Country	Average No. of Years at School (2010)	Literacy Rate as % of People Older Than 15 Years	Government Spending as % of GDP (2010)	No. of Scientific and Technological Journal Activities (2007)
Mauritius	7.2	88.6%	3.6%	18
South Africa	8.2	89.3%	5.1%	2,805
African average	5.6	71.2%	4.7%	316
BRIC average	7.0	88.0%	3.7%	25,209
Developed countries average	11.2	98.8%	5.2%	34,700

Source: United Nations (UN), Human Development Index (HDI): 2010 Rankings, 2010, http://hds.undp.org/en/statistics (accessed April 12, 2011); World Bank, The World Bank Indicators, 2010, http://data.worldbank.org/indicator (accessed April 20, 2011).

(Ethiopia the lowest) and 99% for most developed countries. Mauritius, with a rate at 88.6%, compares well with South Africa and the BRIC countries. Government spending on education is an indicator of the level of educational facilities and ultimately the education level in a country. Mauritius spends less on education (as percent of GDP) than Africa on average, but is on par with spending by BRIC countries. South Africa's spending on education is on par with developed countries and exceeds by far the level of spending if compared to Mauritius. The number of journal articles originating from Mauritius is limited compared to South Africa, BRIC countries, and the developed world, even if compared per capita (UN 2010; World Bank 2010).

Economic Policy Reforms

Background

Significant and far-reaching economic changes are sweeping across the globe, making it imperative for Mauritius to minimize the negative impacts of these changes in order to survive as a small island. Not a single country in the world should consider itself immune to these changes. The statistics, as reflected in the previous section, are a clear indication of Mauritius's ability to position itself strategically to compete in the global marketplace. The government's ongoing commitment to structural reforms and policies that promote integration into the global marketplace since the 1970s has positioned the island's economy as a world leader in economic freedom. In the 2012 Index of Economic Freedom, Mauritius has become the first sub-Saharan African country ever to advance into the top 10 in the world rankings (Heritage Foundation 2012).

A vital part of understanding the current economic successes of Mauritius is to provide a historical overview of the country's economic reforms.

Historical Overview of Economic Policy Reforms

Unlike many African economies, Mauritius did not subscribe to the prevailing orthodoxy of inward-oriented, state-dominated development strategies of the 1960s and 1970s, which focused on stringent import substitution combined with active state intervention in the economy. Starting in 1970, Mauritius followed a mixed-trade policy of import substitution coupled with incentives for exports (e.g., duty-free access to raw material for exports; low corporation tax rates; free repatriation of capital, profits, and dividends; and permanent residence permits) through the export processing zone (EPZ) policy. In the early 1980s Mauritius introduced a stronger market-oriented approach (Wignaraja 2001).

According to Wignaraja (2001) and Peerun-Fatehmamode et al. (2006) economic reforms in the country can be divided into three distinct phases. The first phase (1983–1985) was characterized by the elimination of most quantitative restrictions on imports and the replacement thereof by tariffs. Moreover, macro economic stability (low inflation and competitive exchange rates) became an explicit policy objective. The second phase (1986–1993) consisted of a gradual reduction in the effective protection of industry and of a more vigorous promotion of exports through preferential interest rates on development loans and tax concessions. Export and investment promotion was greatly strengthened by the establishment of the Mauritius Export Development and Investment Authority (MEDIA) in 1985 to provide global marketing support. Emphasis was also placed on maintaining macro economic and price stability. These reforms resulted in the economy becoming more outward-oriented and private sector focused than in the past.

The third phase (1994–2005) focused on the further reduction of protection by lowering import tariffs and on the development of new areas of comparative advantage. New institutions were also established in 2000 to promote new high-skill exports (e.g., Mauritius Productivity and Competitiveness Council).

The above phases can be regarded as a first generation of reforms, championed and executed mostly by the local minister of finance (World Bank 2009).

Forming part of the economic reforms is the diversification of Mauritius's economy. Over the past three decades economic growth has been principally driven by three main sectors—sugar, tourism, and textiles—while financial services, particularly offshore banking, a fourth sector, played a more prominent role over the last decade (Sobhee 2009). More recently the economy was further diversified toward information and communication technology (ICT), business outsourcing, small and medium enterprise development, tertiary-level technical skills development, and greater growth potential for its tourism industry. The latter is being stimulated in part by reducing duties on products, such as clothing, food, jewelry, and electronic equipment (Noury 2011; Duclos and Verdier-Chouchane 2011).

Recent Economic Policy Reforms (2006–2012)

Since 2006 Mauritius has moved from a first generation of reforms to a second generation of reforms, focusing on coordination among multiple ministries/departments and broader institutional capacity in the public sector. Reforms that both are politically feasible and have the potential to unlock growth with equity have become a priority of the Mauritian government. The government has invited various development partners (the African Development Bank, European Commission, United Nations Development Program, Agence Francaice de Developpement, and World Bank) to actively participate in the process.

Given the fact that the world economy impacted Mauritius at the very moment (2008) in which implementation of second-generation reforms was being intensified, the country was forced to balance its long-term objectives with a more immediate focus on socioeconomic consequences from the crisis. This required more emphasis on proactive management of risks and real-time policy responses, while keeping the reform agenda on track. The World Bank was part of this process, providing timely assistance at the request of the Mauritian Government (United Nations Development Program (UNDP) 2009).

Since 2006, Mauritius has been implementing a comprehensive 10-year economic reform program based on four pillars: fiscal consolidation and improving public sector efficiency, enhancing trade competitiveness, improving the investment climate, and widening the circle of opportunities through participation, social inclusion, and sustainability. The main instrument for introducing these reforms is the budget. Consultation and engagement of stakeholders in the design and formulation of reforms assist to mold budgetary targets and spending plans in the right direction (World Bank 2009; Sobhee 2009).

These reforms are embedded in a three-year performance-based budget (PBB) introduced in the 2008–2009 budget in an attempt to strengthen the resilience of the economy. Strategic planning and PBB aim to strengthen accountability, improve performance in public finance and administration, and improve the effectiveness of policies and strategies designed for the implementation of the 10-year economic reform program (UNDP 2009).

The PBB is one of the main interventions of the UNDP Strategic Budgeting Project. Another intervention is the Social Registry of Mauritius (SRM), which constitutes a core element of Mauritius's antipoverty policy. It is a large database of social program beneficiaries with the objectives to (1) better target beneficiaries of social programs and (2) manage social programs in an integrated manner (UNDP 2009).

The above reform program is in line with Mauritius's "Vision 2020: The National Long-Term Perspective Study," which contains Mauritius's long-term development goals. Vision 2020 takes a holistic view of development and addresses economic growth, environment, agriculture, industry, tourism, international financial services, ocean exploration, science and technology, employment, social cohesion, and political stability. It focuses strongly on education to transform Mauritius into a highly skilled and efficient economy (African Development Bank 2009).

The reform program of Mauritius is in line not only with Vision 2020, but also with the Mauritius Strategy for the Further Implementation of the Program of Action for the Sustainable Development of Small Island Developing States (SIDS), which was adopted by 129 countries and territories at the global conference held in Port Louis, January 10–14, 2005. This strategy, covering the decade 2005–2015, is the only global development strategy that addresses the unique development problems of small island developing states and sets out the basic principles and specific actions required at the national, regional, and international levels to ensure sustainable development (United Nations ESCAP 2012).

Forming part of Mauritius's response to sustainable development is the *Maurice Ile Durable*—referred to as the MID program that was introduced in 2008. The objective of this program is to turn the island into a model sustainable island. The document demonstrates that the scope for sustainable development, previously energy-oriented, is now open to economic, social, and environmental considerations, with the main thrust around the five Es: energy, environment, employment, education, and equity (Mauree 2011).

From the above section it is clear that economic reforms have become a recurrent feature of the Mauritian economic landscape to ensure a sustainable path. Mauritius has demonstrated that continued commitment to economic reforms is necessary, but not the only condition for long-term economic success. Good governance and strong institutions are essential for economic success.

Good Governance and Strong Institutions

Good governance involves far more than the power of the state or the strength of political will. The rule of law, transparency, and accountability are not merely the results of administrative procedure or institutional design. They are outcomes of democratizing processes driven not only by committed leadership, but also by the participation of, and contention among, groups and interests in society—processes that are most effective when sustained by legitimate institutions (Johnston 2005).

Mauritius has a very good track record of good governance and strong institutions. Recent legal and regulatory reforms have focused on creating an enabling environment for enhanced business practices and ensuring good governance, transparency, rule of law, and accountability. The 2008 Ibrahim Index of African Governance scored Mauritius the highest in sub-Saharan Africa (African Development Bank 2009).

This section does not contend that the economic reforms of Mauritius are to be a blueprint for African countries. However, valuable lessons can be learned, which will be discussed in the next section.

Lessons Learned for Africa

A number of key lessons can be learned from the Mauritius experience.

Good Governance and Strong Institutions

Recent research has identified good democratic governance and strong, effective institutions as a key to the Mauritius economic success. A government needs to continuously search for new economic drivers, with ongoing adaption to changing environments. Government acts as a facilitator for private sector expansion. Forming part of Mauritius's good track record of good governance is the fact that the country has never had a government focusing on confiscation and nationalization policies (Zafar 2011).

Coherent Competitiveness Strategy

A coherent competitiveness strategy is an important ingredient of economic success in a small state such as Mauritius. According to Wignaraja et al. (2004), six principles seem to underlie such a strategy:

- Focus on evolving comparative advantages
- Best-fit approach
- Link with regional markets and institutions
- Combine incentives and supply side measures
- Involve all stakeholders (partnership formation); and
- Prioritize interventions and actions

Furthermore, it is important to include a wide range of support measures in such a strategy. The main strategic thrusts for support measures can be identified as follows (Wignaraja et al. 2004):

- Maintain credible macro economic policies and exchange rate flexibility
- Persist with outward-oriented trade policies
- Foster small business start-up and growth
- Invest in human resources and skills training
- Ensure adequate technical support
- Encourage and increase inflows of foreign direct investment
- Strengthen public-private sector dialogue and partnerships

Mauritius has a comparative advantage in terms of the textile and clothing industry. In such an industry a country needs to identify specialized products and be a reliable producer of quality products (Ancharaz 2009: 14). In its drive to expand exports, Mauritius has invested in upgrading of its physical infrastructure, such as ports and harbors in support of exports (OECD 2011).

Consolidation of Physical, Human, and Social Capital

Although Mauritius has beautiful natural assets, such as rich marine resources, beaches, and volcanic topography, the country does not have any other form of physical resources that would ensure sustainable economic growth and development. Given this situation, Mauritius has opted for the optimal use of its social and human capital for progress. Human capital formation has focused on health and education, while investing in and adapting to technical change (Sobhee 2009). The lack of natural resources has forced the government to focus on its people and ensure a skilled workforce with a strong service sector (African Business 2011). Skills training policies are in place. Appropriate skills training starts at the school level, and a new educational system was introduced in 2011 in Mauritius to align skills training to skills shortages. Skills shortages currently exist in tourism, ICT, and other sectors (OECD 2011).

Diversification of the Economy

Though Mauritius benefited from the sugar sector, the government recognized early the advantages of diversification. Mauritius has embraced new sectors such as light manufacturing, financial services, and information and communication technology. Diversification has the potential to prevent economies from becoming stagnant and affected by global shocks such as recession.

Private Sector Involvement

Public-private partnership formation is of key importance for the economic success in Mauritius. Mauritius has a set of informal and formal mechanisms guiding the interaction between the public and private sector. This has resulted in the private sector playing an active role in the policy formulation process. The important role the private sector plays in the formulation of economic policy, especially through the Joint Economic Council, is unique in Africa. All Mauritian government delegations to international organizations have a private sector member (Zafar 2011).

Fiscal Management Reforms

As part of fiscal management reforms, a number of fiscal measures have been introduced by the Mauritian government to align its processes to best international practices and ensure effective implementation of the country's 10-year economic reform program. The two most notable measures are

- The development of a medium-term expenditure framework to cast the budget within a three-year rolling basis
- Moving from the traditional line budgeting system to a performance-based budgeting framework

The focus for government budgeting should be on reducing budget deficits, restructuring public spending, and improved budget control and processes. The new budget system must focus on results and performance. The Mauritian government has recently adopted a policy regarding the containment of wages and salaries of the public sector (OECD 2011).

Generous and Broad-Based Social Security Policies

Social security policies have been an important element of the development strategies in Mauritius. These development strategies have not been about the poor, but rather creating economic transformation, employment, and social security for the whole population. Countries where social security policies cater solely to the poor do not succeed in reducing poverty and inequality, as the nonpoor do not benefit from such policies and are therefore less willing to help cover the costs. More effective redistribution is a positive result of social security policies also benefiting the nonpoor (Ulriksen 2012).

Foreign Direct Investment (FDI)

Mauritius has good relations and trade agreements globally. It is a member of the African Union, the World Trade Organization (WTO), the Commonwealth, La Francophonie, the South African Development Community, the Common Market for Eastern and Southern Africa (COMESA), and the Indian Ocean Rim Association (U.S. Department of State 2012).

Conclusion

This chapter provides for an analysis of the Mauritius model for economic success. It provides hope for other, especially small African countries. Mauritius has achieved, against strong odds, sustainable economic development. Although the country is isolated with a small economy, it has not allowed these stumbling blocks to impact negatively on the development of the country. Based on the three main aspects of development, which include effective ports, harbors, and infrastructure, reliable telecommunication facilities, and an effective financial sector, Mauritius has proven to be competitive, even if compared to China (Sobhee 2009).

The Mauritian government has successfully consolidated the physical, human, and social capital of the country. Furthermore, a successful drive toward improved diversification of the economy has been implemented. A diversified economy is less affected by global economic impacts, climate change, natural disasters, and political threats. Diversification allows for a more resilient economy, and the concept also allows for product specialization and value-added products. The local economy is driven by continuous diversification and high levels of employment generation (Sohbee 2009).

International relations and local partnerships with the private sector are of key importance for the government and have contributed to the local economic success. Fiscal incentives to attract foreign investors have also played a vital role in allowing for a comparative advantage for this country. Fiscal incentives successfully attracted investors on a global scale and ultimately supported employment levels and the export-led growth strategies of the government (Sobhee 2009).

Mauritius is known for its high levels of good governance and strong government institutions. Democratic values, stable political systems, and good international relations exist in Mauritius and allow for a positive perception and image of the country, and ultimately foreign investment. The government of Mauritius has actively attempted to reduce hurdles for foreign investment, such as reduction in bureaucracy, red-tape regulations, and corruption (Sobhee 2009)

Mauritius, like any other developing country, needs to continue with the good governance of the past decade. Continuous adaption to rapidly changing economic, political, and social environments is required to maintain economic growth. The concept of "fast" government, as identified by the World Economic Forum, needs to be the continued focus of government. An agile, flexible, and streamlined government, with strong technology research, is required (WEF 2011b).

Mauritius, however small, is a world leader in terms of good governance (ranked number 1 in Africa in terms of the Mo Ibrahim Index in 2011), ease of doing business (ranked number 1 in Africa in the Doing Business Report by the World Bank in 2011), and competitiveness (ranked third in Africa in terms of the Global Competitiveness Report by the World Economic Forum (2011a)).

The challenges for Mauritius are to maintain and expand on current success. Major challenges such as infrastructure backlogs, demand for skilled manpower, and global competition need to be the focus of future policy. Mauritius needs to build on existing strong partnerships, its strong macro economic strategies, and ensuring a positive economic climate for the private sector to thrive (Zafar 2011).

Every country in Africa has its own challenges, strengths, and opportunities. No economic development strategy could be copied from one country to another. But best practice policies and processes could be adopted from the successes implemented in Mauritius to the African countries to best fit specific localities.

References

African Business. 2011. *Lessons in evolution: Special report on Mauritius.* October.
African Development Bank. 2009. *Mauritius: 2009–2013 country strategy paper.*
Ancharaz, V. 2009. David vs Goliath: Mauritius facing up to China. *European Journal of Development Research* 21: 4.
Duclos, J., and Verdier-Chouchane, A. 2011. Analyzing pro-poor growth in southern Africa: Lessons from Mauritius and South Africa. *African Development Review* 23(2): 121–146.
Heritage Foundation. 2012. Index of economic freedom. From http://www.heritage.org/index/ (accessed March 15, 2012).
International Monetary Fund (IMF). 2011. Data and statistics. From http://www.imf.org/external/data.htm. (accessed March 20, 2012).
Johnston, M. 2005. Good governance: Rule of law, transparency, and accountability. Department of Political Science, Colgate University. http://scholoar.google.com/.../Paper1.pdf+Definition+of+good+governance+Africa+and+NEPA (accessed March 24, 2012).
Mauree, P.P. 2011. Maurice Ile Durable: Sustainability and sustainable development. *Le Mauricien*, August 17. From http://www.lemauricien.com/article/maurice-ile-durable-sustainability-and-sustainable (accessed March 15, 2012).
Mo Ibrahim Foundation. 2011. The Ibrahim Index: 2011. From http://www.moibrahimfoundation.org (accessed March 20, 2012).
Noury, V. 2011. Lessons in evolution. *African Business* 79.

OECD. 2011. *African economic outlook: Mauritius.* From http://www.africaneconomicoutlook.org/en (accessed February 12, 2012).
Peacock, B. 2011. Wide-awake economy of a sleepy island. *Sunday Times*, September 18, p. 10.
Peerun-Fatehmamode, R., Bundoo, S., and Jankee, K. 2006. *Competition scenario in Mauritius.* Consumer Unity and Trust Society (CUTS International). Japir, India. From http://www.cuts-international.org (accessed March 25, 2012).
Sobhee, S.K. 2009. The economic success of Mauritius: Lessons and policy options for Africa. *Journal of Economic Policy Reform* 12(1): 29–42.
Ulriksen, M. 2012. How social security policies and economic transformation affect poverty and inequality: Lessons for Africa. *Development Southern Africa* 29(1): 3–18.
United Nations (UN). 2010. Human Development Index (HDI): 2010 rankings. http://hds.undp.org/en/statistics (accessed April 12, 2011).
United Nations Development Program. 2009. Strategic budgeting in the government of Mauritius.
United Nations ESCAP. 2012. Mauritius strategy: Sustainable development of small island developing states.
U.S. Department of State. 2012. Bureau of African Affairs. Diplomacy in action, background notes on Mauritius. From http://www.state.gov/r/pa/ei/bgn/2833.htm (accessed March 25, 2012).
Wignaraja, G. 2001. *Firm size, technological capabilities and market-oriented policies in Mauritius.* London: Commonwealth Secretariat.
Wignaraja, G., Lezama, M., and Joiner, D. 2004. *Small states in transition: From vulnerability to competitiveness.* London: Commonwealth Secratariat.
World Bank. 2009. International Bank for Reconstruction and Development Program document for a proposed loan in the amount of US$50 million to the Republic of Mauritius for a fourth trade and competitiveness development policy loan.
World Bank. 2010. The World Bank indicators. http://data.worldbank.org/indicator (accessed April 20, 2011).
World Bank. 2011. Doing business: Measuring business regulations. From http://www.doing business.org/rankings (accessed March 28, 2012).
World Economic Forum (WEF). 2011a. The global competitiveness report, 2010–2011. From http://weforum.org/reports (accessed September 20, 2011).
World Economic Forum (WEF). 2011b. The future of government. From http://www.weforum.org (accessed September 28, 2011).
Zafar, A. 2011. Mauritius: An economic success story. Paper for part of the African Success Stories Project. World Bank.

Chapter 10

A Comparative Analysis of Local Government in Ghana and South Africa

Ernest Peprah Ababio and Kwame Asmah-Andoh

Contents

Introduction 188
Concept of Local Government 188
Decentralized Ghana and Devolved South Africa 190
Local Government in Modern Constitutions...193
    Relevant Legislative Framework 196
Intergovernmental Relationships and Political Scenarios..................................197
Local Institutional Arrangements 198
Categories of Municipalities in South Africa..198
    Chief Executive Officer.. 200
    Financial Autonomy 202
    Service Provision and Participation 203
Conclusion..205
References 205

Introduction

Local government is generally a nationally recognized jurisdiction with delegated authority to deliver basic services. In many developing countries service provision functions formerly carried out by the central government are being turned to local governments in forms of decentralization as part of political reform due to economic imperatives, and are sometimes occasioned by influence of donor agencies, including the World Bank. Advocates argue that central government's ability to effect meaningful social and economic development in which beneficiary communities fully participate has its limits. Decentralization may take different forms, depending on the extent to which local government is accorded constitutional recognition or the levels of autonomy provided to subnational governments in a given state.

Decentralization, devolution, and deconcentration are sometimes used uncritically to describe the enabling statutory and policy environments that set the structures and mandates created for local government institutions. At other times, these are used as a description of the powers and functional relationships between local government and other higher orders of government in that state. This comparative study is intended to assist with better understanding of the complexities associated with decentralization and devolution of local government as pursued under the existing constitutions in Ghana and South Africa.

This analysis looks specifically at the debate on decentralized and devolved local government; the constitutional, legislative, political, and administrative environment of decentralization; and the process of devolution to local government in Ghana and South Africa. The aim is to provide a lens through which to analyze the institutions and processes supporting decentralization of powers and functions to local government in a specific context, and to examine the core principles that underpin decentralization in order to strengthen local democracy and governance as well as service provision and local economic development.

Concept of Local Government

The form of any particular state and the subnational organizational structure decided upon may vary, but three levels of government seem to be common among state systems: central, state/provincial, and local government levels (Steytler 2005). Though local government predates modern states as the oldest form of government in civilized society, currently the concept of local government denotes political institutions or entities created by national constitutions or specific legislation to deliver a range of specified services to a relatively small geographically delineated area (Shah and Shah 2006). From its Latin root *municipium*, "a free town" or municipality has been a constituent part of local government since ancient Roman times. It relates to a city, town, or village possessing corporate status and enjoying its own local self-government (Craythorne 1997). This and Meyer's definition of local government as "vested with prescribed, controlled governmental powers and sources of income to render specific local services, control and regulate the social and economic development of defined local areas" indicate a certain degree of autonomy to act (in Reddy 1999, p. 10). It is a justified political, representational, and administrative reality that local areas require local decision making for realism and for efficiency in matters that affect inhabitants of that particular area (Meiring 2000).

A measure of autonomy is necessary for local government to provide services consistent with voters' preferences because they are expected to understand the needs, desires, and demands of the communities they serve. Being the units of government closest to the people, local government institutions and processes provide opportunities for communities to participate in the democratic process and for their interests and perspectives to be incorporated in decision making. Total and absolute autonomy for local government cannot exist in a state, whether a centralized (unitary) or federal system; however, decentralization and constitutional recognition are seen as providing some guarantee for the effective performance of functions. This could take the form of

- Being separate constitutionally from central government and being responsible for a significant range of services
- Having control over a separate budget and accounts, and having powers of taxation to produce a greater part of revenue and other resources
- Being an elected council with powers to perform governing functions, such as the ability to make decisions on services provision, public expenditure, and the acquisition of resources, including the appointment and promotion of personnel
- Being subject only to limited interference by central and provincial orders of government based on determined intergovernmental relationship processes (cf. Mawhood 1993)

The traditional status and role of local government remain, but the trend is to defer many functions previously performed by higher orders of government to local government institutions. The rationale for this is explained as bringing government closer to the people in the hope of giving citizens, especially the poor, a greater voice in their well-being and making government more effective and more accountable. This trend is driven not only by democracy, but also by economic imperatives, that is, the quest for local decision making power that will facilitate efficient provision of infrastructure and services demanded by the citizens. The principle of local democracy requires that local decisions should be made by elected local representatives and be as close as possible to the citizens. There is also the assertion that oftentimes the central state apparatus is relatively unwieldy and lacks capacity in rural areas. Decentralization of powers and functions to local government is thus intended to bring government and governmental processes close to citizens, and promote political participation and efficient provision of services to meet citizens' expectations (Wunch and Olowu 1990).

The trend in both developed and developing countries has been toward increasing the role of local authorities in the provision of services in the form of downloading more and more functions onto local government, a process generally described as decentralization. Decentralization has been implemented to varying degrees in both Ghana and South Africa since the early 1990s. Dubois and Fattore (2009) classify the concept of decentralization into political, administrative, fiscal, and market decentralization. The degree to which local government authority is guaranteed minimum interference, clear mandates, the ability to acquire financial and human capital talent, including the transfer of resources and empowerment to operate efficiently, and political space to carry out their functions may be used as a basis for a comparative study (Manor 1999). Local government in Ghana can be described as decentralized, while South African local government is seen as a form of devolution. Both countries give recognition to local government in their respective constitutions. This typology will be used as an analytical framework for the discussion on decentralization in Ghana and devolution in South Africa.

Decentralized Ghana and Devolved South Africa

Decentralization is advanced on the grounds that a local government understands the concerns of local residents, and a strong local government enhances efficiency, responsiveness, accountability, manageability, and autonomy (Shah and Shah 2006). However, the decentralization and devolution debate revolves around the challenges associated with establishing effective local-level institutional and politico-administrative arrangements for services provision to meet the needs and expectations of citizens. Transferring functions and powers to local government, however, is a fundamental feature of both decentralization and devolution.

The concepts of decentralization and devolution tend to defy acceptable or standard definitions. The difficulty has been summed up by Antwi-Boasiako (2010), who wrote that "the concept of decentralization and its interpretations have become a battleground for a variety of disciplines and theories" (p. 169). Ahwoi (in Sharma 2010) does little to sort out the confusion over definitions when he blurs the distinction between the two concepts. He expresses the view that decentralization and devolution are closely aligned when authority over and responsibility for resources are ceded to local governments. Litvack (2010) sees decentralization as a complex, multifaceted concept, and defines it as the transfer of authority and responsibility for public functions from the central government to subordinate or quasi-independent government organizations or the private sector. The authority and responsibility package, in this case, are classified as political, administrative, fiscal, and market decentralization. Antwi-Boasiako concurs when he maintains that decentralization is a process where central government transfers political, fiscal, and administrative powers to lower levels in an administrative and territorial hierarchy. Similarly, Smith (in Hattingh 1988, pp. 28–29) identifies a number of contexts within which the concept decentralization can be applied, providing an indication of its diverse meanings:

- When a central authority establishes subordinate authorities and assigns functions to them, this is referred to by some as a decentralization of functions.
- Decentralization may also denote the assignment of powers to specific subordinate government bodies by the central authority.
- [It can also be seen as the] allocation of discretionary powers to specific political office-bearers by the legislative authority.

A motive in Ghana, as pointed out by Ayee (2008), is that since independence, successive governments in Ghana have preoccupied themselves with decentralization because they regarded it as a necessary condition for not only the socioeconomic development of the country, but also as a way of achieving their political objectives, such as the recentralization of authority. Functionally, therefore, as captured by the Institute of Local Government in Ghana (2011, p. 4), decentralization is envisioned to transfer functions, powers, means, and competence to district assemblies from the central government ministries and departments.

In many respects, South African municipalities, as constituents of local government compared to the district assemblies in Ghana, denote an essential feature of greater devolution to local government than at any time in the country's history. Local government in South Africa no longer comprises "corporate bodies with defined powers and functions" (Craythorne 1997). A feature of the constitution of the Republic of South Africa (1996) is that it laid down the framework for maximum devolution of authority to the local sphere within the constitutional spheres of government. This is accompanied by electoral and new public management (NPM) reforms, political leadership, and political accountability at the local government level.

What may be of interest in the above discourse on definitions is that decentralization is a central government prerogative, and not a constitutional imperative. This distinction, in our view, is what makes the difference between the concepts of decentralization and devolution. In effect, local government decentralization approaches create territorially organized political and administrative institutions, while the policy and operational autonomy are allocated through devolved constitutional statutes or parliamentary legislation.

Thus, on the one hand, in terms of Section 240 of the constitution of the Republic of Ghana (1992), Ghana has a system of local government and administration that, as far as is practicable, is decentralized. Among other provisions, parliament enacts appropriate laws to ensure that functions, powers, responsibilities, and resources are at all times transferred from central government to local government units in a coordinated manner. On the other hand, the constitutional version of the case of South Africa is as follows, in terms of Section 151 of the constitution of the Republic of South Africa (1996):

- The local sphere of government consists of municipalities, which must be established for the whole of the territory of the republic.
- The executive and legislative authority of a municipality is vested in its municipal council.
- A municipality has the right to govern, on its own initiative, the local government affairs of its community, subject to national and provincial legislation, as provided for in the constitution.
- The national or a provincial government may not compromise or impede a municipality's ability or right to exercise its powers or perform its functions.

The distinguishing features of local government systems in Ghana and South Africa, in terms of respective constitutional provisions, are therefore:

- Local government in Ghana is a creation of central government; in South Africa, local government is created by the 1996 constitution.
- Local government in Ghana implements policies of the central government, albeit with discretion. In South Africa, local government is not an adjunct, a tier of central government. It is recognized as a sphere, about parallel to provincial and national governments.

At this stage of semantic exploration, the viewpoint that comes closest to explanation of devolution is one offered by Antwi-Boasiako (2010, p. 169):

> Political decentralization, which is manifested in the degree and types of political autonomy and accountability ... is a situation where local people in the districts and regions elect their own legislative and executive personnel so that those units will be able to hire, pay and dismiss administrative personnel without reference to central authority.... This gives citizens and their elected representatives the political power in the public policy process.

It can therefore be argued that whereas powers and functions transferred by the central government can also at any time be withdrawn by the transferring institution, that is, in a decentralized relationship, the same cannot be said of devolutionary status where institutions are created by constitutions and accorded a much greater degree of autonomy. It is our view, therefore, that the local government system in Ghana is a function of decentralization, that is, the creation of tiers of institutions by the central authority, which has discretion to assign, transfer, and withdraw these. Comparatively, local government in South Africa functions on devolution; that is, municipalities are a creation of the constitution that accords autonomy comparable to other spheres of government (constitution of the Republic of South Africa 1996; hereafter referred to as the 1996 constitution).

Given the nature of local government, the autonomy accorded to local government in a state cannot be absolute, even under a federal system. The constitutions of both South Africa and Ghana are classified as unitary systems. The concepts of decentralization and devolution in practical terms thus provide analytical descriptions on the extent to which local government is given political space within the state to carry out local service provision functions. The historical development of local government itself provides some argument for delegating service provision functions formerly carried out by the central government. Oates (1972) argues that for local decision making to be responsible to the people for whom the services are intended, each public service needs to be provided with jurisdiction over the relevant geographical area.

Local Government in Modern Constitutions

Just as in most Western democracies, the constitutional recognition of local government in Ghana and South Africa is very recent. In both countries, the turning over of expanded service provision functions to local government, together with constitutional recognition and decentralization, is part of the ongoing democratization initiatives and management reforms that began in the early 1990s. The objectives include an effort to increase the capability of communities and individuals to take advantage of the opportunities created. The question remains whether decentralization or devolution will indeed enhance the performance of the expanded role and functions of the local government sphere in these two countries. This also harks back to the conceptualization of local government and the theory of decentralization and devolution in the modern constitution.

The Union of South Africa was established on May 31, 1910, and the South Africa Act (1909) made the provincial councils responsible for municipal and other local authorities (Botes, Brynard, Fourie, and Roux 1997). The far-reaching implications of the apartheid era are still evident on geographical settlements. Institutional and infrastructural development meant that the Local Government Negotiating Forum (LGNF), as part of the multiparty negotiations, concentrated on ways to establish nonracial local democracy that accommodates both majority and minority communities (Razin 2003). Constitutional recognition and devolution to local government in South Africa was premised on creating a statutory environment to enable the promotion of local economic development in response to the negative effects of the socioeconomic or settlement patterns. In the early years of democratic rule, local government still manifested the effects of past racial policies but was adjudged to be better positioned than central government to redress racial discrimination at the grassroots level, while at the same time deepen democratic accountability and responsiveness to the citizenry (van de Walle 2003). Thus devolution (or so-called democratic decentralization) was actively pursed to enable communities to avail themselves of political empowerment and promote maximum political participation in a manner that responded to the challenges of the immediate apartheid past.

By way of comparison, the local government system in Ghana is the product of the country's colonial past. A study of its political development shows that while under colonial rule, rudimentary local government institutions were established in urban areas, while traditional authorities and institutions were variously utilized in rural areas. The current local government system in Ghana is regulated by Chapter 20 of the constitution of the Republic of Ghana (1992) (hereafter referred to as the 1992 constitution). The legislative framework that has shaped local government in Ghana dates back to 1859 in a municipal ordinance that established municipalities in the coastal towns of the then Gold Coast. These were extended in 1943 with elected town councils for Accra, Kumasi, Sekondi-Takoradi, and Cape Coast. The trend of establishing local government institutions mainly in urban centers continued even after independence in 1957 with the Local Government Act, No. 54 of 1961. As pointed out by ILGS (2010), the legislation always made a distinction between two different machineries for the administration of Ghana, namely, one based in the capital Accra, with branches at the local/district level, and another separate and district level, based in well-defined localities and referred to as local government. From 1949 to 1974, no less than 10 commissions and committees of inquiry attempted to shape local government structures in Ghana. However, recommendations by these initiatives into the restructuring of local government yielded little impact on decentralization. In contrast, the 1992 constitution was to make a bold revamp.

Proponents in favor of a measure of constitutional recognition for local government argue that central government's ability to effect social and economic development has its limits, and that meaningful development efforts require full participation of the beneficiary communities (Steytler 2005; *White Paper on Local Government* 1998). Olowu (in Cameron 2004) notes that decentralization to local government as part of the reform process in Africa has been influenced by economic imperatives, which has led to political and management reforms. The development of local government in both Ghana and South Africa indicates the quest to achieve viable, democratic, and functional local government institutions and thus deepen democracy. There are also discernible impacts occasioned by donor agencies, most notably the World Bank, which has stepped in to provide support once decentralized institutions have been established (Manor 1999).

In South Africa, the 1996 constitution recognized the status of local government as a distinctive sphere alongside the provincial and national government. This is also reflected in a number of provisions of the constitution. The whole of Chapter

7 of the 1996 constitution and sections of the chapter on cooperative government give constitutional guarantees to local government in South Africa.

In comparison, Chapter 20 of the 1992 constitution of Ghana is straightforward in intent. Entitled "Decentralization and Local Government," the cardinal features of decentralization are outlined as follows:

- Assurance that functions, powers, responsibilities, and resources are at all times transferred from the central government to local government units in a coordinated manner
- Enhancement of the capacity of local government authorities to plan, initiate, coordinate, manage, and execute policies in respect to all matters affecting the people within their areas
- Establishment of, for each local government unit, a sound financial base with adequate and reliable sources of revenue
- Promotion of accountability through formal control measures and by public participation

It may therefore be argued that decentralization and devolution in both Ghana and South Africa are indicative not so much of differences in the degree to which the individual countries have acknowledged local government, but how the differing decentralization constitutional and political policies are given effect.

Issues of governance processes impact on the decentralization or devolution and influence the legislative framework adopted in particular countries. Manor (1999) suggests that there are four necessary conditions if decentralized institutions are to succeed: sufficient constitutional or statutory powers to influence the local environment, including significant development activities; sufficient financial resources; adequate administrative capacity; and reliable accountability mechanisms. The latter condition includes accountability of elected politicians to citizens, as well as accountability of bureaucrats to elected officials. Above all, creating viable and independent democratic local government institutions with decentralized or devolved powers requires the transfer of resources to buttress efficient and sustainable provision of local government services.

There appear to be some differences in the development of local government in South Africa and Ghana. The transformation of local government in South Africa during the multiparty negotiations was aimed at de-racializing society and making local government an instrument for integration and equitable redistribution of resources. The objective of creating institutions of local government with devolved powers to improve democratic participation and responsiveness is in line with *inter alia* the rights contained in the bill of rights in the 1996 constitution. Decentralization of local government in Ghana is part of constitutional development and is possibly influenced by the International Monetary Fund (IMF) and other donor agencies' Structural Adjustment Program, imposed on the country from the 1990s. The value of constitutional recognition of local government in

Ghana and South Africa finds meaningful manifestation in the relevant legislative and administrative powers granted. Constitutional recognition and policies to buttress the functioning of local self-government institutions are undertaken to broaden and deepen inhabitants' participation in democratic processes and increase governmental responsiveness and accountability to communities. Thus in their present constitutional environments and the transfer of a broader range of competencies, the success of local self-government will depend on the manner and allocation of their powers and functions.

Relevant Legislative Framework

The expanded roles for local government flowing from constitutional recognition in the form of decentralization and devolution have been given enabling legislation. Giving effect to Chapter 20 of Ghana's 1992 constitution is the Local Government Act, No. 462 of 1993. The 14 component parts of 163 sections translate the vision of the government of Ghana on local government decentralization. Part 1, comprising 45 sections, deals with the focal point of decentralization, namely, the district assemblies. These are either metropolitan (with a population of over 250,000), municipal (over 95,000), or district (75,000). Ten regional coordinating councils exercise oversight functions of the district assemblies for the 10 regional administration units in Ghana. The Ministry of Local Government and Rural Development promotes the establishment of "a vibrant and well-resourced decentralized system of local government for the people of Ghana to ensure good governance and balanced rural based development" (Goel 2010, p. 2). Similar legislations have been enacted to provide a framework for local government in South Africa.

The legislative basis for the current local government system in South Africa can be traced from the Local Government Transition Act (1993) and the relevant provisions of the interim constitution (1993), which saw the establishment of the embryonic institutions for metropolitan, urban, and rural local government. Subsequently, the 1996 constitution buttressed the maximum devolution envisaged for local government by entrenching municipalities as constituent parts of the local sphere of government in constitutional cooperative government as distinctly independent, although interrelated with the other spheres.

Section 151(1) of the 1996 constitution stipulates that "the local sphere of government consists of municipalities, which must be established for the whole of the territory of the Republic." Comparatively, not only is the status and role of local government in South Africa changed with the constitutional recognition, but there appears to be a reconceptualization as developmental local government because "local government is committed to working with citizens and groups within the community to find sustainable ways to meet their social, economic and material needs and improve the quality of their lives."

Sections 17–20 of the *White Paper on Local Government* (1998) state that developmental local government has four interrelated characteristics, including *inter alia*:

> maximising social development and economic growth; integrating and co-ordinating development plans to enhance the provision of services; empowering poor communities, redistributing services and democratising development; as well as learning and providing strategic visionary leadership in mobilising resources to meet basic needs and achieve developmental goals.

Other legislative and policy instruments, including the *White Paper on Local Government* (1998), the Local Government: Municipal Structures Act (1998), and the Local Government: Municipal Systems Act (2000), are all devoted to creating an environment for devolved local government. These give municipalities administrative and legislative power with regard to 38 listed functional areas in the annexures, and also entrench fiscal powers.

The fact that local government in Ghana is a creation of the central government is underlined by Section 241(2), which states that "Parliament may by law make provision for the redrawing of the boundaries of districts or for reconstituting the districts." The focal point for local government decentralization is the district assemblies. These have the status of being the highest political authority in the district, and have legislative and executive powers. District assemblies are primarily responsible for the implementation of development policies and programs coordinated by a National Development Planning Commission.

The constitutional recognition of local government within the constitutional sphere meant a shift from the traditional role of municipal services provision to include local political and socioeconomic development (Parnell, Pieterse, Swilling, and Woodridge 2000). Institutionally, the decentralized and devolved local government is designed to assist policy makers and program managers in all spheres to support participatory, decentralized planning and development. Devolution could have the disadvantage of obstructing unity and proper alignment of national policies with local government implementation, especially in unitary systems. Legislative functional allocation is required for the proper management of intergovernmental relationships.

Intergovernmental Relationships and Political Scenarios

In considering roles and responsibilities for decentralized local government, two important issues need further discussion. First, the role of higher levels of government will be very important in signaling directions on where local government is going and how efficiently it is functioning. The continuous erosion of the powers of local government and its autonomy signals the emergence of neocentralism. But it should not be forgotten that the objective of decentralization or devolution is to allow local governments to develop and thus become effective partners with other levels of government. This will also ensure local government's relevance in society and allow it to deliver effectively. Decentralization is also about partnerships and the right to develop partnerships.

Second, a key factor identified in comparative studies of local government is the role of the broader national political and legal environment in which local government decentralization is embedded and in which local governments operate. Local governments in a state are regarded as best-equipped units to provide services in defined areas; however, in unitary states such decisions have interrelational and interdependence implications. The extent of autonomy ceded to the local government and the qualified control of higher orders of government determine the functional relationship. Devolution of more powers and functions to local government could create potentially difficult intergovernmental relationships, especially between metropolitan municipalities and provincial governments. Decentralization by nature does not incur the challenges of managing intergovernmental relations or the question of party political control. Devolution may prove more problematic and thus require management of intergovernmental relationships, as in the case of South Africa.

Local Institutional Arrangements

An important factor for the success of devolution or decentralization is the type of institutional arrangement established for local government. The institutions of the devolved local government in South Africa mainly sought to undo the hitherto racially based structures and create democratic local authorities in their place to redistribute and provide services equitably. South Africa's constitutional categories of municipalities capture the rural-urban divide and the multilayered systems that seem to be present in most democracies. The transformation of nearly 1,000 race-based and 843 somewhat unviable local authorities to the current arrangement for 284 municipalities followed a three-phased process.

Categories of Municipalities in South Africa

The constitution of the Republic of South Africa (1996), Section 155(1), provides for three categories of municipalities in the country, as shown in Table 10.1.

The category A metropolitan municipality system was premised on the creation of an institutional framework to promote strategic planning in a coordinated

Table 10.1 Categories of Municipalities in South Africa

Category A municipalities: 8	A municipality that has exclusive municipal executive and legislative authority in the area
Category B municipalities: 232	A municipality that shares municipal executive and legislative authority in its area with a category C municipality within the area of which it falls
Category C municipalities: 46	A municipality that has municipal executive and legislative authority in an area that includes more than one municipality
Total: 286	Wall-to-wall municipalities covering the whole of the territory of the Republic of South Africa

fashion for physical and infrastructural development and for marketing the metropolis as a whole (Provincial Affairs and Constitutional Development 1998).

Though structurally different, the aim was that district municipal institutions would improve the coordination and strategic linkages between urban and rural settlements, which is not far from the argument adduced for the creation of the single metropolitan municipal system. Both were influenced, first, by the distorted legacy of apartheid policies based on racial settlements, and second, by the need for economic viability and enhanced citizens' participation. The municipal institutions in South Africa (as shown in Table 10.1) are classified into metropolitan, district, and local, with the latter two sharing territorial and jurisdictional functional authority.

From a constitutional perspective, the role of local government is primarily to provide essential services such as water, sanitation, and electricity to all local residents. However, decentralization or devolution introduce secondary roles, such as the promotion of economic and social uplifting/development, which call for their participation in national and provincial development programs that require appropriate constitutional and legislative institutions with the necessary capacity.

The focal points for local government decentralization in Ghana are the district assemblies (Figure 10.1). These have the status of being the highest political authority in the district and have both legislative and executive powers. District assemblies are primarily responsible for the implementation of development policies and programs coordinated by a National Development Planning Commission. Types of district assemblies have been outlined above. At the grassroots level there are two-tier subdistrict structures, namely, zonal and town/area councils and unit committees (UCs) that perform duties delegated to them by the assemblies but do not have their own budgets.

From the provisions of Ghana's Local Government Transition Act, No. 209 of 2003, up to the system now in place, a clear distinction is made between municipalities in metropolitan areas and those in the nonmetropolitan areas.

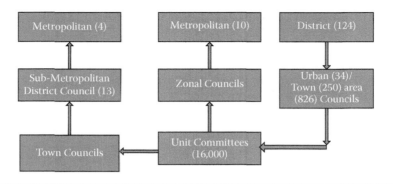

Figure 10.1 Structure of local government in Ghana.

Currently, South African municipalities in metropolitan areas are structured as single-tier, autonomous local authorities. Outside metropolitan areas there are two layers of municipalities: the district municipality and the local municipality (1996 constitution). The objective was to create institutions that have the flexibility to embrace different settlement types and administrative capacity (or lack of it) in many rural areas of the country. The local municipality is the primary local authority in these areas. The district municipality integrates a number of local municipalities in a broader geographical area, which includes a district council and its administrative unit. The establishment of this model of district municipality is premised on the search for effectiveness and efficiency of service delivery, and for political responsiveness. In effect, the local municipality, as the primary local authority, is charged with maintaining political responsiveness, while the broader district municipality takes responsibility for economic efficiency.

Chief Executive Officer

A strategic feature of Ghana's local government decentralization arrangement is the position of the district chief executive (DCE) in each district. In terms of Section 243 of the 1992 constitution, the DCE is appointed by the president with the prior approval of not less than two-thirds majority of the district assembly. This differs from a devolved local government, as is the case in South Africa, where in terms of Section 55 of the Municipal Structures Act of 1998, the executive mayor is elected and appointed by relevant council. What is more, in Ghana, the DCE, as mayor, is responsible for the day-to-day performance of the administrative and executive functions of the district assembly. The DCE is also the chief representative of the central government. Further, under PNDC Law 327, the local government personnel have to function under a single centralized public service. In other words, officials implement the decisions and programs of the central government in a decentralized district. Among other tasks, the head of the civil service is responsible for the posting of administrative officers, secretarial personnel, and executive officers in the districts. This undoubtedly makes the process of decentralization tread a very fine line between central and local governments.

In contrast, the two main types of executive systems functioning in South African local government are as follows:

1. The *collective executive system*, which vests leadership of the municipality in a collective executive committee, with the position of the mayor as a *primus inter pares* in a cabinet system.
2. The *mayoral executive system*, which vests the executive authority in an executive mayor who is assisted by a mayoral committee of councillors. The *White Paper on Local Government* (1998) indicates a preference for the mayoral system and subsequent legislation; the Local Government: Municipal Structures Act (1998) adopted this system of a strong mayoral presence. This mandates the executive mayor or the mayoral committee to assume responsibility for strategy and policy, with ordinary councillors having little involvement in the detailed administration and management of the day-to-day affairs of the council. Unlike the executive mayor in the United States, the South African mayor is not directly elected. His or her candidature is indicated prior to the elections, and the winning party's candidate is elected at the first sitting of the council. Notably, rural councils make provision for 20% representation of traditional rulers on the council.

Comparatively, the contrasting positions of chief executive officer in the two countries are also linked to the public service systems. Ghana has a unified public service compared to what is theoretically referred to as a fragmented system in South Africa. The head of the civil service in Accra appoints, and can transfer, local government personnel from the district to the central government. In South Africa, a municipal council in a given municipality has the power to appoint and dismiss all officials from the municipal manager to the gravedigger. The argument is that the latter could be prone to political patronage and nepotism, while the former has the disadvantage of being "alien" to local needs.

Section 156(1) of the 1996 constitution provides municipalities with executive authority and the right to administer the local government matters listed in Part B of Schedule 4 and Part B of Schedule 5. The role and powers of the executives of municipalities in South Africa may also be determined by the type of municipality. In practice, different types of local government have different responsibilities. Larger metropolitan and urban municipalities have responsibility for a range of functions and services, while rural local governments generally provide fewer services. Category A metropolitan municipalities have all the above-listed functions.

However, Sections 154(3)(c) and 229 of the 1996 constitution, and Section 84 of the Municipal Structures Act (1998), divide the powers and functions between categories C and B municipalities. In addition, in terms of Section 155(3)(c), a division of powers and functions between a category B municipality and a category C municipality may differ from the division of powers and functions between another category B municipality and that of a category C municipality.

Financial Autonomy

Most local governments in South Africa were established as bodies corporate, and thus historically, the bulk of revenue has been from property taxes and surcharges on the provision of services such as water, electricity, refuse removal, and other user charges. In terms of the 1996 constitution, rates on property are a constitutionally guaranteed source of revenue for local governments, while Sections 228 and 229 explicitly prohibit provinces from introducing such tax.

Section 214(1) of the 1996 constitution requires an act of parliament to provide for the equitable division of revenue raised nationally among the national, provincial, and local spheres of government; and any other allocations to provinces, local government, or municipalities from the national government's share of that revenue; and any conditions on which those allocations may be made. Additionally, Section 229 of the 1996 constitution provides municipalities with power to impose taxes, rates on property, surcharges on fees for services provided, and other sundry taxes, levies, and duties. Section 227(2) makes it clear that additional revenue raised by a municipality may not be deducted from a municipality's share of revenue raised nationally and other allocations made by national government.

The ability to generate revenue from one's own sources determines the extent of autonomy for a constitutionally devolved local government. Municipalities in South Africa are expected to generate a greater percentage of their revenue. However, reliable and relatively better generating sources, such as income tax and value-added tax, are controlled by the central government. This, though, has the potential for worsening inequalities between municipalities, especially in the case of rural municipalities with a low property tax base and simultaneously poor infrastructural bases. Budgetary and decision-making flexibility for local services provision will be impaired if local expenditure decision making falls outside the control of the municipal council. Predictability of fiscal transfers and fiscal independence of municipalities is, in theory at least, necessary for financial accountability.

The financial provision for the local government system in Ghana is contained in Sections 245 and 252 of the 1992 constitution. Virtually similar to the equitable share of revenue in South Africa, Ghana's 1992 constitution creates a so-called District Assemblies' Common Fund, which comprises not less than 5% (it currently stands at 7%) of the total revenue of Ghana to the district assemblies. Further, the assemblies are empowered to generate revenues locally. These are in the form of rates, property taxes, licenses, trading, and miscellaneous sources. Central government assumes full responsibility for salaries and other remunerations to staff who serve on the district assemblies. The statutory stipulations for both the annual Division of Revenue Act (which governs the distribution of nationally raised revenue to the spheres of government) and the constitutionally mandated District Assemblies' Common Fund envisage a degree of fiscal independence for local government. These regulations exist to provide a basis for a rational and predictable source of revenue, structured intergovernmental relationships, and therefore enhanced accountability of local government to citizens.

As is pointed out by Goel (2010), there are significant weaknesses in the financial decentralization process in Ghana. Notably, there is a lack of policy on fiscal decentralization to guide local government. Consequently, existing legislation and administrative procedures on local government finance have led to centralization of the management of public finances. Crawford (in Goel 2010) adds that despite the extensive responsibilities decentralized to district authorities, their financial position is weak. Local government has little fiscal independence, remaining overwhelmingly dependent on central government for its financial resources and its own limited revenue-raising ability. Gyimah-Boadi (2010) sums it up when he maintains that although local governments are given autonomy over finance, control from the central government takes away that power from the local people. The districts do not have the capacity to manage their own finances, and even the District Assemblies' Common Fund is controlled by the central government.

Service Provision and Participation

The NPM reforms that accompanied the introduction of the developmental local government concept in South Africa are concerned with how better to achieve the objectives of expanded, sustainable public services delivery. The maximum devolution is also aimed at creating a local government environment in which municipalities (and their public managers) are given flexibility in the use of resources but held accountable by citizens for results (Shah and Shah 2006). Top-down control by higher orders of government is to be replaced with bottom-up focus on results.

According to Atkinson (in Cameron 2004) the developmental local government concept and South Africa's flagship integrated development plan for local government call for a shift from basic service provision to a focus on infrastructural services toward local socioeconomic development. To a large extent, this is in line with devolution of authority. However, due to the dearth of capacity and skills within most municipalities, planning has tended to be short term and often reflects isolated projects instead of programs that give meaning to integrated development. It could also have the negative side effect of exacerbating inequalities, especially those between the rural and urban municipal areas. A coordinating role for the provincial government, in line with decentralization, may be necessary.

Part of their autonomy depends on the control of delivery of services within the political jurisdiction that underpins accountability and responsiveness to the communities they serve. Community-driven development initiatives and programs are at the epicenter of decentralization and devolution. Some researchers are of the view that community-initiated and -driven programs hold the promise for meaningful community empowerment, poverty reduction efforts, and sustainability. However, institutional and investment arrangements that are needed to support such initiatives could be detrimental to devolution or public sector reform. This requires analysis of the core concepts and principles that undergird decentralization and devolution for local participatory development. Such analysis includes how the various political and institutional reforms undertaken at the local government level relate to each other and cumulatively contribute to producing the desired political, social, and economic impact on residents in the local government areas.

Developmental local government in South Africa has certain fundamental blueprints. First, there should be a local planning and development framework to support participatory planning, decentralized development with flexibility for public-private partnerships, and market-style management principles. Second, developmental local government should promote institutional restructuring of municipalities as constituents of local government, including the creation of categories of municipalities. Third, from its aim of working with communities, developmental local government is intended to give direct attention to resident communities. It should empower the historically marginaliszd, the poor, and other community groupings, improving local governance and broadening community participation in local democracy (Local Government: Municipal Systems Act 2000).

The local government restructuring following the multiparty dispensation in 1994 has also brought to the fore the role of traditional authorities in the democratic local government systems. The critique against the undemocratic nature of traditional customary systems of kings and chiefs cannot be overlooked, and the processes of reincorporation of these continue to pose long-term implications for the functioning of municipalities in rural areas. It may be argued that decentralization could accommodate the role of traditional rulers, especially in rural municipalities.

Another feature of public participation in local government in Africa and especially in South Africa is the participation of the youth. Young people are an important demographic and represent an intriguing group for local government participation and electoral mobilization because of their high-profile militancy and their numerical significance. The political participation of the youth in South Africa may be due to the important position the ANC Youth League enjoys in the ruling party.

In Ghana, the apolitical nature of district assemblies' representation offers room for comment. In a political environment that is as historically highly charged as Ghana's, any assumption that local government elections will be conducted without political implications is frankly unrealistic. The objective of having government nominees was to provide a balanced representation for categories such as women, traditional authorities, and technocrats. However, as pointed out by Goel (2010), in many cases, party activists are appointed, thus killing the noble objective of the provision. On average, women represent less than 15% of electoral candidates and are discouraged from running for office by monetary requirements, gender bias, lack of political will, and male-dominated political parties (Carter Center, in Goel 2010). Azongo (2009) also criticizes the district assembly system as a major conceptual challenge in Ghana's decentralization program, with its "lop-sidedness and unilateral focus" on district assemblies as a central government creation at the local level. Also under strain is the perceived nonpartisan aspect of election of members of district assemblies. In the opinion of Gyimah-Boadi (2010), the nonpartisan concept of decentralization has become enmeshed with party politics.

Decentralized and devolved local government systems are designed to enable citizen participation of individuals, households, and community groups in processes and decision making for improved service provision. Meaningful participation refers to a real possibility for communities, groups, and individuals to express choices and realize desired actions and outcomes (World Bank 2004).

Conclusion

Examining comparable local institutions performing similar functions in the formulation and execution of the collective will at the local level in different countries is to comprehend the complexities of political and governmental processes. Public demands and expectations have focused attention on the enabling environment for local government and how effectively these governance structures meet community needs. The decentralization literature argues for a strong local government role in grassroots economic development, public services provision, and accountable governance to improve the quality of life. We argue that Ghana has a decentralized system, compared to a devolved system in South Africa. The devolution of authority to local government in South Africa is provided with more extensive constitutional protection than the decentralized Ghanaian system, which is significantly weaker in many respects.

However, the constitutions of both countries acknowledge the relative importance of local government in the provision of public services, broadening of democratic ethos, and enhancement of public accountability in the performance of public functions. There are also variations in the established institutions and their respective responsibilities in Ghana and South Africa.

References

Antwi-Boasiako, K.B. 2010. Public administration, local government and decentralization in Ghana. *Journal of African Studies and Development* 2: 166–175.

Ayee, J.R.A. 2008. The balance sheet of decentralization in Ghana. In *Foundations for local governance. Decentralization in comparative perspective*, ed. F. Saito. Accra: Book Chaper International.

Azongo, N. 2009. Local government and decentralized Ghana. From http://www.ghanaweb (accessed May 8, 2012).

Botes, P.S., Brynard, P.A., Fourie, D.J., and Roux, L. 1997. *Public administration and management: A guide to central, regional and municipal administration and management.* Pretoria: Kagiso Tertiary.

Cameron, R. 2004. South African local government: The limits of institutional reform? Paper presented at Hurst Seminar on Reform and Democracy in Local Government of Countries in Transition, Ben Gurion University of the Negev, Beer Sheva, Israel, May 23–24, 2004.

Craythorne, D.L. 1997. *Municipal administration: A handbook.* 4th ed. Cape Town: Juta.

Dubois, H.F.W., and Fattore, G. 2009. Definitions and typologies in public administration research: The case of decentralization. *International Journal of Public Administration* 32(8): 704–727.

Goel, P.R. 2010. Other country decentralization experiences: Ghana. In *National Council of Applied Research*, April 2010.

Gyimah-Boadi, E. 2010. Reflection on Ghana's decentralization programme: Progress, stagnation or retrogression. From http://www.ghanaweb.com.

Hattingh, J.J. 1988. *Governmental relations: An introduction.* Pretoria: Unisa Press.

ILGS. 2010. Local government system in Ghana.

Litvack, J. 2010. Different forms of decentralization. From http://www.ciesin.org/decentralization (accessed May 9, 2012).

Manor, J. 1999. *The political economy of democratic decentralisation. Directions in development.* Washington, DC: World Bank.

Mawhood, P., eds. 1993. *Local government in the third world: Experiences of decentralisation in tropical Africa.* 2nd ed. Pretoria: African Institute of South Africa.

Meiring, M.H. 2000. Evaluation of inter-governmental relationships in South Africa with specific reference to local authorities. In *Handbook of global political policy*, (pp. 105–128), ed. S.S. Nagel. New York: Marcel Dekker.

Oates, W. 1972. *Fiscal federalism.* New York: Harcourt Brace Jovanovich.

Parnell, S., Piterse, E., Swilling, M., and Wooldridge, D. 2002. *Democratising local government: The South African experiment.* Landsdowne: University of Cape Town Press.

Razin, E. 2003. Needs and impediments for local government reform: Lessons from Israel. Unpublished paper. Jerusalem: The Hebrew University.

Republic of Ghana. 1992. Constitution of the Republic of Ghana. Accra: Government Printer.

Republic of Ghana. 1993. Local Government Act, No. 462. Accra: Government Printer.

Republic of South Africa. 1996. Constitution of the Republic of South Africa. Pretoria: Government Printer.

Republic of South Africa. 1998a. *The white paper on local government.* Pretoria: Government Printer.

Republic of South Africa. 1998b. Local Government: Municipal Structures Act. Pretoria: Government Printer.

Republic of South Africa: Department of Provincial Affairs and Constitutional Development. 1998. *The white paper on local government.* Pretoria: Government Printer.

Shah, A., ed. 2005. *Public services delivery.* Washington, DC: World Bank.

Shah, A., and Shah, S. 2006. The new vision of local governance and the evolving roles of local governments. In *Local governance in developing countries*, (pp. 1–46), ed. A. Shah. Washington, DC: World Bank.

Sharma, K.C. 2010. Book review: Local government and decentralization in Ghana. *Commonwealth Journal of Local Governance* 7: 240–245.

Steytler, N., ed. 2005. *The place and role of local government in federal systems*. Occasional papers. Johannesburg: Konrad-Adenauer-Stiftung.

van de Walle, N., Ball, N., and Ramachandram, V. (Eds). 2003. *Beyond structural adjustment: The institutional context of African development*. New York: Palgrave Macmillan.

World Bank. 2004. *Measuring empowerment: An analytical framework*. PREM Empowerment Team. Washington, DC: World Bank.

Wunsch, J., and Olowu, D. (Eds). 1990. *The failure of the centralised state: Institutions and self-governance in Africa*. Boulder: Westview Press.

Chapter 11

Integrating Traditional Leadership Structures with Contemporary Public Administration Machinery for Innovative Governance and Improved Service Delivery

Shikha Vyas-Doorgapersad and
Lukamba-Muhiya. Tshombe

Contents
Introduction..210
Overview of Traditional Leadership...211
Traditional Leadership Structures versus Modern Governance............................212
    Traditional Leadership Structures: The Case of Selected African Countries ...212

Paradigm Shift in Traditional Leadership 215
Integration of Traditional Leadership Structures in Modern Systems of
Governance... 217
Traditional Leadership and Local Governance... 218
The Way Forward 219
Conclusion.. 220
References 221

Introduction

Diverse forms of governance institutions exist globally to deal with issues such as traditional customs, rules, and traditions in indigenous systems and ethnic groups where chiefs or traditional leaders have exercised leadership functions for generations. These structures were established to express the belief systems of particular societal groups. In a changing modernizing sociopolitical environment, the need has arisen to bring the essence of traditional leadership into the mainstream of democracy for improved governance.

A debate is ongoing to identify ways to integrate traditional leadership into the modern public administration. Representatives from diverse indigenous communities, including organizations and networks from Latin America and the Caribbean, Asia, Africa, and North America, all of them part of the global indigenous community, met in Rio de Janeiro in 1992 at the Rio 92 Convention to explore the significance of indigenous communities in the process of sustainable development of their communities and their countries. At this conference, the Global Indigenous Peoples' Caucus issued the Kari-Oca Declaration of Indigenous Peoples, which accords recognition to traditional leaders as one of the important role players in sustainable development.

A follow-up of the Rio 92 Convention was held in Johannesburg, South Africa, in 2002, and at this conference more than 100 heads of state gave their consensus to implement the Kimberley Declaration and the Indigenous People's Framework for Sustainable Development. A major landmark of this convention was the listing of the phrase "indigenous people" by the United Nations Declaration on the Rights of Indigenous Peoples (UNDRIP), which was officially adopted in 2007.

The latest development in the process is a global preparatory meeting of indigenous peoples at Kari-Oca 2 held in Brazil in 2011. The aim of this meeting was to bring indigenous people into the preparatory process of the UN Conference on Sustainable Development. This decision of engaging indigenous people in the process of sustainable development is a crucial milestone toward integrating them into the public administration realm.

This chapter describes the meaning of traditional leadership, and makes careful use of the available literature to explore the significance of traditional leadership for improved governance and public services. The chapter holistically explains the historical background of traditional leadership as a foundational milestone to explore the status and role of traditional leaders in society in the promotion of sustainable development. The chapter will focus on traditional leadership in African countries.

Overview of Traditional Leadership

African communities (and later countries) were originally ruled by traditional leaders; they were political heads with strong family orientation, and they imposed customary laws to maintain order among their people and rule their communities. This precolonial era, when the economy was regulated on a family basis, can therefore be considered an era of communalism. The family orientation began to fade with time, when family members gradually became scattered geographically for better occupation prospects and, in the process, developed their own territorial authorities.

Because of a degree of failure experienced in the traditional communal approach, in the 1960–1970 period of the post-colonial era, most African countries followed a socialist-oriented system of governance. This also proved largely unworkable because socialism tended to cause ethnic tension between communities. A paradigm shift occurred during the 1980s, when some African states considered adopting the neoliberal approach and implemented a range of Structural Adjustment Programs for development. However, this approach brought dissatisfaction because of the failed implementation of development initiatives.

Moreover, colonialism had brought with it "two contrasting systems for ruling the indigenous African population. The first system was to try and weaken the institution of chieftaincy and govern through the colonial bureaucracy ... the second was to rely on local indigenous rulers to administer and control the local population in a system of 'indirect rule'" (Beall and Ngonyama 2009, p. 8). Traditional leadership structures were therefore weakened and destabilized by the scramble for Africa and the onset of colonialism.

The outcome of this was that distant and remote government structures in urban centers became inaccessible to scattered rural African communities, creating the necessity to reconsider the values and cultures of indigenous approaches to governance and to integrate them into the modern administrative and state structures. This is an area of continuous debate. There are neotraditionalists who argue that traditional leadership structures should be set up to regulate matters of concern to local community members, and thus ensure that they enjoy a safe and secure environment. On the other hand, there are neoliberalists who argue that in the post-colonial era the communities that fell under traditional leaders were not accorded basic representative rights, and this goes against the notion of democracy.

Traditional Leadership Structures versus Modern Governance

Traditional Leadership Structures: The Case of Selected African Countries

There are various existing structures that recognize the values of the traditional tribal culture of indigenous ethnic communities, including traditional leaders, chiefs, amakhosi, and kings (the names vary from country to country). These structures were established to give credence to the belief systems, values, and practices of particular societies.

The traditional organogram in the African continent incorporates the king as the supreme authority. In some African chieftaincies there are certain levels of authority below that of the king, known variously as mambo, thobela, tautona, and ngwenyama. Below these vertical levels, there is a horizontal level that includes the chief. The chief is head of the khosi, kgosi, and inkosi. Below this horizontal level there is another sphere of authority that includes the ward head, legota, nduna, and tona. These structures independently (at their levels) and collectively serve the administrative, judicial, civil, and political portfolios.

A traditional leadership title in Africa is not elected; instead, it is based on hereditary rule and passes, according to custom, from one generation to the next. The traditional leadership structure in Africa differs from one tribe to another. There are tribal or ethnic groups where there are kings and other dignitaries, but in sub-Saharan Africa not all tribal societies have kings.

In the Democratic Republic of Congo (DRC) there are over 400 ethnic groups, making it one of the most diverse countries on the continent. When the colonial powers and missionaries arrived in the DRC in the late nineteenth century they relied largely on traditional authorities as a link with the indigenous people at large. According to Kostner (2005) traditional authorities were first undermined by the Mobutu government. However, with time a close relationship developed between traditional leaders and their constituency; thus their position was reinforced through cooperation during the later years of the second republic (1965–1997).

Currently, all the ethnic groups or tribes in the DRC are organized into collectivities, with each collectivity being based on a specific lineage. Collectivities are in turn divided into group and villages. Collectivities are monoethnic groups, but often tribes have blood ties with neighboring collectivities. The tribe's traditional boundaries are the basis for the modern administrative boundaries (Kostner 2005). The collectivity is the lowest administrative structure and is headed by a chief (called *mfumu* in Kikongo); it has been established in different tribal societies in the province of Bas-Congo. These traditional authorities play a double role in the village because in addition to their traditional powers, they represent the state in the village. The new DRC constitution that came into force in 2006 formally recognized this dual role of traditional leaders. Article 207 in the DRC constitution (2006) stipulates (in the original French):

> L'autorité coutumière est reconnue. Elle est dévolue conformément a la coutume locale, pour autant que celle-ci ne soit pas contraire à la constitution, a la loi, à l'ordre public et aux bonnes mœurs. Tout chef coutumier désireux d'exercer un mandat public électif doit se soumettre a l'élection, sauf application des dispositions de l'article 198 alinéa 3 de la présente constitution.

The English translation follows:

> The traditional authority is acknowledged by the DRC constitution. It follows the local custom. Without contravening the constitution, all traditional authorities that want to be member of parliament should go through an electoral process. They must respect the law and have good manners, except the application of ACT 198 Section 3 of the current constitution.

For example, if a traditional leader in the DRC wishes to be involved in a political career, he or she must go through an electoral process to be elected by the relevant constituency. In the case of the DRC the traditional authority does not play a significant role in the governance of the country as a whole.

The case of Uganda is completely different from that of the DRC. In Uganda there is a monarchy, a kingdom of the Ganda people, called Buganda. It is the largest of the traditional kingdoms in Uganda that still exists today. The Buganda Kingdom comprises the entire central region of the country and includes Kampala, the capital city. This ethnic group is the largest in Uganda, with a population of 5.5 million Buganda. In the singular form individuals are called a Muganda, which is an adjective derived from Ganda (Basheka 2012).

Buganda has a long, extensive history. The kingdom was unified in the fourteenth century under the first king, King Kato Kintu, the founder of Buganda's Kintu Dynasty. Buganda grew to become one of the largest and most powerful states in East Africa during the eighteenth and nineteenth centuries. During the scramble for Africa, and following unsuccessful attempts to retain its independence against Britain, Buganda became the central region of the Uganda Protectorate in 1894; the name of Uganda, the Swahili term for Buganda, was subsequently adopted by the British authorities. Under British rule, many Buganda acquired the status of colonial administrators, and Buganda became a major producer of cotton and coffee.

The organizational structure of the Buganda Kingdom's administration is as follows:

- His majesty the king (Kabaka)
- Prime minister (Katikkiro)

- Parliament (the Lukiiko)
- Executive (the secretariat of the Buganda Kingdom)
- Hierarchy of lower councils and their executives, down to the village level
- The Buganda Investment and Commercial Undertakings Ltd. (BICUL)
- The Buganda Cultural and Development Foundation (BUCADEF)

In Uganda there is also another kingdom, the Bunyoro Kingdom, which is located in midwestern Uganda. Bunyoro was once a powerful empire, and at the height of its glory it included parts of present-day western Kenya, northern Tanzania, and the eastern part of DRC (Tumusiime 2007). Both Buganda and Bunyoro play a major role in influencing local authorities' decisions, especially in matters concerning service delivery in their kingdoms.

Turning to the situation in South Africa, the central government recognizes the role of traditional leaders. There is Act No. 41 of 2003, which recognizes the kingships and the king per se. There are many traditional kings in South Africa, for example, the well-known Zulu Kingdom in South Africa under King Zwelithini Goodwill Ka Bhekuzulu. The South African constitution (1996) stipulates the role of the king as a ceremonial leader. Besides the king there are also princes, such as Chief Mangosuthu Buthelezi, the leader of the political party (with strong cultural roots) called the Inkatha Freedom Party. He plays a role similar to that of premier in the Zulu Kingdom and acts as a special adviser to the king.

There is also a wealthy kingdom in the North West Province, the Bafokeng Kingdom, ruled by a king who is known as Kgosi Leruo Tshekedi Molotlegi. The Bafokeng Supreme Council is made up of hereditary headmen; elected and appointed men and women who form the traditional legislature must abide by Bafokeng customary law and the South African constitution (1996).

According to Kgosi Leruo Tshekedi Molotlegi (2004) in the case of South Africa, traditional leaders, including members of traditionally governed communities, are not opponents of the national government, but are rather its constituents, ready to participate in the wider national debate. What is needed is a good mindset, in which traditional structures are viewed as valuable partners rather than as competitors or opponents of African democracies.

It has been observed that many African countries find it difficult to cooperate fully with traditional leaders. Some have reduced the authority of traditional leaders and take little if any cognizance of their input in government decision making.

The role of traditional leaders in South Africa is recognized in the constitution (1996). Most of them play a significant role in the integrated development planning process, which is a five-year program involving local municipalities. Their advice and input is taken into consideration by the relevant local authorities, especially for the development of their constituencies.

Looking at the Ghanaian experience in terms of traditional leadership, since the colonial period the traditional leaders in Ghana have been involved in local governance of their communities. According to Ayee (2007, pp. 1–2) there is no controversy about the role of traditional authorities in local governance and the development of Ghana:

> Those who favour the membership of chiefs in local government units in general, argue that traditionally, the traditional authority is the leader of his people and that despite the decline of chieftaincy as an institution, traditional authorities still command great influence in their areas of jurisdiction.

The Ghanaian constitution recognizes the role traditional leaders play for the development of their people. In all five constitutions of Ghana (in 1957, 1960, 1969, 1979, and 1972), the local leaders do feature (Republic of Ghana, 1992). Furthermore, the Chieftaincy Act, No. 370 of 1971, was passed by Busia's Progress Party government in September 1971 to change the statute law on chieftaincy to align it with the provisions of the 1969 constitution. The same constitution made certain provisions on the role of the chieftaincy and also created a National House of Chiefs, which was duly included in the 1979 and 1992 constitutions (Ayee 2007). The Ghanaian constitution (1992) also established a system of chiefly councils. This has three levels: (1) the National House of Chiefs, (2) the Regional Houses of Chiefs, and (3) traditional councils.

The National House of Chiefs comprises five paramount chiefs elected by each of the 10 Regional Houses of Chiefs. In other words, there are 50 members in the National House of Chiefs. Furthermore, in the provinces where there are fewer than five paramount chiefs, the Regional Houses of Chiefs is authorized to elect such number of divisional chiefs to make up the required representation of the chiefs for the region (Ayee 2007).

Looking at the structure and significance of traditional leadership in these selected African countries, it is clear that their role differs from one state to another. The examples provided show that in some of the countries, especially those in former British colonies in sub-Saharan Africa, a great deal has been done to promote the role of traditional leaders at the local government level. By the use of a comparative approach in selected countries, the level of accommodation of traditional authority into the modern state governance has been indicated.

Paradigm Shift in Traditional Leadership

To bring traditional leaders into the mainstream of modern public administration has proved to be a challenge to democratic nation-states in Africa. On the one hand, conferences are being held to bring increased recognition to traditional leaders. On the other hand, bureaucratic portfolios are being restructured and new bodies being established to enhance public administration structures to meet the new social and political demands of modern states. There is a paradigm shift from being localized to becoming globalized. In this changed scenario of excessive administrative, managerial, and political demands, it is imperative to reassess the role of traditional leadership in the process of governance. This paradigm leads to a number of critical questions: Is traditional leadership equipped to deal with the demands of twenty-first-century public administration? Will traditional leaders be considered "co-role-players" in public policy making? Will the modern bureaucracy adopt the traditional leadership approaches in the decision-making processes? What is the point of commonality to integrate traditional leadership into the modern public administration for improved governance and enhanced public services?

In order to look for answers to these questions, a number of treaties were signed to recognize the role of traditional leaders in modern bureaucratic systems. An agreement known as the Treaty of Waitangi was signed between the government of New Zealand and indigenous societies, with the aim of enhancing tribal participation in the affairs of governance. A treaty of a similar nature was signed between the government of Canada and certain indigenous societies to recognize the status of their so-called first nation people. In terms of this agreement the government is responsible for settling tribal claims by granting them land or cash compensation. In its constitution, the United States recognizes the indigenous Indian societies as "domestic dependent nations." The U.S. government has furthermore signed a treaty with the Native American people whereby a federal trust is established to enhance the relationship between the government and the traditional communities.

As for the African continent, Botswana's constitution makes provision for a National House of Chiefs that has an advisory role to participate in the executive and legislative branches of government. A similar constitutional obligation is supported by Ghana, where a National House of Chiefs and Regional Houses of Chiefs have been established. Kenya also recognizes the customary laws in its magistrate courts. Namibia, too, gives due recognition to traditional leaders and respects their customary laws. In terms of its constitution, the traditional institutions and authories in Namibia are obliged to participate in the affairs of governance by supporting public policies. As for South Africa, the government has established a National House of Traditional Leaders and Provincial Houses of Traditional Leaders to recognize the significance of traditional leadership, particularly in rural areas. The Swazi Administration Order of 1998 obliges traditional leaders (chiefs) in Swaziland to act as a catalyst between the central government and indigenous communities.

Furthermore, significant workshops are being organized to explore the issue of integrating traditional leadership into the modern public administration. Among these the United Nations Economic Commission for Africa (UNECA) organized the Fourth African Development Forum in 2004 on the theme "Governance for a Progressing Africa." Here the roles and responsibilities of traditional leadership systems in the modern state were discussed at length. The delegates agreed that it is not an issue of whether "the traditional and modern systems of governance are competing against each other, but how to integrate the two systems most effectively to better serve citizens in terms of representation, participation and public service delivery" (Kargbo 2011, p. 6). Moreover, in 2007 a workshop was organized in Johannesburg, South Africa, on harnessing traditional governance in Southern Africa to explore mechanisms of integrating traditional leadership structures into the mainstream of modern government structures. The idea behind this workshop was to improve governance and public services through incorporation of two diversified systems of governance.[*] At another international conference on traditional leadership in Durban, South Africa, also in 2007, the premier of KwaZulu-Natal, S.J. Ndebele (2007, p. 1), stressed the necessity for integration of traditional leadership into the modern governance structure. He emphasized that traditional leadership is an

> institution that works for development in partnership with the rest of government, civil society and communities; an institution that relentlessly promotes the values of Ubuntu,[†] and in every way helps to deepen our democracy and expand the access of our people to its benefits.

Integration of Traditional Leadership Structures in Modern Systems of Governance

In African countries traditional leadership plays an important role in the social, economic, political, and cultural aspects of communities. Indeed, chieftaincy has the capacity to work effectively alongside modern government structures. This assertion was discussed at length at a workshop organized by the United Nations Economic Commission for Africa in Addis Ababa in 2006. The underlying principle of the workshop was to discuss the significance of harmonizing traditional and modern governance structures for social and economic transformation in Africa. The consensus was that the official, formal, or prescribed establishments of the state are that

> rules regulating the structure of polity, property rights, and contracting, cannot be effective if they fail to advance the interests of large segments of the population and disregard or contradict the traditional institutions which govern the lives and livelihoods of large segments of the population. (Kidani 2006, p. 1)

---

[*] Comprehensive and detailed information on both these workshops is provided in J. Kargbo, "Harnessing Traditional Governance in Southern Africa: South Africa," United Nations Economic Commission for Africa, 2011, http://www.hsrc.ac.za/research/output/outputDocuments/4922_Amoateng_Harnessingtraditionalgovernance.pdf.

[†] Ubuntu is a belief that emerged in the southern region of Africa. Its emotional meaning is well expressed in the statement "I am because we are and because we are, you are. [Ubuntu] … encapsulates a profound understanding of human interconnectedness. It is a statement of being" (Naidoo 2010, p. 1).

Moreover, at the 2007 Johannesburg conference on traditional governance (mentioned above), the objective was to identify ways to integrate traditional leadership structures into central government structures. The core focus of the discussion between traditional leaders and other stakeholders was to amalgamate the traditional and modern government structures for improved governance and enhanced delivery of localized services.

The workshop paved the way for exploring the role of traditional leaders in modern governance, and there was extensive discussion on how they could be drawn into policy-making processes in an advisory capacity. The decentralized system of local government, as in South Africa, offers opportunities for these leaders to play a participatory role in grassroots governance. With the advancement of technologies, particularly in urban areas but also to some extent in most rural areas, the possibility has emerged for traditional leaders to perform a developmental role, offering feedback comments on projects and improvements in their communities. Furthermore, their traditional role in conflict resolution could be utilized; traditional leaders could become an integral part of the modern judicial system. Another of the leading arguments at the Johannesburg workshop was that traditional leaders and municipalities must cooperate closely by sharing information and resources for improved service delivery. There should also be cooperation between these authorities to conduct a needs assessment. When the needs of the various communities have been identified, traditional leaders should be given the opportunity to participate in strategic policy-making processes at the grassroots level. In other words, traditional leaders must be given mandates to participate in community-based projects.

Traditional Leadership and Local Governance

Traditional leaders can play an important developmental role in the local government sphere. In most African countries chieftaincy is still seen as the core of the local political milieu. There are

> still wide areas in Africa where no development is possible unless it is routed through the traditional leaders and is backed by them. It may be necessary to re-examine the position of chiefs in decentralization efforts and consider a meaningful role for chiefs in local affairs. (ADF IV Traditional Governance Focus Group 2003)

This can be witnessed in some African countries, notably Botswana, Ghana, Ivory Coast, Liberia, Sierra Leone, South Africa, and Zambia, where the paramount chieftaincy plays an important role in the affairs of local governance. The responsibilities of traditional leaders in these countries are predominantly conflict resolution, complemented by the implementation of customary laws to manage local justice; consultation on matters of governance; lobbying; and other advisory responsibilities.

At a conceptual level, it is suggested that "poly-centric decentralized democratic governance" be adopted to provide "an appropriate model for integrating the traditional into the modern. This is a system with 'multiple decision-making centres' which interact to solve common problems and the management of collective resources" (ACE Electoral Knowledge Network 2011, p. 1). This approach has the potential to promote an integrated relationship between the traditional and modern African governance structures, given that many indigenous societies have a "tradition of collectively sharing responsibilities within a common framework" (ACE Electoral Knowledge Network 2011, p. 1).

The Way Forward

In the precolonial era, traditional leaders in Africa held sway over administrative, cultural, social, and political aspects of daily life in indigenous societies. Over time, with the onset of colonialism followed by decolonization, the formation of new democracies, and the introduction of modern, decentralized systems of governance, traditional African leaders faced the challenge of becoming an integral part of modern bureaucracies. This challenge was exacerbated by a lack of resources and capacity-building programs to train and prepare them to adopt and adapt to the new environment of governance.

Discussions are ongoing, but there is a need to implement strategic decisions to incorporate traditional leadership into the mainstream of governance in the modern state. Relevant recommendations include steps to encourage the acceptance of traditional leadership by modern bureaucracies and the recognition of traditional leadership by the political authorities at all levels. In particular, the involvement of traditional leaders in the policy-making process must be sped up because they are important stakeholders for development and improved service delivery, particularly in rural areas. Mechanisms must be established to offer capacity-building programs so that traditional leaders are able to enhance their understanding of how modern public administration functions. It is important, for example, that they become accountable in the fulfillment of the norms of good governance and are consulted on the formulation of local by-laws and other grassroots policies. They must also be drawn into the implementation of development projects that are of benefit for their communities.

Miles (1993, p. 31) suggests that "linkage or 'brokering' between grassroots and capital; extension of national identity through the conferral of traditional titles; low-level conflict resolution and judicial gate-keeping; ombudsmanship; and institutional safety-value for overloaded and sub-apportioned bureaucracies" may be used as the means of integrating traditional leaders into the structures of modern public administration. He adds that "creating educated chieftaincies significantly enhances the effectiveness of traditional rulers' contributions to development and administration."

Conclusion

This debate is ongoing. There is a need to reach a consensus on whether, in Africa,

> traditional chiefs and elders [are indeed] the true representatives of their people, accessible, respected, and legitimate, and therefore still essential to politics on the continent, and especially to the building of democracies. Or is traditional authority a gerontocratic, chauvinistic, authoritarian and increasingly irrelevant form of rule that is antithetical to democracy? (Logan 2008)

In most African countries, especially in the sub-Saharan region, the traditional customs and practices are indeed significant and are necessary to understand and accommodate the needs of the disadvantaged members of society. One of these traditional customs is known as the *mafisa system*[*] and is a valued practice in rural communities, where it fulfills an economic and development objective. Due to the emergence of colonial rule, the rising demands of globalization, and the inconclusive debate on traditionalist versus modernist outlooks, many of the age-old traditional customs have fallen into disuse.

African countries are culturally rich; indigenous people set great store by the belief systems that have become enmeshed in their ethnic and traditional structures. With the changed social, political, economical, and technological environment, pressure has been imposed on traditional authorities to adapt to a new and ever-changing sociopolitical environment and be prepared to adopt new strategies in order to become an integral part of the modern system of governance. There is often a misinterpretation of the concept of adoption while implementing the term in practice. Adoption does not mean changing, abandoning, altering, or moving away from existing beliefs and values. Instead, it means reworking, accepting that "new innovations from outside [can] ... be replaced by strategies of endogenous development, 'development from within' ... [and that] outsiders can build up relationships with traditional leaders" (Haverkort, Millar, and Gonese 2011, p. 152). This implies discussing local/tribal/rural issues on agriculture, the utilization of natural resources, farm management, etc. Furthermore, this requires adaptation so that new innovations can be initiated and new ideas generated about traditional leadership structures. Concerted deliberations with all stakeholders must generate new thoughts, concepts, and innovations. This will enable traditional societies to "incorporate new ideas into their body politic without loosing the essential elements of their own traditions, and also make the new concepts understandable" (Senyonjo 2012, p. 5).

---

[*] The mafisa system is a Basotho traditional custom of loaning economic resources (usually cattle) to others, who are able to make claim to some of the produce and (in the case of cattle), to the offspring, but do not have ownership rights of the original loaned resources.

References

ACE Electoral Knowledge Network. 2011. Paramount chieftaincy as a system of local government. http://aceproject.org/electoral-advice/archive/questions/replies/177154637 (accessed April 12, 2012).

Ayee, J.R.A. 2007. Traditional leadership and local governance in Africa: The Ghanaian experience. Paper presented at the Fourth National Annual Local Government Conference "Traditional Leadership and Local Governance in a Democratic South Africa: Quo Vadis?" Durban, July 30–31.

Basheka, B. 2012. Traditional leadership structure in Uganda (email correspondence). Kampala: Uganda Management Institute.

Beall, J., and Ngonyama, M. 2009. Indigenous institutions, traditional leaders and developmental coalitions: The case of Greater Durban, South Africa. Developmental Leadership Programme: Policy and Practice for Developmental Leaders, Elites and Coalitions. From http://www.dlprog.org (accessed April 7, 2012).

Constitution de la République Démocratique du Congo. Kinshasa: Government Congolais.

Ghana, Republic of (1992). Constitution of the Republic of Ghana, 1992. Tema: Ghana Publishing Corporation.

Haverkort, B., Millar, D., and Gonese, C. 2011. Knowledge and belief systems in sub-Saharan Africa. From http://www.compasnet.org/blog/wp-content/uploads/2011/03/ARNS/arns_14.pdf (accessed April 10, 2012).

Kargbo, J. 2011. *Harnessing traditional governance in Southern Africa.* Cape Town: United Nations Economic Commission for Africa.

Kidani, A.B. 2006. Human development: Relevance of African traditional institutions in governance. *Sudan Vision—An Independent Daily.* From http://www.sudanvisiondaily.com/modules.php?name=News&file=article&sid=49770 (accessed April 12, 2012).

Kostner, M. 2005. *Toward inclusive and sustainable development in the Democratic Republic of the Congo.* Washington, DC: World Bank. From http://www.worldbank.org (accessed June 10, 2012).

Logan, C. 2008. Traditional leaders in modern Africa: Can democracy and the chief co-exist? Afrobarometer Working Paper 93. Cape Town: Institute for a Democratic Alternative for South Africa (IDASA).

Miles, W.F.S. 1993. Traditional rulers and development administration: Chieftaincy in Niger, Nigeria and Vanuatu. *Studies in Comparative International Development* 28(3): 31–50.

Molotlegi, L.T. 2004. *Traditional leadership for a progressing Africa.* Addis Ababa: Africa Union.

Naidoo, M. 2010. The meaning of Ubuntu. From http://www.muthalnaidoo.co.za/articles-and-papers-othermenu-86/244-the-meaning-of-ubuntu (accessed April 15, 2012).

Ndebele, S.J. 2007. *South African Ndebele: International conference on traditional leadership.* Pietermaritzburg: KwaZulu-Natal Provincial Government.

Senyonjo, J. 2012. Traditional leaders. Introduction, Part I. From https://docs.google.com/viewer?a=v&q=cache:TwdXRwpf43YJ:www.federo.org (accessed February 2, 2012).

South Africa. 2003. Traditional Leadership and Governance Framework Amendment Act, No. 41 of 2003. Pretoria: Government Printer.

Traditional Governance Focus Group. 2003. ADF IV Traditional Governance Focus Group. Issues Paper. From https://docs.google.com/viewer?a=v&q=cache:XODu5dRvSuwJ:www.uneca (accessed April 10, 2012).

Tumusiime, J. 2007. *Uganda the pearl.* Kampala: Tourguide Publication.

Index

A

Ababio, Ernest P., *ix–x*, 153–164, 187–205
Abidine Ben Ali, Zine El, 163
Accelerated and Shared Growth Initiative for South Africa (ASGI-SA), 101
"Accelerating Decentralization and Local Governance for National Development," 140
acceptance of solicitations, 71–72
accountability
    administrative systems context, Uganda, 57
    cornerstone of democracy, 62
    good governance, 155
    health care sector, 89
    ministers, executive authority, 19
    public sector dysfunction, 90
Accra, 194
Accra Agenda for Action, 123
ACCU, *see* Anticorruption Coalition Uganda (ACCU)
Act 81-003/17/07/1981, 36–37
Act 82-006/25/02/1982, 37
activities and employment, informal sector, 104–107
adaptability, 114
administrative capacity, building, 19–20
Administrative Staff College of Nigeria (ASCON), 91
administrative systems context, 54–59
AFDL, *see* Alliance des Forces Democratiques pour la liberation du Congo (AFDL)
Africa Day, 111
African Development Bank, 141, 148–149, 179
African Governance Report II, 136
African National Congress (ANC), 127, 129, 204
African Peer Review Mechanism (APRM)

    benefits of process, 160–161
    democracy and governance, 155
    historical developments, 153–155
    lapses of process, 160–161
    losses, 50
    matrix, promoting public service reform, 158–159
    objective, 160
    overview, 156
    promoting public service reform, 158–159
    public service reform, 156, 158–160
    states without review, 161, 163
    structural functioning, 157–159
    successes and failures mechanisms and initiatives, 6
    summary, 163–164
African Peer Review Ombuds (APRO), 161
African Union (AU)
    foreign direct investment, 184
    governance, 15, 155
    media role, 123
    policy-making process, 9
    revamping, 154
Afrobarameter, 6, 142
Agence Francaise de Developpement, 179
agricultural land, 173
Agricultural Revolution, 129
Algeria, 158, 161, 170
Ali, Zine El Abidine Ben, 163
alleviation paradigms, 101–102
Alliance des Forces Democratiques pour la liberation du Congo (AFDL), 40
All Media Product Study (AMPS), 127
alternative service delivery (ASD) model, 13
Alure people, 29
Amin, Idi, 56–57
AMPS, *see* All Media Product Study (AMPS)
Anany, Jerome, 34

223

ANC, *see* African National Congress (ANC)
Anglo-Belgian Indian Rubber Company, 30
Angola, 29, 158
Ankole Kingdom, 56
Annan, Kofi, 160
annual income and expenditure survey (IES), 14
antibribery ideal, 59
Anticorruption Act (2009), 71–72
Anticorruption Coalition Uganda (ACCU), 76
apparatus defined, 2
apparatus of government
  executive authority, 17–20
  judiciary authority, 21–22
  legislative authority, 20–21
  overview, 16–17
applications, government apparatus architecture, 5
APRO, *see* African Peer Review Ombuds (APRO)
APR panel, *see* Panel of Eminent Persons (APR panel)
arable agricultural land, 173
Arab spring, 154
architecture, governance apparatus, 4–8
Aristotle (philosopher), 2, 46
artisanal products, 105–106
Aruwimi, 32
ASCON, *see* Administrative Staff College of Nigeria (ASCON)
ASD, *see* Alternative service delivery (ASD) model
ASGI-SA, *see* Accelerated and Shared Growth Initiative for South Africa (ASGI-SA)
Asians, forceful expulsion, 57
Asmah-Andoh, Kwame, 187–205
AU, *see* African Union (AU)
Auditor-General Department, 148
Australia, 94
autonomy, 189, 198
Ayida, Alison, 84

B

Babangida, Ibrahim, 84
Bafokeng Kingdom, 214
Bafokeng Supreme Council, 214
Bamba, Emmanuel, 34
Bambili, 32
Bandundu, 28, 32
Bangala, 32
Banjo, Adewale, 83–130

Bantu-based languages, 29
Basankusu, 32
Bas-Congo
  background development, 28
  first reform measures (1914), 32
  history and political context, public administration, 30
  tribal societies, 212
Basheka, Benon C., 45–78
Basoko, 32
Basotho traditional custom, 220
Bas-Uele, 28, 32
Bas-Zaire, 36
BBC, *see* British Broadcasting Corporation (BBC)
Ben Ali, Zine El Abidine, 163
benefits
  African Peer Review Mechanism, 160–161
  informal sector, South Africa, 113–114
Benin, 158
Berelson, Bernard, 122
Berlin Conference (1885), 30
best practice case, *see* Mauritius
Bhekuzulu, King Zwelithini Goodwill Ka, 214
Binaisa, Godfrey, 57
Bloemfontein, 16, 22, 105
Boma, 32
Botswana
  health issues, 177
  human development index, 170
  traditional leadership integration, 216, 218
  transitional period, 41
bottom-up approach, 148
Brazil, *see* BRIC countries
bribes, *see* Corruption
BRIC countries
  agriculture, 184
  education and research, 177–178
  government financial control, 173
  health issues, 176, 177
  macro economic aspects, 172, 174
  population analysis, 171
  poverty and inequality index, 170
  rural development, 173
  safety and security, 175, 176
  unemployment, 172
  water and sewer access, 175
British Broadcasting Corporation (BBC), 120, 123
Broadcasting Act, No. 64 (2002), 125
brokering grassroots efforts, 219

Index ■ 225

budget considerations, *see* Service delivery and budget implementation plans (SDBIPs)
Buganda Kingdom, 56, 213
Bukenya, Gilbert, 59
Bunyoro Kingdom, 56, 214
bureaucratic corruption, 68–69, 71
Burkina Faso, 158
Burundi
    border with DRC, 29
    corruption perception, 48, 49
    human development index, 170
    South Africa's governance, 16
Busia's Progress Party, 215
Buta, 32
Buthelezi, Chief Mangosuthu, 214

C

Cameroon, 158, 172
Capacity Building Forum, 120–121
Cape Coast, 194
Cape Town, 16
capital, consolidation of, 182–183
car wash enterprises, 111
categories of municipalities, 198–205
Center for Management Development (CMD), 91
Central African Republic, 29
centralized decentralization, 148
central state apparatus, 189–190
Chad, 170
challenges, 62, 129
characteristics, informal sector, 103
chief executive officer (CEO), 200–202
Chieftaincy Act, No. 370 (1971), 215
child support grants, provider model, 101
China, 169, *see also* BRIC countries
Chisano, Joachim, 161
CHOGM, *see* Commonwealth Heads of Government Meeting (CHOGM)
Chokwe, 29
Cicero (philosopher), 3
citizens
    bearing burden, 63, 65
    civic education, 77
    corruption as normal way of life, 53–54
    decentralized and devolved systems, 205
    deracializing, 195
    government as virtual organization, 67
    media, socialization of people, 120
    participation in governance, lack of, 143
    social exclusion, poverty, 143
civic rights, 16
CMD, *see* Center for Management Development (CMD)
codes of conduct, 77
collective executive system, 201
colonial governance, 31–33
COMESA, *see* Common Market for Eastern and Southern Africa (COMESA)
commercialization, 13
Common Market for Eastern and Southern Africa (COMESA), 184
Commonwealth Heads of Government Meeting (CHOGM), 76, 184
Commonwealth Media Development and Capacity Building Forum, 120–121
Commonwealth Secretariat, 120
communalism, 211
communication
    media, constitutional mandates, 125–126
    public sector reform, 93
    two-step flow of, 122
community food gardens, 102
comparative analysis, Ghana and South Africa
    chief executive officer, 200–202
    decentralization and devolution, 190–193
    district chief executive officer, 200–202
    financial autonomy, 202–203
    intergovernmental relationships, 197–198
    local government, 188–190, 193–197
    local institutional arrangements, 198–205
    modern constitutions, 193–197
    municipality categories, 198–205
    overview, 188
    political scenarios, 197–198
    relevant legislative framework, 196–197
    service provision and participation, 203–205
    summary, 205
compensation, *see* Salaries and wages
Competition Act, No. 89 (1998), 125
competitiveness strategy, 182
complementary school of thought, 88
compliance report, 89
compliance school of thought, 87
Conference on Sustainable Development, 210
confiscation policies, focus on, 181
Congo, *see* Democratic Republic of Congo (DRC)
Congo-Central, 36
Congo-Kasai, 32
consolidation of capital, 182–183

constitution
- decentralization, 189–193
- financial autonomy, 202
- judiciary authority, 21
- local government recognition, 21
- mandates, 125–126
- media and good governance, 125–126
- municipalities with executive authority, 201
- municipality categories, 21
- recognition of languages, 16
- relevant legislative framework, 196
- role in Uganda, 74
- South African governance apparatus, 2–4, 16–17
- traditional leaders role, 214–215

contracting, 13
cooperative government, 22–23
coping strategies, 103
Coquilhatville, 32
core task, media, 124
co-role-players, 216
corporatization, 14
corrective basis for reforms, 87
corruption
- determinants of, 60–68
- education sector, 69–71
- effects of, 75–77
- elements of, 60
- endemic nature, 52, 55
- environment, 50–51
- institutional, 71
- judiciary sector, 71–73
- law and order sector, 71–72
- political, 71
- reports, Uganda, 49–50

Corruption Perception Index, *see also* Corruption
- Ghana, 142, 148
- Uganda, 48, 49

Cote d'Ivorie, 16, 161–163, 218
Countries at the Crossroads report, 52
Country Review Report, 136
courts, 22
credibility, 161
crops, 56
cyber-labs, 128

D

DAC, *see* Development Assistance Committee (DAC)
day laborers, informal, 104–105

DCE, *see* District chief executive (DCE) officer
decentralization and devolution
- comparative analysis, 188–190
- Democratic Republic of Congo, 37
- Ghana and South Africa comparative analysis, 190–196
- Ghana governance reform, 136–137, 140–142, 148
- modern constitutions, 193–197
- public service, DRC, 39
- relevant legislative framework, 197

"Decentralization and Local Government," 195
decision processes, two judgments, 35
Declaration on Democracy, Political, Economic and Corporate Governance, 157, 158
democracy
- African Peer Review Mechanism, 155
- concept of, 119, 155
- corruption threat to public institutions, 48
- Nigeria, 87–89, 91–93
- waves of, 126

Democratic Republic of Congo (DRC)
- background developments, 28–30
- colonial governance and government, 31–33
- ethnic groups, 29, 212
- first phase of reform (1960–1965), 33–36
- first reform measures (1914), 32
- historical context of public administration, 30–31
- human development index, 170
- independence, public administration after, 33–36
- overview, 28
- peer review, 158
- political context of public administration, 30–31
- public administration after independence, 33–36
- public administration structure in 1981, 36–40
- second phase of reform (1965–1997), 36
- second reform measures (1924), 32
- South Africa's governance, 16
- status of media, 126
- summary, 41–42
- third reform measures (1933), 32–33
- transitional period (1999–2011), 40–41

Demographic and Health Survey (2008), 137
demographic profile, respondents, 107
Deneysville, 100
Department of Communication (DoC), 128

Department of Cooperative Government and
    Traditional Affairs, 23
Department of Public Service and
    Administration, 158
dependence on foreign aid, 16
deracializing society, 195
determinants of corruption, 60–68
Development Assistance Committee (DAC), 16
devolution, see Decentralization and devolution
dictatorships, effect on media, 126
digital communications and media, 126, 128
Digital Terrestrial Television, 128
disability grants, provider model, 101
discrimination, 16
District Assemblies Common Fund Act (1993),
    137, 202–203
district chief executive (DCE) officer, 200–202
district courts, judiciary authority, 22
District Governance Citizen's Report Checklist,
    141
district municipalities, 21
diversification of economy, 179, 183
diversity, 14
Division of Revenue Act, 203
Djibouti, 158
documents, 68, 127
Doing Business Report, 185
domestic dependent nations, 216
DRC, see Democratic Republic of Congo
    (DRC)
dress code, 56
dressmakers, 109
dual role, traditional leaders, 213
Dubai, 107
Durban, 100, 217
duties on products, 179

E

earnings, see Salaries and wages
ease of doing business, 185
East African Bribery Index (2011), 50
Eastern Cap, 14
Easy African Submarine Cable Systems, 128
ECA, see Economic Commission for Africa
    (ECA); Electronic Communications
    Act, No. 36 (2005) (ECA)
Economic and Financial Crimes Commission
    of Nigeria (EFCC), 94
Economic Commission for Africa (ECA), 136
economic costs, corruption, 75–76
economic policy reform, Mauritius
    background developments, 178
    competitiveness strategy, 182
    consolidation of capital, 182–183
    diversification of economy, 183
    economic aspects, 172–173
    education and research, 177–178
    fiscal management reforms, 183
    foreign direct investment, 184
    good governance and strong institutions,
        181
    government, 171–172
    health issues, 175, 177
    historical developments, 178–179
    human development index, 170
    infrastructure, 175
    key indicators, 169–170
    lessons learned, 181–184
    macro economic aspects, 172–173
    overview, 168–169
    population analysis, 171
    poverty and inequality index, 170–171
    private sector involvement, 183
    recent policy reforms (2006–2012), 179–181
    rural development, 173
    safety and security, 175
    sewer access, 175
    social security policies, 183–184
    socioeconomic comparisons, 169–178
    summary, 184
    unemployment, 171
    water access, 175
Economic Policy Research Center, 49
education and research
    acquisition, 93
    administrative systems context, 55
    complaints against school authorities, 69
    corruption in, 51
    forms of corruption, 69–71
    human capital focus, 182
    information technology, 129
    public sector reform, 93
    socioeconomic comparisons, 177–178
EFCC, see Economic and Financial Crimes
    Commission of Nigeria (EFCC)
effects of corruption, 75–77
e-government
    alternative service delivery, 13
    media, constitutional mandates, 126
    South Africa Online, 127–128
Egypt, 158, 161, 163
EIC, see L'Etat Independent du Congo (EIC)
Ekurhuleni Metropolitan Municipality, 109

El Abidine Ben Ali, Zine, 163
electricity access, 51
Electronic Communications Act, No. 68 (2002)
Electronic Communications Act, No. 36 (2005) (ECA), 126
Electronic Communications and Transaction Act, No. 68 (2002)
embezzlement, 60
employment
    combating poverty, South Africa, 112
    informal sector, South Africa, 104–107
enabling strategy, support model, 102
engagement, process of, 160–161
EPZ, see Export processing zone (EPZ)
Equateur
    background development, 28
    first reform measures (1914), 32
    second phase of reform (1965–1997), 36
    second reform measures (1924), 32
    third reform measures (1933), 32
Equatorial Guinea, 158
L'Etat Independent du Congo (EIC), 30
ethical values, 67
Ethics IASIA working group, 68
Ethiopia, 158, 178
ethnic groups, number of, 29
European Commission, 179
European Union, 41, 156
Evaton, 100
executive authority, 17–20, 58
expenditures, see Income and expenditure survey (IES)
export, products for, 105–106
export processing zone (EPZ), 169, 178

F

factors of corruption, 60–68
"fast" government, 185
FDI, see foreign direct investment (FDI)
Federation of Women Lawyers (FIDA), 139
fictitious affidavits, 65
FIDA, see Federation of Women Lawyers (FIDA)
financial autonomy, 202–203
financial management and system
    Ghana, 138–139
    Mauritius, 183
    Nigeria, 87
first phase of reform (1960–1965), 33–36
first reform measures (1914), 32

FOAT, see Functional Organizational Assessment Tool (FOAT)
food gardens, 102
food sellers/traders, 109
foreign aid, dependence on, 16
foreign direct investment (FDI), 169, 184
foster care grants, provider model, 101
Fourth African Development Forum, 216
"Fourth Estate" metaphor, 120
France, 169
franchising, 13
freedoms
    attack of, 58
    corruption resembling, 59
    judiciary authority, 22
    media role, 130
Free State, 98, see also Poverty
French language, 29
Fuchs, Michael, 89
Functional Organizational Assessment Tool (FOAT), 141
functioning of colonial government, 31
future developments, 219

G

Gabon, 158, 170
Gaddafi, Muammar, 163
Gambia, 121
Gaudet, Hazel, 122
Gauteng
    day laborers, 105
    demographic profiles, 107
    informal sector, 98, 109
    poverty rates, 14
Gbagbo, Laurent, 163
GEAR, see Growth, Employment, and Redistribution (GEAR)
gender issues, 38, 113
geographical public policy perspective, 11
Ghana
    Demographic and Health Survey, 137
    financial management, 138–139
    governance overview, 62
    as model, 94
    peer review, 158
    reform commissions, 138
    traditional leadership integration, 216, 218
Ghana, governance reform
    good governance overview, 137–139
    local governance, 139–142, 147–149
    overview, 136–137

performance management, 142–144
poverty reduction, 142–147
Ghana and South Africa comparative analysis
  chief executive officer, 200–202
  decentralization and devolution, 190–193
  district chief executive officer, 200–202
  financial autonomy, 202–203
  intergovernmental relationships, 197–198
  local government, 188–190, 193–197
  local institutional arrangements, 198–205
  modern constitutions, 193–197
  municipality categories, 198–205
  overview, 188
  political scenarios, 197–198
  relevant legislative framework, 196–197
  service provision and participation, 203–205
  summary, 205
Ghana Integrity Initiative (GII), 139
Ghana Poverty Reduction Strategy (GPRS I), 142–147
Ghana Shared Growth and Development Agenda (2010–2013) (GSDA), 139, 142–147
Ghana Statistical Service (GSS), 147
ghost workers, 41
Gini Index, 171
Global Competitiveness Report, 173, 185
Global Corruption Barometer
  Ghana governance reform, 142
  indicators of good governance, 6
  reported bribes, 63
Global Indigenous Peoples' Caucus, 210
globalization, 215–216
Global Program on Capacity Development for Democratic Governance Assessments and Measurements, 6
goodness of countries, 5
governance
  African Peer Review Mechanism, 155
  characteristics of good, 6
  corruption in, 52
  overview, Ghana, 137–139
  and strong institutions, 181
  surveys, 6
governance, traditional leadership integration with
  cases of selected countries, 212–215
  future developments, 219
  local governance, 218–219
  overview, 210–211, 217–219
  paradigm shift, 215–217
  summary, 220
  traditional leadership overview, 211
governance and media, South Africa
  challenges, 129
  constitutional mandates, 125–126
  good governance defined, 119–120
  media and society, 124–125
  media defined, 119
  nexus, media–government–society, 121–125, 127–129
  overview, 118, 120–121
  role of media, 125–129
  status of media, 126–127
  summary, 129–130
  theories of media, 122–124
governance apparatus, South Africa
  apparatus of government, 16–22
  architecture of, 4–8
  cooperative government, 22–23
  executive authority, 17–20
  governance overview, 14–16
  judiciary authority, 21–22
  legislative authority, 20–21
  overview, 2
  policy and service delivery, 10–12
  service delivery innovations, 12–14
  state, society, and constitutionalism, 2–4
  summary, 23–24
  value chain clarification, 8–14
  value chain integration, 22–23
"Governance for a Progressing Africa," 216
governance reform, Ghana
  good governance overview, 137–139
  local governance, 139–142, 147–149
  overview, 136–137
  performance management, 142–144
  poverty reduction, 142–147
government, socioeconomic comparisons, 171–172
Government Gazette, 10
GPRS II, *see* Growth and Poverty Reduction Strategy (GPRS II)
grand scale corruption
  most corrupt sectors, 75
  overview, 68
  procurement, 73–74
grants, provider model, 101
grassroots participation, 124, 219
Growth, Employment, and Redistribution (GEAR), 101
Growth and Poverty Reduction Strategy (GPRS II), 142–147

GRPS I, *see* Ghana Poverty Reduction Strategy (GPRS I)
GSDA, *see* Ghana Shared Growth and Development Agenda (2010–2013) (GSDA)
GSS, *see* Ghana Statistical Service (GSS)

H

hair salons, 111
handwriting experts, 68
harmony, South Africa's governance, 16
Haruna, Peter Fuseini, 135–149
Haut-Katanga, 28
Haut-Lomami, 28
Haut-Luapula, 32
Haut-Uele, 28, 32
Haut-Zaire, 36
HDI, *see* Human development index (HDI)
health issues and health care sector
   administrative systems context, 55
   corruption in, 51
   human capital focus, 182
   information technology, 128–129
   Nigeria, 88–89
   public sector reform, 92
   socioeconomic comparisons, 175, 177
hereditary rule, 212
heritage month, 111
hierarchical structures
   public policy perspective, 11
   public service, DRC, 37–38
high-level corruption
   most corrupt sectors, 75
   overview, 68
   procurement, 73–74
historical developments
   African Peer Review Mechanism, 153–155
   Democratic Republic of Congo, 30–31
   Mauritius economic policy reform, 178–179
human capacity, 15
human development index (HDI), 170
human rights, 17, 22, *see also* Citizens
Hume, David, 3
hypodermic needle theory, 122

I

IBA, *see* Independent Broadcasting Authority (IBA)
Ibrahim Index of African Governance (2008), 181
ICASA, *see* Independent Communications Authority of South Africa (ICASA)
ICASA Amendment Act, *see* Independent Communications Authority of South Africa Amendment Act, No. 3 (2006) (ICASA Amendment Act)
ICPC, *see* Independent Corrupt Practices Commission of Nigeria (ICPC)
IDP, *see* Integrated development plans (IDPs)
Idris I (King), 163
IG, *see* Inspectorate of Government (IG)
illegal sales, 60
ILO, *see* International Labor Organization (ILO)
impetus for reform, 90–91
income and expenditure survey (IES), 14
independence, public administration after, 33–36
Independent Broadcasting Authority (IBA), 125
Independent Communications Authority of South Africa Amendment Act, No. 3 (2006) (ICASA Amendment Act), 126
Independent Communications Authority of South Africa (ICASA), 125
Independent Corrupt Practices Commission of Nigeria (ICPC), 94
Index of Economic Freedom, 178
India, 169, *see also* BRIC countries
Indian Ocean Rim Association, 184
Indian Rubber Company, 30
indicators
   goodness of countries, 5
   socioeconomic comparisons, 169–170
   sustainable governance indicators, 6
Indigenous Peoples' Framework for Sustainable Development, 210
indigenous societies, 216
indirect rule, 211
Indonesia, 107
Industrial Revolution, 129
Industrial Training Fund (ITF), 91
inequalities
   exacerbating, 203
   and poverty index, 170–171
   South Africa's governance, 14
influence, 15–16
informal day laborers, 104–105
informal producers, 104
informal sector
   activities and employment, 104–107
   benefits, 113–114

characteristics, 103
demographic profile, respondents, 107
framework, 102–103
gender dimensions, 113
infrastructure, 113
innovative skills, 112
locality, 106–107
operation, 109–112
participants, 112
products, 105–106
remuneration, 113
results of research, 107–112
sector business operations, 110–111
skills development, 109
working conditions, 113
informal service providers, 104
informal traders, 104
Information Age, 129–130
Information and Communication Technology (ICT), 128–129
information technology, 127–129
infrastructure
administrative systems context, 55
informal sector, South Africa, 113
public sector reform, 92
socioeconomic comparisons, 175
Inkatha Freedom Party, 214
inkosi, 212
innovative skills, 112, 114
Inongo, 32
Inspectorate of Government Act (1999), 67
Inspectorate of Government (IG)
corruption in Uganda, 48, 69, 75
procurement integrity, 74
Institute of Local Government (Ghana), 191
institutional corruption, 71
institutional roles, poverty reduction, 146
integrated development plans (IDPs), 12
integration, cooperative government, 23
integration, traditional leadership and modern governance
cases of selected countries, 212–215
future developments, 219
local governance, 218–219
overview, 210–211, 217–219
paradigm shift, 215–217
summary, 220
traditional leadership overview, 211
integrity, 157, *see also* African Peer Review Mechanism (APRM)
integrity initiative, 139
intelligence operatives, 58

Intergovernmental Framework Act 13 (2005), 23
intergovernmental relationships, 197–198
International Labor Organization (ILO), 98
International Monetary Fund (IMF), 87, 143, 156, 169, 195
International Telecommunication Union (ITU), 93
issues, problems conversion to, 8–9
ITF, *see* Industrial Training Fund (ITF)
ITU, *see* International Telecommunication Union (ITU)
Ituri, 32
Ivory Coast, *see* Cote d'Ivoire

J

job creation, 15
Johannesburg
conference, 217, 218
judiciary authority, 21
Johnson, Sir Harry H., 56
Joint Education Council, 183
journal articles, 178
Journal Elima, 39–40
judiciary authority, South Africa, 21–22
judiciary sector, 65, 71–73

K

Ka Bhekuzulu, King Zwelithini Goodwill, 214
Kabila, Laurent, 40
Kabinda, 32
Kadaga, Rebecca, 48
Kafukumbu, 32
Kambove, 32
Kananga, 29
Kannae, Lawrence Akanweke, 135–149
Kantor, Mickey, 46
Kari-Oca Declaration of Indigenous Peoples, 210
Kasai, 32
Kasai-Occidental, 28, 36
Kasai-Oriental, 28, 36
Katanga, 28, 32–33, 36
Kato Kintu (King), 213
Kenlloyd Logistics, 74
Kenya
corruption perception, 48, 49
peer review, 158
traditional leadership integration, 214, 216

232 ■ *Index*

key indicators
    goodness of countries, 5
    socioeconomic comparisons, 169–170
    sustainable governance indicators, 6
kgosi, 212
Kgosi Leruo Tshekedi Molotlegi, 214
Khan, Abaul Waheed, 124
khosi, 212
kickbacks, 60
Kikongo language, 29, 212
Kilokele language, 29
Kimba, Evarist, 34
Kimberley Declaration, 210
Kingdom of Kongo, 30
Kinshasa, 28, 29, 36
Kintu Dynasty, 213
Kisangani, 29
Kiswahili language, 29
Kivu, 32, 36
Kongo-Central Province, 28
Kongolo, 32
Kumasi, 194
Kwango, 28, 32
KwaZulu-Natal, 98, 217, *see also* Poverty
Kwilu Province, 28

L

Lac Leopold II, 32
La Francophonie, 184
languages
    complexity, source of corruption, 65
    constitutional recognition, 16
    ethnic groups, 29
    forceful use, 56
lapses of process, 160–161
law and order sector, 71–72
laws
    being above, 47
    executive authority, 18
    first phase of reform (1960–1965), 33
Lazarsfeld, Paul F., 122
legal sanctions, 77
legislation, Ghana, 138
legislative authority, South Africa, 20–21
legota, 212
lekgotlas, 9
Leopold II (King), 30, 31
Leopoldville, 32
les adminstrateurs de territoires et les bougmestres, 38
Lesotho, 158

lessons learned, 181–184
L'Etat Independent du Congo (EIC), 30
LGNF, *see* Local Government Negotiating Forum (LGNF)
Libenge, 32
Liberia, 158, 218
liberty, fundamental rights, 4
Libya, 160–161, 163, 170–171
life, fundamental rights, 4
limited effects theory, 122
limited resources, maximization, 168
Limpopo, 14, 98, *see also* Poverty
Lines, Kathy, 123
Lingala language, 29
linking grassroots efforts, 219
Lisala, 32
local governance and government
    concept, 188–190
    experience, 139–142
    in modern constitutions, 193–197
    summary, 147–149
    traditional leadership and modern governance integration, 218–219
Local Government: Municipal Structures Act 117 (1998), 21, 197, 201
Local Government: Municipal Systems Act (2000), 197
Local Government Act (1961), 194
Local Government Act (1993), 145, 196
Local Government Negotiating Forum (LGNF), 193
Local Government Service Act (1993), 137
Local Government Transition Act (1993), 196
Local Government Transition Act (2003), 199
local institutional arrangements, 198–205
locality, informal sector, 106–107
local municipalities, 21
Locke, John, 3
Lomami, 28, 32
Lowa, 32
low-scale corruption, 68–69, 73
Lualaba Province, 28
Lubumbashi, 29
Luebo, 32
Lukamba, Muhiya Tshombe, *ix,* 27–42, 209–220
Lule, Yusuf, 57
Lulonga, 32
Lulua, 28, 32
Lumumba, Patrice Emery, 33
Lunganda language, 56
Lusambo, 32

M

macro economic aspects, 172–173
mafisa system, 220
magistrates' courts, 22, 65
Mahamba, Alexandre, 34
Mai-Ndombe Province, 29
Makerere University, 49
Malan, Frans, 127
Malawi, 158, 171
Malaysia, 107
Mali, 158
Maniema, 32
Maniema Province, 28–29
Manufacturers Association of Nigeria (MAN), 88
matrix, promoting public service reform, 158–159
Matsuura, Koichiro, 124–125
Maurice Ile Durable (MID) program, 180–181
Mauritania, 158
Mauritius
  agriculture, 184
  background developments, 178
  competitiveness strategy, 182
  consolidation of capital, 182–183
  diversification of economy, 183
  economic aspects, 172–173
  education and research, 177–178
  financial control, 173
  fiscal management reforms, 183
  foreign direct investment, 184
  good governance and strong institutions, 181
  government, 171–172
  health issues, 175, 176, 177
  historical developments, 178–179
  human development index, 170
  infrastructure, 175
  key indicators, 169–170
  lessons learned, 181–184
  macro economic aspects, 172–174
  overview, 168–169
  peer review, 158
  population analysis, 171
  poverty and inequality index, 170–171
  private sector involvement, 183
  recent policy reforms (2006–2012), 179–181
  rural development, 173
  safety and security, 175, 176
  sewer access, 175
  social security policies, 183–184
  socioeconomic comparisons, 169–178
  summary, 184
  unemployment, 171–172
  water access, 175
Mauritius Export Development and Investment Authority (MEDIA), 179
Mauritius Productivity and Competitiveness Council, 179
Mauritius Strategy for the Further Implementation of the Program of Action for Sustainable Development of Small Island Developing States (SIDS), 180
mayoral executive system, 201
Mbandaka, 29
Mbeki, Thabo, 160, 163
Mbuji-Mayi, 29
MDG, *see* Millennium Development Goals (MDGs)
MEC, *see* Members of executive councils (MECs)
MEDIA, *see* Mauritius Export Development and Investment Authority (MEDIA)
media and governance, South Africa
  challenges, 129
  constitutional mandates, 125–126
  core task of media, 124
  good governance defined, 119–120
  media and society, 124–125
  media defined, 119
  nexus, media–government–society, 121–125, 127–129
  overview, 118, 120–121
  role of media, 125–129
  status of media, 126–127
  summary, 129–130
  theories of media, 122–124
media–government–society nexus
  media and society, 124–125
  overview, 121–122, 127–129
  theories of media, 122–124
members of executive councils (MECs), 17, 19
members of provincial legislature (MPL), 19
methodology of research, 99–100
metropolitan municipalities, 21
Meyer, Daniel Francois, 167–185
mfumu, 212
m-government, 13
Midrand, 157
Millennium Compact, 141, 147
Millennium Development Goals (MDGs)
  Ghana governance reform, 141

Nigeria, 88
poverty, 100
poverty reduction experience, 144
Millennium reforms, 89–91
minerals contracts, 51–52
ministers, executive authority, 19
Ministry of Finance and Economic Planning, 147
Ministry of Local Government and Rural Development, 141, 196
Ministry of Planning and Regional Cooperation, 143
Ministry of Regional Cooperation, 158
Mobile Telecommunication (M-Tel), 93
Mobutu, Joseph-Desire, 28, 34–35, 40
models
   alternative service delivery, 13
   combating poverty, 102
modern governance and traditional leadership integration
   cases of selected countries, 212–215
   future developments, 219
   local governance, 218–219
   overview, 210–211, 217–219
   paradigm shift, 215–217
   summary, 220
   traditional leadership overview, 211
Mo Ibrahim Foundation/Index, 6, 171, 185
Molotlegi, Kgosi Leruo Tshekedi, 214
monetary grants, provider model, 101
Mongala, 29
moral dilemma, 55
Moscow, 107
motivation, 40, 90–91
Moyen-Congo, 32
Mozambique, 158, 170
MPL, *see* Members of provincial legislature (MPL)
M2PressWire, 89
M-Tel, *see* Mobile Telecommunication (M-Tel)
Mubarak, Hosni, 163
Muganda, 213
multiparty negotiations, 195
municipality categories
   chief executive officer, 200–202
   district chief executive officer, 200–202
   financial autonomy, 202–203
   overview, 21, 198–200
   service provision and participation, 203–205
Museveni, Yoweri, 49
Muwanga, Paulo, 57

Mzini, Loraine Boitumelo (Tumi), 97–115

N

Namibia, 149, 170
National Anticorruption Strategy (2008–2013), 50
National Assembly
   legislative authority, 20
   media, constitutional mandates, 125
   ministers accountability, 19
   policy-making process, 10
National Consultative Council (NCC), 57
National Council of Provinces (NCOP)
   executive authority, 20
   legislative authority, 20
   media, constitutional mandates, 125
   policy-making process, 10
National Development Plan, 76
National Development Planning Act (1994), 145
National Development Planning Commission
   categories of municipalities, 199
   local governance experience, 141
   poverty reduction, 143, 145
   relevant legislative framework, 197
National House of Chiefs, 215
National House of Traditional Leaders, 216
National Interagency Monitoring Group, 145, 147
nationalization policies, focus on, 181
National Medium Term Development Policy Framework (2010–2013), 137
National Policy for Strategic Partnership, 139
National Program of Action, 136
National Resistance Army (NRA), 57
National Resistance Movement (NRM), 48, 57, 58
NCC, *see* National Consultative Council (NCC)
Ndebele, S.J., 217
nduna, 212
neocentralism, 198
Neotel, 128
New Partnership for Africa's Development (NEPAD)
   Ghana governance reform, 141
   peer review mechanism, 154
   promoting public service reforms, 158
   successes and failures mechanisms and initiatives, 6
new public management (NPM) reforms, 191

New Year's address, Uganda, 49
New Zealand, 216
nexus, media–government–society
   media and society, 124–125
   overview, 121–122, 127–129
   theories of media, 122–124
Niger, 170
Nigeria
   democracy reforms (1999–2009), 91–93
   Millennium reforms, 89–91
   overview, 83–86
   peer review, 158
   population analysis, 171
   recommendations, 94
   reform commissions, 86
   review of studies, 86–89
   summary, 94
Nigerian Telecommunications (NITEL), 88, 93
Noelle-Neumann, Elisabeth, 122
Nord-Kivu Province, 28, 29
Nord-Ubangi, 29
normal way of life, corruption, 53–54, *see also* Citizens
North West Province, 214
NPM, *see* New public management (NPM) reforms
NRM, *see* National Resistance Movement (NRM)

O

Obama, Barack, 164
Obasanjo, Olusegun, 88, 89, 160
objectives of research, 99
Obote, Apollo Milton, 56
OECD, *see* Organization for Economic Cooperation and Development (OECD)
offerings, 59
Office of Head of Civil Service, 141
Office of the President, 147
oil sector, 75
Oke, Ayodele, 120–121
old-age pensions, provider model, 101
operation, informal sector, 109–112
opportunism, 53
O'Regan, Kate, 127
Organization for Economic Cooperation and Development (OECD), 16, 61
Organization of African Unity, 154
organizations, formation and design, 7

Oriental Province
   background development, 28
   second phase of reform (1965–1997), 36
   second reform measures (1924), 32
   third reform measures (1933), 32
Orme, William, 123–124
Orombi, Luke, 50
Oubangui, 32
outcomes, 61, 181
outsourcing, 13
Outtara, Alassane, 163

P

PAJA, *see* Promotion of Administration of Justice Act, No. 3 (2000) (PAJA)
Pan-American Parliament, 159
Panel of Eminent Persons (APR panel), 157
paradigm shift, 215–217
Paris Club, 88
Paris Declaration on Development Effectiveness, 141
parliament, 20, 147
participants, informal sector, 112
partnerships, 13, 198
pay for work, *see* Salaries and wages
PBB, *see* Performance-based budget (PBB)
Peace and Security Council, 159
peacefulness, South Africa's governance, 16
performance-based budget (PBB), 180
performance management, poverty reduction, 144–147
petty corruption, 68–69, 73
pharmaceutical products, 105–106
PHCN, *see* Power Holding Company of Nigeria (PHCN)
Plato (philosopher), 2, 3, 4
police, 65, 72
policy and service delivery, 10–12
policy-making process, 9–10
policy reforms (2006–2012), 179–181
political context, 30–31, 71
political corruption, 71, *see also* Corruption
political ombuds, 161
political scenarios, 197–198
poly-centric decentralized democratic governance, 219
population, 29, 171
portfolios, executive authority, 18–19
Postal Services Act, No. 124 (1998), 125
poverty
   activities and employment, 104–107

alleviation paradigms, 101–102
background developments, 100–101
benefits, 113–114
characteristics, 103
demographic profile, respondents, 107
effect of corruption, 47
experience, 142–144
framework, 102–103
gender dimensions, 113
inequality index, 170–171
informal sector, 102–114
infrastructure, 113
innovative skills, 112
institutional roles, 146
locality, 106–107
methodology of research, 99–100
need for employment, 112
objectives of research, 99
operation, 109–112
overview, 98–99
participants, 112
performance management, 144–147
products, 105–106
provider model, 101
recommendations, 114
reduction, 142–147
remuneration, 113
results of research, 107–112
sector business operations, 110–111
skills development, 109
social exclusion, 143
South Africa's governance, 14
summary, 114–115
support model, 102
survey findings, 112–114
working conditions, 113
Power Holding Company of Nigeria (PHCN), 88
power supply, 92
PPDA, see Procurement and Disposal of Assets Authority (PPDA)
PPP, see Public-private partnerships (PPPs)
Pretoria, 16
Principe, 158
private sector involvement, 183
privatization, 14
problems, conversion to issues, 8–9
process of engagement, 160–161
Procurement and Disposal of Assets Authority (PPDA), 74
procurements, 60, 73–74
producers, informal, 104
products, informal sector, 105–106
promoting public service reform, 158–159
Promotion of Access to Information Act, No. 2 (2000), 125
Promotion of Administration of Justice Act, No. 3 (2000) (PAJA), 125
property, fundamental rights, 4
Protection of Public Information Act, 129
provider model, 101
Province-Oriental, 36
Provincial Houses of Traditional Leaders, 216
PSR, see Public service/sector reform (PSR)
public administration, 27–42, 45–78
Public Integrity Index, 6
public policy, 11
public-private partnerships (PPPs), 13
Public Procurement Agency, 148
public revenue and expenditure management, 73
Public Services Commission, 141
public service/sector reform (PSR)
    commonalities and specific types, 159–160
    concepts, 156
    Ghana, legislation, 138
    goals of, 84
    matrix for promoting, 158–159
    review of studies, Nigeria, 86–89

Q

Qalabotjha, 100
questioned documents, 68
quiet corruption, 60, see also Silent corruption

R

"Ready to Govern" document, 127
rebureaucratization, 142, 146
recentralization, 142, 146, 191
recommendations, 94, 114
Reconstruction and Development Program (RDP), 101
recruitment, public service, DRC, 38
reform commissions, 86, 138
regional courts, 22
Regional House of Chiefs, 215
regulatory sanctions, 77
relevant legislative framework, 196–197
religion, 58, 67
remediation basis for reforms, 87
remuneration, 113, see also Salaries and wages
reports, corruption in Uganda, 49–50

Republic of Congo, 29
Republic of South Africa Act 108 (1996), 3, see also South Africa
resources contracts, corruption, 51–52
respectability, 139
results of research, 107–112
retirement, compulsory, 37
review of studies, 86–89
Rio 92 Convention, 210
risks, informal sector participation, 112, 113
road services, 51
role of media, 125–129
Rousseau, Jean-Jacques, 3
rowing vs. steering, 12
Royal Netherlands Embassy, 73
RPD, see Reconstruction and Development Program (RDP)
rubber exploitation, 30
rule of law, threat to, 47, see also Laws
rural areas
    exacerbating inequalities, 203
    population, DRC, 29
    poverty rates, 14
    socioeconomic comparisons, 173
Russia, see BRIC countries
Rwanda
    border with DRC, 29
    corruption, 48, 49, 53
    governance overview, 62
    peer review, 158
    status of media, 126

S

SAARF, see South African Advertising Research Foundation (SAARF)
SABC, see South African Broadcasting Corporation (SABC)
SACU, see South African Customs Union (SACU)
SADC, see Southern African Development Community (SADC)
safety and security, 175
salaries and wages
    corruption in Uganda, 67
    fair pay undermined, 76
    fiscal management reforms, 183
    informal sector earnings, 113
    public service, DRC, 40
    transitional period (1999–2011), 41
Sankuru, 29, 32
São Tome, 158

SAP, see Structural Adjustment Program (SAP)
Sasolburg, 100, 105
science education acquisition, 93
SDBIP, see Service delivery and budget implementation plans (SDBIPs)
Seacom, 128
Sebokeng, 100
Second Annual Report on Corruption Trends in Uganda: Using the Data Tracking Mechanism, 49
second phase of reform (1965–1997), 36
second reform measures (1924), 32
secretariat, functions of, 157–158
sector business operations, 110–111
sectors, corruption environment, 50–52
Sedibeng District Municipality (SDM), 98, see also Poverty
Sekondi-Takoradi, 194
self-reformation, 90–91
Senegal, 124–125, 158
service delivery, 10–14
service delivery and budget implementation plans (SDBIPs), 12
service providers, informal, 104
service provision and participation, 203–205
service shedding, 13
sewer access, 175
SGI, see Sustainable Governance Indicators (SGIs)
Shaba, 36
Sharpeville, 100
Sibasa-Thohoyandou, 100
SIDS, Small Island Developing States (SIDS)
Sierra Leone, 158, 218
silence theory, spiral of, 122
silent corruption, 47, 67, see also Quiet corruption
Singapore, 94
skills, 109, 112, 114
Small Island Developing States (SIDS), 180
small-scale corruption, 68–69, 73
social exclusion, 143
social fabric of life, 52, 55
social grants, 15
socialism, 211
social management process, 155, see also Governance
Social Registry of Mauritius (SRM), 180
social security policies, 101, 183–184
societal problems, 7
society and media, 124–125
socioeconomic comparisons

economic aspects, 172–173
education and research, 177–178
government, 171–172
health issues, 175, 177
human development index, 170
infrastructure, 175
key indicators, 169–170
macro economic aspects, 172–173
overview, 169
population analysis, 171
poverty and inequality index, 170–171
rural development, 173
safety and security, 175
sewer access, 175
unemployment, 171
water access, 175
sociological impact of corruption, 54
solicitations, 71–72
Somalia, 62
South Africa
    agriculture, 184
    education and research, 177–178
    governance overview, 62
    government financial control, 173
    health issues, 176, 177
    human development index, 170
    macro economic aspects, 172, 174
    as model, 149
    peer review, 158
    poverty and inequality index, 170–171
    rural development, 173
    safety and security, 175, 176
    traditional leadership integration, 216, 218
    transitional period (1999–2011), 41
    unemployment, 171–172
    water and sewer access, 175
South Africa, combating poverty
    activities and employment, 104–107
    alleviation paradigms, 101–102
    background developments, 100–101
    benefits, 113–114
    characteristics, 103
    demographic profile, respondents, 107
    framework, 102–103
    gender dimensions, 113
    informal sector, 102–114
    infrastructure, 113
    innovative skills, 112
    locality, 106–107
    methodology of research, 99–100
    need for employment, 112
    objectives of research, 99
    operation, 109–112
    overview, 98–99
    participants, 112
    products, 105–106
    provider model, 101
    recommendations, 114
    remuneration, 113
    results of research, 107–112
    sector business operations, 110–111
    skills development, 109
    summary, 114–115
    support model, 102
    survey findings, 112–114
    working conditions, 113
South Africa, governance apparatus
    apparatus of government, 16–22
    architecture of, 4–8
    cooperative government, 22–23
    executive authority, 17–20
    governance overview, 14–16
    judiciary authority, 21–22
    legislative authority, 20–21
    overview, 2
    policy and service delivery, 10–12
    service delivery innovations, 12–14
    state, society, and constitutionalism, 2–4
    summary, 23–24
    value chain clarification, 8–14
    value chain integration, 22–23
South Africa, media and governance
    challenges, 129
    constitutional mandates, 125–126
    good governance defined, 119–120
    media and society, 124–125
    media defined, 119
    nexus, media–government–society, 121–125, 127–129
    overview, 118, 120–121
    role of media, 125–129
    status of media, 126–127
    summary, 129–130
    theories of media, 122–124
South Africa Act (1909), 193
South Africa and Ghana comparative analysis
    chief executive officer, 200–202
    decentralization and devolution, 190–193
    district chief executive officer, 200–202
    financial autonomy, 202–203
    intergovernmental relationships, 197–198
    local government, 188–190, 193–197
    local institutional arrangements, 198–205
    modern constitutions, 193–197

municipality categories, 198–205
overview, 188
political scenarios, 197–198
relevant legislative framework, 196–197
service provision and participation, 203–205
summary, 205
South African Advertising Research Foundation (SAARF), 127
South African Broadcasting Corporation (SABC), 125
South African Customs Union (SACU), 16
South African Development Community, 184
South African Human Rights Commission (SAHRC), 130
South African Institute of Race Relations, 15
South Africa Online, 127–128
Southern African Development Community (SADC)
    media opportunities, 127
    policy-making process, 9
    South Africa's governance, 15
space-binding relationship, 121
spiral of silence theory, 122
SRM, *see* Social Registry of Mauritius (SRM)
stability, 16
standards distortion, 47
Stanleyville, 32
state, society, and constitutionalism, 2–4
State Journal, 36
Statesman, 4
states without APRM review, 161, 163
Statistics South Africa, 14
status of media and good governance, 126–127
steering *vs.* rowing, 12
strategic sessions, 9
street level corruption, 68–69
strong institutions, 164, 181
Structural Adjustment Program (SAP), 87, 195, 211
structural functioning, 157–159
structure, public administration in 1981, 36–40
successes and failures, 6, 77
Sudan, 29, 158
Sudan language, 29
Sud-Kivu Province, 28, 29
Sud-Ubangi, 29
summaries
    African Peer Review Mechanism, 163–164
    combating poverty, South Africa, 114–115
    comparative analysis, Ghana and South Africa, 205

corruption, 77–78
economic policy reform, Mauritius, 184
governance apparatus, South Africa, 23–24
media and good governance, South Africa, 129–130
public administration, 41–42, 77–78
public sector reforms, Nigeria, 94
traditional leadership and modern governance integration, 220
support model, 102
supreme court of appeal, 22
surveys
    combating poverty, 112–114
    public administration and corruption, 73–75
sustainable governance indicators (SGIs), 6
Swazi Administration Order (1998), 216
Swaziland
    health issues, 177
    traditional leadership integration, 216
    unemployment, 171, 172

T

Tanganyika, 29
Tanganyika-Moero, 32
Tanzania
    border with DRC, 29
    corruption perception, 48, 49
    overthrow of Amin, Idi, 57
    peer review, 158
    traditional leadership integration, 214
tax base, 15
tax treaties, 169
technology education acquisition, 93
telecenters, 128
Telkom, 128
"The Impact of Public Participation on Poverty Alleviation: A Case of Promoting Self-Reliance through Community Food Gardens," 99
The New Vision newspaper, 76
theories of media, 122–124
The Politics, 46
Thipanyane, Tseliso, 130
third reform measures (1933), 32–33
Three Rivers, 105
Thusong Service Centers, 128
TI, *see* Transparency International (TI)
time-binding relationship, 121–122
Tobago, 94
Toffler, Alvin, 129

Togo, 158
tolerance, 16
tona, 212
top-down relationships and control, 142, 203
Toro Kingdom, 56
traders, informal, 104
trading zones, 113
traditional leadership integration
    cases of selected countries, 212–215
    future developments, 219
    local governance, 218–219
    overview, 210–211, 217–219
    paradigm shift, 215–217
    structures, 213
    summary, 220
    traditional leadership overview, 211
training, support model, 102
transitional period (1999–2011), 40–41
transparency, 88, 91
Transparency International (TI)
    bribery index, 50
    corruption perception, 48, 142, 148
    Ghana, surveys, 139
    procurement corruption, 76
transportation, 51, 92–93
Treaty of Waitangi, 216
trias politica prinicple, 4
Trinidad, 94
Tshiluba language, 29
Tshombe, Moise, 33–34
Tshopo, 29
Tshuapa, 29
Tunisia, 161, 163, 170, 172
two-step flow of communication, 122

U

Uganda
    border with DRC, 29
    exiles, overthrow of Amin, Idi, 57
    as model, 149
    peer review, 158
    traditional leadership structures, 213
Uganda, public administration and corruption
    administrative systems context, 54–59
    bureaucracy, 52–53
    concept of, 59–60
    democratic public institutions, threat to, 48
    determinants of corruption, 60–68
    education sector, 69–71
    effects of, 75–77
    forms of, 68–75
    institutional, 71
    judiciary sector, 71–73
    law and order sector, 71–72
    nation's New Year's address, 49
    as normal way of life, 53–54
    opportunism, 53
    overview, 45–54
    political, 71
    reports, 49–50
    rule of law, threat to, 47
    sectors, corruption environment, 50–52
    sociological impact, 54
    summary, 77–78
    surveys, 73–75
Uganda Investment Authority, 63
Uganda People's Congress (UPC), 57
Uganda Revenue Authority (URA), 73
Uganda's Anticorruption Act (2009), 71–72
u-government (ubiquitous government), 126
UNDRIP, *see* United Nations Declaration of Human Rights of Indigenous Peoples (UNDRIP)
unemployment, 14–15, 171, *see also* Informal sector
Union of South Africa (1910), 193
unitary systems, 193
United Kingdom, 169
United Nations Conference on Sustainable Development, 210
United Nations Declaration of Human Rights, 12
United Nations Declaration of Human Rights of Indigenous Peoples (UNDRIP), 12
United Nations Development Program (UNDP)
    architecture, government apparatus, 5
    indicators of good governance, 6
    media role, 123
    recent economic policy reforms, 179–180
    transitional period (1999–2011), 41
United Nations Economic Commission for Africa, 216, 217
United Nations Economic Commission for Africa (UNECA), 5
United Nations Millennium Declaration (2000), 137, 141, *see also* Millennium Development Goals (MDGs)
United States, 169, 216
Universal Primary Education (UPE) program, 49

Universal Secondary Education (USE) program, 49
Universal Service Obligations, 128
Universal Services Access Agency of South Africa, 128
University of Stellenbosch, 127
unofficial earnings, 103
unprocessed products, 105–106
UPC, *see* Uganda People's Congress (UPC)
UPE, *see* Universal Primary Education (UPE) program
URA, *see* Uganda Revenue Authority (URA)
U.S. Agency for International Development (USAID), 74
U.S. Department of State Investment Climate Statements (2009), 73
USE, *see* Universal Secondary Education (USE) program
Uturi Province, 28

V

Vaal Show Grounds, 109
value chain
  integration, 22–23
  overview, 8–10
  policy and service delivery, 10–12
  service delivery innovations, 12–14
Vanderbijlpark, 100, 105
van der Waldt, Gerrit, 1–24
Venda, 100
Venter, Annelise, 167–185
Vereeniging, 100, 105, 109
Villiers, 100
"Vision 2020: The National Long-Term Perspective Study," 180
Vubu, Joseph Kasa, 33, 34
Vyas-Doorgapersad, Shikha, *ix,* 117–130, 209–220

W

wages, *see* Salaries and wages
ward head, 212
watch dog organizations, 77, 118, 121, 127
water access
  administrative systems context, 55
  corruption in, 51
  Ghana governance reform, 142
  informal sector, 111–112
  socioeconomic comparisons, 175
waves of democracy, 126

Weberian image and mode, 52–53, 60
Western Cape, 14
WGI, *see* World Governance Index (WGI)
whistle-blowing, 77
White Paper on Local Government, 194, 197, 201
WISE, *see* Women's Initiative for Self-Empowerment (WISE)
Women's Initiative for Self-Empowerment (WISE), 139
working conditions, informal sector, 113
World Bank
  alternative vision, 85
  architecture, government apparatus, 5
  comparative analysis, 188
  development policy credit, 89
  Doing Business Report, 185
  governance surveys, 6
  local governments, modern constitutions, 194
  opportunism, 53
  poverty reduction experience, 143
  public revenue and expenditure management, 73
  public sector reform, 84, 87
  recent economic policy reforms, 179–180
  reform strategies experimentation, 90
  rural development, 173
  socioeconomic indicators, 169
  successes and failures mechanisms and initiatives, 6
  transitional period (1999–2011), 41
  Uganda performance, 74
World Economic Forum, 173, 185
World Freedom Day, 124–125
World Governance Assessment, 6
World Governance Index (WGI), 6
World Summit on Information Society, 128
World Trade Organization (WTO), 184
World Values Survey, 6
WTO, *see* World Trade Organization (WTO)

Y

youth participation, 204

Z

Zaire, 28, 36, *see also* Democratic Republic of Congo (DRC)
Zambia
  border with DRC, 29
  health issues, 177

peer review, 158
  traditional leadership integration, 218
  transitional period (1999–2011), 41
Zande, 29
Zimbabwe
  dysfunctionality, 62
  health issues, 177
  population analysis, 171
  status of media, 127
Zulu Kingdom, 214

An environmentally friendly book printed and bound in England by www.printondemand-worldwide.com

This book is made of chain-of-custody materials; FSC materials for the cover and PEFC materials for the text pages.

#0163 - 150616 - C0 - 234/156/14 [16] - CB - 9781439888803